The Height of Summer:
New Plays from Williamstown
Theatre Festival 2015–2021

The Height of Summer:
New Plays from Williamstown
Theatre Festival 2015–2021

Paradise Blue

Cost of Living

Actually

Where Storms Are Born

Selling Kabul

Grand Horizons

Edited and with a Foreword by
MANDY GREENFIELD

methuen | drama

LONDON • NEW YORK • OXFORD • NEW DELHI • SYDNEY

METHUEN DRAMA
Bloomsbury Publishing Plc
50 Bedford Square, London, WC1B 3DP, UK
1385 Broadway, New York, NY 10018, USA
29 Earlsfort Terrace, Dublin 2, Ireland

BLOOMSBURY, METHUEN DRAMA and the Methuen Drama logo are trademarks of
Bloomsbury Publishing Plc

First published in Great Britain 2022

Foreword Copyright © Mandy Greenfield, 2022

Paradise Blue © Dominique Morisseau, 2022
Cost of Living © Martyna Majok, 2022
Actually © Anna Ziegler, 2022
Where Storms Are Born © Harrison David Rivers, 2022
Selling Kabul © Sylvia Khoury, 2020
Grand Horizons © Beth Wohl, 2020

The authors have asserted their right under the Copyright, Designs and Patents Act, 1988,
to be identified as authors of this work.

Cover design by Rebecca Heselton
Cover image © James Hardy/ Getty Images

All rights reserved. No part of this publication may be reproduced or transmitted in any form or by any means, electronic or mechanical, including photocopying, recording, or any information storage or retrieval system, without prior permission in writing from the publishers.

Bloomsbury Publishing Plc does not have any control over, or responsibility for, any third-party websites referred to or in this book. All internet addresses given in this book were correct at the time of going to press. The authors and publisher regret any inconvenience caused if addresses have changed or sites have ceased to exist, but can accept no responsibility for any such changes.

No rights in incidental music or songs contained in the work are hereby granted and performance rights for any performance/presentation whatsoever must be obtained from the respective copyright owners.

All rights whatsoever for these plays are strictly reserved. Application for performance, etc. should be made before rehearsals begin to the respective playwrights' representatives listed on page 437. No performance may be given unless a licence has been obtained.

A catalogue record for this book is available from the British Library.

Library of Congress Cataloging-in-Publication Data
Names: Greenfield, Mandy, editor. | Williamstown Theatre Festival.
Title: The height of summer : new plays from Williamstown Theatre Festival 2015–2021 : new plays from Williamstown Theatre Festival, 2015-2021 / edited by Mandy Greenfield.
Description: London ; New York : Bloomsbury Publishing, 2022. | "Cost of living, Actually, Selling Kabul, Grand horizons, Paradise blue, Where storms are born." | Identifiers: LCCN 2022002185 | ISBN 9781350289314 (hardback) | ISBN 9781350289307 (paperback) | ISBN 9781350289321 (epub) | ISBN 9781350289338 (pdf) | ISBN 9781350289345
Subjects: LCSH: American drama–21st century.
Classification: LCC PS634.2 .H45 2022 | DDC 812/.608—dc23/eng/20220331
LC record available at https://lccn.loc.gov/2022002185

ISBN: HB: 978-1-3502-8931-4
PB: 978-1-3502-8930-7
ePDF: 978-1-3502-8933-8
eBook: 978-1-3502-8932-1

Typeset by RefineCatch Limited, Bungay, Suffolk
Printed and bound in Great Britain

To find out more about our authors and books visit www.bloomsbury.com
and sign up for our newsletters.

Contents

Foreword 1
Williamstown Theatre Festival 10
Paradise Blue by Dominique Morisseau 13
Cost of Living by Martyna Majok 79
Actually by Anna Ziegler 155
Where Storms Are Born by Harrison David Rivers 191
Selling Kabul by Sylvia Khoury 245
Grand Horizons by Bess Wohl 365
Performance Rights 437

This anthology of plays is dedicated to my husband, Matt Fassler, and our sons, Gabriel and Ezra, for embracing adventure each summer while I made art.

Foreword

A few months into my first year as artistic director of Williamstown Theatre Festival, the then Chairman of the Board of Trustees, Matt Harris, called me to check in about how my first season was coming together. After some light banter, his tone changed dramatically when he—a career venture capitalist—asked me, of my first season: are you going to play it safe or are you going to go for it, artistically?

I am going to go for it; in fact, I am going to risk it all. That is the only way I know how to do this. That is the only way I know how to make theater. That is the job: to take the entirety of who each of us is, embrace it, and throw it, with abandon, discipline, and skill, into work on stage. In the theater—just as our ancestors did, just as our progeny will—we probe the condition of being alive to understand what it means to be alive. Our contours must be excavated, interrogated, illuminated if we are to properly and thoroughly use the resources of the theater to connect with and transform an audience and shed a small light on the condition of being human. Playing it safe was never under consideration.

From 2015 until 2019, I programmed five summers of theater at the Williamstown Theatre Festival; in 2020, we made an entire season of work, originally intended for the stage (but cancelled due to the global health pandemic) with Audible, the world's leading creator and provider of audio storytelling. In 2021, we produced an entirely outdoor theater season to ensure the safety of our artists, staff, and audiences during the ongoing pandemic. Seven years of work—fifty-two world premiere plays and musicals and revivals of existing plays—which garnered theatrical accolades from Lucille Lortel Awards to Tony Awards to the Pulitzer Prize in Drama. Seven summers within the sixty-seven year history of Williamstown Theatre Festival. Many of the finest world premiere plays during the time I enjoyed the privilege of being artistic director of the company appear in this anthology.

As soon as I took the helm and every year I held it, I sought the best new plays I could find. I searched for extraordinary dramatic writing which breathed new life or perspective into familiar stories or which told new stories rarely if ever seen on stage. I did not program to a rubric or to an agenda; I sought exquisite writing for the stage. I did not nor do I know how to separate excellence from diversity. Excellence is not possible without diversity—to create any piece of work, let alone a season or seasons of work, without harnessing the plurality of perspectives and experiences across all silos of identity—race, gender, sex, ability, to name a few—is to miss the purpose and the opportunity before us and doom the work to mediocrity, at best. I cast a wide net for plays from every corner of the field and I read voraciously. I let plays happen to me. And, in happening to me, I imagined them in three dimensions, on stage. It is in this moment—the imagination of what a play can be on stage—that an artistic director does her most important work; it is in this moment that she conjures how an audience might experience the world premiere production of a play.

The role of artistic director demands aesthetic, cultural, and artistic arrogance. The act of curation and the acts of molding, shaping, editing an artistic process can only be done with confidence and clarity, with the certainty that one's taste and artistic instincts are sharp, unique, and vital. It is terribly arrogant to declare—through a series of bold and definitive, inclusive choices—what matters, what *should* matter, what stories will be elevated to a platform with global impact, what constitutes artistic excellence, what an audience needs or wants, and, finally, perhaps most importantly what will work on stage.

At the same time, the role of artistic director requires deep humility to be executed correctly. First and finally, the choice to produce a play is a choice not for one's own edification but for an audience's experience. There are many measures of a play's success, yes: critical response, press features, awards, accolades, advance ticket sales, philanthropic support, commercial success, the artists' satisfaction with the work and a resulting desire to collaborate again. But there is no measure greater than what happens in the theater each night when humans on one side of the footlights offer a story to humans on the other side of the footlights. This is the ancient ritual we still enact. The best plays speak to an audience because they are about the resolution or impossibility of resolution of conflict internal to the lives of the characters on stage; and, they are equally about conflict in the lives of the audience. We laugh or we cry, we leap to our feet and cheer, we leave the theater transfixed and also transformed, when we imagine how our own lives will carry on, or not, in the world outside the theater, when the show comes down . . .

What I couldn't fully see until the occasion of this anthology is that what connects these six plays is their prescience. These six plays are as much about the time in which we are alive as they are about their characters and plots. Each play utilizes the dramatic form—and the ancient obligation to engage civically—to unearth a timely and pressing concern in American culture, in a global culture. These plays will stand the test of time because they are dramatically potent. But they are also a record of our time. They will continue to help us understand who we were in the years between their birth on the page and then on the stage; and, I suspect, they will offer revelations about who we will be for years to come.

Audiences at the Williamstown Theatre Festival and well beyond loved these plays. There were world premiere musicals—Matt Gould and Carson Kreitzer's *Lempicka*, directed by Rachel Chavkin and choreographed by Raja Feather Kelly and Daniel Goldstein, and Michael Friedman's *Unknown Soldier*, directed by Trip Cullman, to name two—equally beloved and embraced but which are not the focus of this anthology. I am grateful to these six playwrights, among so many others, who trusted and took the leap of creative faith required to create a world premiere production. Dominque Morisseau, Martyna Majok, Anna Ziegler, Harrison David Rivers, Sylvia Khoury and Bess Wohl were, like me, willing to risk it all—to put their whole selves into the work, in the northwest corner of Massachusetts—to premiere a play.

I read Dominique Morisseau's *Paradise Blue* in the first weeks of my appointment as artistic director in the fall of 2014 and I remember weeping at the end of the play. I wept for Pumpkin, the protagonist, who loses both the love of her life and her way of life—neither idealized by the play but rendered complex throughout. Pumpkin must navigate a future as a Black woman, on her own, during a time and in a place increasingly inhospitable to her success. But I recall weeping also in part simply because the play ended; the end meant I had to leave the Paradise Club—the characters, the music, the poetry, the joy, and the seduction of all its possibility and promise, grandeur and beauty—and return to the world fashioned by the forces outside that Black Bottom neighborhood club in 1949.

Dominique's music—the rhythm and specificity of her language—conspire with her sense of humor and deep feeling to theatricalize a vivid world of Black lives being lived fully and unapologetically. The music in the play—quite literally, the way in which the play deploys music as a character—enlarges and abstracts the emotional scope of the storytelling. When Ruben Santiago Hudson enthusiastically agreed to direct the premiere, the first choice he made was to invite renowned blues musician and composer Bill Sims, Jr. to co-write the music with award-winning trumpet player Kenny Rampton who would also record it for the show. The music inside that club was hot. But it is the world outside that club, the one we never see but are forced to imagine—a racially motivated body politic destroying Black neighborhoods in the interest of "economic redevelopment"—that is the powerful achievement of this play on the page and, also, it turns out, in production. The audience is forced to confront how white Americans, not in this play, work each day to destroy the lives and livelihoods of Black Americans, in this play. The play dramatizes the resilience, strength, and creativity in Black communities to resist and overcome those historical and sadly, persistent realities. Part of the "Detroit Project" trilogy, *Paradise Blue* announced itself as a major play on that first read: a play that demanded a big canvas because it tells an urgent story about the moment in which we all live.

When I programmed *Paradise Blue* on the Main Stage I learned that the only other play by a Black female or female-identifying playwright to be produced on the Main Stage in the Festival's six-decade history had been Lorraine Hansberry's 1959 classic *A Raisin in the Sun*, in 1999. The *New York Times* critic who reviewed *Paradise Blue* noted her discomfort at hearing the intimate, unswitched code of Black characters in front of an entirely white audience in Williamstown in 2015; at the time, I internalized the critic's discomfort more as a function of her own insecurity, than as a critique of the American theater. In 2020, the Black Lives Matter movement, in the wake of George Floyd's murder, seismically shifted discourse throughout American culture and especially in the American theater. Today, one might argue that it was irresponsible or harmful to have created the world premiere of this play on the Festival Main Stage in 2015 for an almost entirely white audience. While there is merit to the argument, its opposite is also valid: for just as my collaboration with Robert O'Hara on the 2019 revival of *A Raisin in the Sun*, the second revival of the play in Festival history, shook Festival audiences awake to the danger of their own participation in systems of racial inequity, Dominique Morisseau's brave and brilliant writing alerted them in 2015—subtly, powerfully, provocatively—of the same. *Paradise Blue* also indicated to the Festival audience that world premiere plays and purposeful revivals in the coming seasons would not only entertain but also engage and challenge them socially, politically, spiritually, and artistically.

In 2020, we were forced to cancel the live theatrical season due to the global health pandemic. As a result, I forged a collaboration with Audible. I approached Dominique about including *Paradise Blue* in the endeavor given how perfectly the piece—in all of its musicality—is suited to the sonic format. But it was also an opportunity to address the problem of a homogenously white audience receiving a play by and with entirely Black artists. While *Paradise Blue* enjoyed an off-Broadway run at Signature Theatre and has gone on to enjoy major productions all over the country, there is an even broader and ever-more diverse audience for this play to reach. The barriers of time, geography, and expense are all torn down on the Audible platform and Dominique's extraordinary music can fill the ears, hearts, and minds of all who wish to listen in America and around the world, moving forward.

I read Martyna Majok's *Cost of Living* before it was finished. At the time, it was a work in progress—both an expansion of her 2015 one-act, "John, Who's Here from Cambridge," and new material. She admitted, at our first meeting together, that she was skittish about the fact that I had read it at all. She was floored, I learned from her agent, when I committed to producing the play on the spot, in that, our first meeting. I had never met characters like Jess and John, Ani and Eddie in a play: fierce, unapologetic, desirous, viciously funny, vulnerable, alive, compromised, and each in search of a better life. These characters—their relationships and their obstacles, what each had and what each lacked—leapt off the page as totally singular, fully formed, and dramatically necessary from that first read. Far too few plays I had encountered included robust, dynamic characters with disabilities and even fewer demanded that actors with disabilities inhabit them. I came into our first meeting knowing I wanted to produce what was then called *Ropes in the Well* and would become, months and drafts later, *Cost of Living*.

Like her characters, Martyna herself was a revelation: she made it clear she would write this play until its claws gripped every person who experienced it. Her unbridled ambition, reverence for the theater as an artform as well as her palpable humility and biting sense of humor were all instantly accessible. That first meeting, and subsequent early ones together, involved a deliberate unfolding of our personal backstories until trust was established. Martyna's play and Martyna made it clear that a play about class and survival, about having and needing, could only be made honestly by collaborators who could say the whole truth to each other. Director Jo Bonney joined us and fused her frank, unsentimental approach to directing actors to the process.

In *Cost of Living*, Jess is a recent college graduate with meaningful debt and no familial, financial support. She takes a survival job as a caregiver to John, an affluent and arrogant graduate student with cerebral palsy. Separately in the play, acid-tongued Ani is rendered quadriplegic as a result of a car accident and allows her philandering ex-husband, trucker Eddie, to care for her during a brief period following the accident. These two stories unfold separately, simultaneously until they converge in real time: Eddie, haunted by his emotional missteps and several missed calls from now-deceased Ani's cellphone number, welcomes Jess, broke, broken, and humiliated, in from the cold.

The play does something extraordinary: it assumes—rightly—that the audiences' sympathies will rest first and, perhaps, fully with the characters with disabilities. That assumption—audacious and subversive in and of itself—is completely hijacked and destroyed by the writing within the first few pages of the first scenes in which we meet the pairs and we understand greater forces are at play—class, race, privilege, and, perhaps, fate. Because we rarely experience a character with cerebral palsy in the theater, Martyna knows we immediately form certain ideas upon meeting one: he is fragile, he is insecure about his body, he is not capable. Not John! Because we rarely experience a character who is authentically working class, the child of an immigrant and a woman of color, Martyna is certain we immediately form certain ideas upon seeing one: she is uneducated, she is not trustworthy. Not Jess! Neither Eddie nor Ani conform to our expectations, deeply held biases, or tendencies to stereotype. The result is a powerful, dramatic tug of rope with sympathy pulling us one way and antipathy another. Who we root for in this play and why tells us something about who each of us is and why. The play blew Festival audiences away and subsequently enjoyed a critically acclaimed run at Manhattan Theatre Club, off-Broadway. In early 2018, *Cost of Living* was awarded the Pulitzer Prize for Drama, the first play to originate on a Williamstown Theatre Festival stage to do so.

Strong two-handers are nearly impossible to find and extraordinary when they work. The vectors of a conflict, between two dramatic entities, must engage to create tension from the opening moments of a play and, over the course of something like one hundred pages, ratchet up to a climax of some consequence. Two-handers seem extraordinary when, by the end, somehow, neither character has left the stage but something remarkable and somehow inevitable happens between them.

In Anna Ziegler's *Actually*, Amber, white and Jewish, and Tom, African-American, both college freshmen at Princeton, meet, drink, and spend a night together. Conflict ignites on the first page: two young people engage romantically and, possibly, sexually but neither is in control because each is intoxicated. The tension builds quickly and steadily. We come to understand that what brings us, the audience, to the proceedings is that we are just like the panel of college disciplinarians before whom Amber and Tom have been called to testify. We are being asked to judge, without the benefit of legal expertise or a formal judicial process, what happened between them. We come to know and sympathize with both characters. One of the most notable features of the writing is that the more access it offers us to Amber and Tom, individually, the less certain we are about what actually, pun intended, happened between them. Director Lileana Blain-Cruz directed actors Joshua Boone and Alexandra Socha with nuance and balance for the Festival and subsequently, when the production ran at Manhattan Theatre Club.

As gripping as the play is from a character standpoint, the play puts its finger on something larger. The question of Anna's play is not the validity of sexual misconduct claims by young women on college campuses nor is it the problem of racial bias against Black men at predominantly white institutions of higher education in America. While the play certainly spends time unpacking both themes as well as the complex nature of consent, the question of Anna's play centers on the integrity, efficacy, and limits of Title IX bureaucracies—and the moving target around the standard for the burden of proof—on college campuses to access truth.

In 1972, the United States enacted Title IX to prohibit discrimination on the basis of sex in educational programs receiving federal financial assistance. Title IX, the people who fought for it and the people who realized it, is widely understood to be and credited as the instrument that achieved equality for women (and also transgender people) in American education. In 2011, under President Barack Obama, a policy statement clarified that Title IX applied also to universities' responses to claims of sexual misconduct and mandated that universities in receipt of federal funds have a Title IX coordinator in place at least part time to adjudicate and resolve matters brought up under this policy. During the Obama administration (at the time of the writing of the play), the standard of proof used to determine the outcome of sexual misconduct cases was articulated as a "preponderance of the evidence" (otherwise known as "fifty percent plus a feather"). Under the Trump administration (at the time of the premiere of the play), schools were given more leeway to decide what standard they deemed appropriate. Universities could adopt a "clear and convincing" standard, if they so chose, but a preponderance of evidence was still permissible.

Anna's play is dramatically intense because Amber and Tom share a conflict we desperately want resolved and each character is both deeply sympathetic and flawed. The play uses the conventions of theatrical storytelling—two characters on stage, dialogue between them and direct-address monologue—to frame a messy problem. And, finally, the play ends not by resolving the conflict but by utilizing theatrical convention to make its point. The audience, like the college panel of administrators and faculty carrying out its Title IX obligation, must decide the truth, and live with it as well as the consequences of it, once the show comes down.

I was gripped by *Where Storms Are Born* on first read but had already cemented the 2016 season when I met this play. Its playwright, Harrison David Rivers, and I mutually committed to its world premiere production in the 2017 season and he graciously agreed to serve as the first Festival Playwright in Residence, a program launched in the summer of 2016.

To have a living writer embedded in the day-to-day operations of the Festival was extraordinary; to have this writer was truly a gift for no artist could have been more fully present, productive, brave, or bold as he. In July of 2016, Alton Sterling and Philando Castile were killed by police in Louisiana and Minnesota, respectively. The inexplicable murder of these two men of color, captured on cell phone video and widely circulated online, brought parts of the country and certainly the Festival to a complete halt. As protests broke out regionally—protests foreshadowing but ultimately dwarfed by the magnitude of civil unrest following the murder of George Floyd in 2020—we paused in Williamstown to try to comprehend and respond to the events unfolding around us. And while most of the Festival paused helplessly, Playwright in Residence Harrison David Rivers hurled into action and began to write a new play. In a matter of days, he had created a dramatic response to these murders. Bravely, without hesitation, he read from that play—now called *This Bitter Earth*—in front of the Festival at what was meant to be a mid-season, full company meeting about the Festival operations but which became a lesson in true human courage and brilliance. His play, not unlike the one we would produce a season later, cautions against the danger of personal and political abdication in the face of unspeakable, horrific racial inequity and racially motivated violence in America.

But the play we would produce a season later, *Where Storms Are Born*, was pushing into themes and ideas that would not dominate headlines for several more years. The play, whose title is borrowed from the language of Arna Bontemp's Harlem Renaissance-era poem "Reconnaissance," shattered me on first read. Lush, expressive, rhythmically dazzling words from Bethea, a mother mourning the loss of her incarcerated adult son, give us access to the interior glut of pain she manages daily. In the play, Bethea charts a recovery from loss and a future filled with hope, alongside her devoted living son, Gideon. Dramatically stirring, the writing fearlessly excavates the loss of a child, for Bethea, and a brother, for Gideon. At the same time, the piece presciently interrogates the fatal consequences of systemic racism in the American judicial system and the tragic results of wrongful incarceration. America is just beginning to reckon with these realities as we move through yet another post-civil rights national movement for equality and justice for Black and Brown people in this country; the play, at the time of this publication, is perhaps even more resonant than when we premiered it. At the heart of Harrison's play is a woman reeling from the senselessness of a world that would ruin and end one of her Black sons' lives. Also at the heart of this play is a woman deeply invested in the possibility that the very same world will empower her other adult son to live and love fully and freely as a gay Black man. The expanse of the play's interests is as vast as the depth of Bethea's love for her boys. Director Saheem Ali directed the play with delicacy and authenticity for the Festival.

In 2020, Harrison David Rivers joined the Festival for an online panel discussion that aimed to define the role that theater might be able to play in the national healing process following the murder of George Floyd, during a health pandemic which disproportionately impacted Black, Brown, and Indigenous Americans. As vividly as I can remember Myra Lucretia Taylor's breathtaking performance of Bethea's words in his play, I recall Harrison offering the phrase that plays have a unique ability to "dream us forward." *Where Storms Are Born* dreams us forward to the version of the world where joy and limitless opportunity for Bethea and Gideon are the rule, not the exception.

Selling Kabul was awarded the 2018 L. Arnold Weissberger New Play Award, administered by the Festival since 1992, and expanded in 2017 to include a commission for a new play. As part of the Weissberger Award, the Festival hosts a reading of the play so in the summer of 2018, we heard the piece read aloud by actors. Sylvia Khoury's taut thriller had me on the edge of my seat as I listened to four Afghan characters survive on the night their lives can no longer be kept safe from the Taliban. Sylvia's technical achievement—the meticulous plotting of a thriller, the delicate insertion of information on a need-to-know basis—is breathtaking. Sylvia also writes with an economy that is rare—her characters say exactly what they can afford—in time, in emotional cost—to say to each other. So, a stage direction—a touch, a look, a hug—can be devastating and always satisfying.

In the play, Afiya returns home from the hospital following the birth of her brother Taroon's first child by his wife. Taroon cannot be at the hospital for the birth because he has been living in hiding in Afiya's (and husband Jawid's) apartment, wanted for dead by the Taliban for working as a translator for the American military. Because the Taliban suspect Taroon will emerge from hiding—wherever he is—on the night his first child is born, each scene of the play masterfully and subtly dramatizes the increasing threat from the offstage Taliban, as reported or enacted by the onstage characters. Tyne Rafaeli's virtuosic directorial additions—sound, light, subtleties of staging—added to the mounting sense of urgency as the dangers of the outside world pierce the walls of Afiya and Jawid's apartment.

The play is set in 2013 as, history reminds us, Afghan forces took the lead in security responsibility for their country and the United States began the long, complicated withdrawal of troops from what would become the longest war in US history. In 2019, when we produced the world premiere of *Selling Kabul*, the way in which it shone a light on the consequences of US intervention in and abandonment of the region felt uniquely illustrative: how were the lives of everyday Afghans who, for example, worked as translators for the military, impacted when the US military gave up on a conflict it had exacerbated but hardly solved?

By the time the next production of the play opened in 2021, off-Broadway at Playwrights Horizons (following a nearly two-year closure of live theater in New York due to the pandemic), it felt both uniquely illustrative, achingly familiar and deeply urgent. In August of 2021, the world witnessed the total collapse of the Afghan government at the forceful hands of the Taliban, following the withdrawal of American troops from the country. The American media was saturated with images and stories of Afghans clinging to planes leaving Kabul for safety, of translators awaiting Special Immigrant Visas falsely promised to them by the US for their service to the US military. The world was saturated with stories of Afiyas, Jawids, and Taroons but Sylvia's play—prescient, gripping, singular—brought the reality, heartbreak and resilience of those lives into intimate and startling clarity for American audiences.

Bess Wohl writes extraordinary roles for women. Bess Wohl has a theatrical imagination ripe and endlessly surprising. Bess Wohl's play *American Hero*, directed by Leigh Silverman, originated on the Nikos stage at the Festival in 2013 and subsequently transferred to the uptown, off-Broadway venue of Second Stage Theatre. When Second Stage artistic director Carole Rothman and I began to discuss the possibility of co-commissioning a playwright to write a play that would be born on the Main Stage of the Festival and then transfer to the Helen Hayes, the Broadway theater of Second Stage, Bess Wohl was the obvious choice.

When I think back on my first read of *Grand Horizons*, I remember laughing out loud, alone, in the library where I read each Friday afternoon and then crying. I was crying so hard I had to leave because I was so loud and messy. I was crying because Bess wrote a play so baldly about the uniquely female frustration of being defined and limited by one's relationship and service to others. In this play, Nancy is and always has been someone's wife, someone's mother, someone's daughter. And in this play, Nancy, at eighty years old, has the courage to defy the expectations imposed on her by a lifetime of those roles and ask to be seen as her own, whole person by the people who most need her in relationship to them. The play is structured impeccably, wildly funny, deeply true, and profoundly moving. I knew, reading it that day, that audiences would embrace it as enthusiastically as imaginable and I feared that the American, patriarchal theater establishment would not.

The powerful, male, critical establishment has openly admitted to being mystified, even offended, by many of the female-authored plays (which often also center the interiority and conflict of female protagonists) within the body of work I have commissioned, developed and produced over two decades. With undeniable frequency, regardless of their genre and independent of their ultimate success, however one measures it, plays by and about women are compared to sit-coms or "Lifetime television movies" (a reference to movies made by the American network geared toward women), and are admonished for being "sentimental." Adjectives such as "manipulative," "brittle," and "shrill," appear to describe the (often) leading, female characters. All one has to do is internet search the prominent American reviews for premieres of plays by many of our most important and gifted American women playwrights—at theaters all over the United States—to tally the frequency of this gendered language. Often, it's not just gendered language, it's overt sexism. Writing for *The Observer* in 2015 about the world premiere of Carey Perloff's *Kinship* at the Festival, a male critic remarked of the production that, "it's another blunted attempt to shine some light on the plight of a liberated woman headed for a collision with the parameters of sexual and psychological social mores (a subject with which Ms. Greenfield has an obvious obsession)."

Yes, yes I do have an obvious obsession with the parameters of sexual and psychological mores; and, it turns out, so do many women who come to the theater. The incomparable experience of listening to 500 people roar with laughter during *Grand Horizons* on the Main Stage of the '62 Center for Theatre and Dance in Williamstown was exceeded only by doing the very same thing with 597 people each night at the Helen Hayes on Broadway. It was both gratifying and a fitting reversal to my anxiety-induced-library-weeping episode to see an influential female critic for *The New York Times* recognize the "full humanity" of *Grand Horizons*, calling it a "clever truth bomb of a play." But the real gift of producing this play was listening to women talk about the play on their way out of the theater each night. Through tears of complex joy, women just like Nancy consistently remarked that they had never seen themselves on stage and felt seen, for the first time, by the uncanny wisdom and unfaltering honesty of the writing. *Grand Horizons*, directed by Leigh Silverman, was wildly successful on Broadway, earning two Tony Award nominations in 2021, including one for Best Play (alongside Adam Rapp's *The Sound Inside*, which also premiered on the Festival stage in 2019, in the same Broadway season).

These six plays—and many of the others we produced at the Festival—are manifestations of living, American playwrights grappling with and breathing dramatic life into the conflicts and questions at the heart of who we were, who we are, and who we will become. These plays imagine and interrogate pieces of the human experience we are still in the midst of unpacking and understanding. These plays came into the world over the course of seven seasons of production at Williamstown Theatre Festival where a small army of brilliant and determined artists, administrators, technicians, artisans, and young theater professionals convened to create theater.

But before they were productions on the Festival stages, before they garnered acclaim and notoriety, they were words on a page, waiting to be heard, seen and felt . . . waiting to transform hearts and minds.

Let them happen to you.

Mandy Greenfield
December 2021

Williamstown Theatre Festival

During the winter of 1954, members of Williams College and local community members had a "Eureka!" moment: use the Adams Memorial Theatre during its summer vacancy to launch a local summer stock theater and bring much-needed economic vitality to the community in the northwestern corner of Massachusetts. With the help of the board of trade, local businessmen, and town residents, including Cole Porter, Williamstown Summer Theatre—later renamed Williamstown Theatre Festival—was formed with $9,000 in the bank.

Intending to produce ten plays in ten weeks, the Williams' Drama Department Chair sought out an associate who could direct half the season. On the recommendation of the Dean of the Yale School of Drama, Nikos Psacharopoulos was appointed. A twenty-six member company was assembled from young New York professionals, Yale actors and alumni, and a few students from Williamstown.

The first season was successful enough for the theater to plan a second.

The following year, Nikos became artistic director, and the Festival's repertory became increasingly ambitious (and notably less summer stock) with productions of Shaw, Giraudoux, Miller, Williams, and Chekhov. A growing family of actors evolved including Mildred Dunnock, E. G. Marshall, and Thornton Wilder (who played the Stage Manager in his own *Our Town* in 1959), later joined by the likes of Kate Burton, Blythe Danner, Olympia Dukakis, Edward Herrmann, James Naughton, Christopher Reeve, and Christopher Walken, whose return year after year gave stability to the Equity company.

In the 1960s and early 1970s, Williamstown became known for innovative, elaborate versions of classics: *The Seagull* (taped for PBS), *Galileo*, *Six Characters in Search of an Author*, *Peer Gynt*, and *The Threepenny Opera*. By this time, more than 100 people worked in the theater every summer. Auxiliary activities began to supplement the Main Stage: the Apprentice Workshop, an experimental Second Company, lively Late-Night Cabarets, Sunday literary events, and new play readings. The 1980s saw some ambitious work, including *The Greeks* and a two-night celebration of Tennessee Williams with the playwright in residence.

After an extraordinary and visionary thirty-three years as the head of WTF, Nikos Psacharopoulos passed away in 1989. From 1990 through 2014, the Theatre Festival was led by several visionary artistic directors including Peter Hunt, Michael Ritchie, Roger Rees, Nicholas Martin, and Jenny Gersten. The Festival was producing ten plays in ten weeks and blossomed to over 300 summer participants. In 2002, Williamstown Theatre Festival received the Tony Award for Outstanding Regional Theatre. In 2011, WTF received the Commonwealth Award for Achievement, the highest cultural honor bestowed by the Commonwealth of Massachusetts. Many of the shows WTF produced transferred for successful runs on and off Broadway in those years.

Mandy Greenfield was appointed artistic director of Williamstown Theatre Festival in late 2014 and served until 2021. The plays showcased in this collection were developed and produced during this time.

Under Mandy's direction, Williamstown Theatre Festival grew support, resources, and a commitment to diverse, generative artists, with a particular focus on playwrights and composers. She created and launched the New Play and Musical Commissioning Program, through which artists such as Aziza Barnes, Jocelyn Bioh, Nathan Alan Davis, Rick Elice, Halley Feiffer, Meghan Kennedy, Sylvia Khoury, Jason Kim, Justin Levine, Matthew Lopez, Marsha Norman, Zoe Sarnak, Benjamin Scheuer, Jen Silverman, Lucy Thurber, Sanaaz Toosi, and Bess Wohl, among others, were supported. Mandy established the position of Playwright-in-Residence, a seat held by writers such as Pulitzer Prize winner Michael R. Jackson, Diana Oh, Mona Pirnot, Max Posner, and Harrison David Rivers.

The plays commissioned, developed, and produced by the Festival during Mandy's tenure garnered every major theatrical honor, including the Lucille Lortel Award, Drama Desk Award, Obie Award, and the Kleban Prize in Musical Theatre. The world premiere of Martyna Majok's *Cost of Living*, which won the Pulitzer Prize for Drama in 2018, was developed and produced at the Festival. In 2021, two plays that originated at the Festival—Bess Wohl's *Grand Horizons* and Adam Rapp's *The Sound Inside*—were nominated for Tony Awards for Best Play.

Mandy co-created and launched important Festival programs, including COMMUNITY WORKS, in collaboration with associate artistic director Laura Savia and playwright Lucy Thurber, and the Early Career BIPOC Theatre-Makers Program, in collaboration with Black Theatre United. She established the J. Michael Friedman Fellowship in honor of the late American lyricist and composer, and she expanded the scope and cash prize of The Arnold L. Weissberger Award, given annually to an emerging playwright. In response to the global health pandemic of 2020, Mandy forged a collaboration with Audible, the leading creator and provider of premium audio storytelling, to create a seven-show season of audio projects available to a global audience.

In the seven decades since its founding, Williamstown Theatre Festival has grown and evolved to meet the unique opportunities and challenges of each moment, yet its overarching goals have remained constant: to attract top talent, cultivate early-career theater-makers, produce reinterpreted versions of classics and new plays from gifted generative artists, and continue to attract audiences with the quality and ambition of the Festival's work.

Paradise Blue

Dominique Morisseau

Introduction

Paradise Blue is a part of my three-play cycle on Detroit, titled "The Detroit Project." The cycle looks at three different eras in Detroit's history that are iconic to the city's development and shaped the core of Detroit as I came to know it growing up. These eras are: 2008, during the auto industry collapse and foreclosure crisis; 1967, during the urban rebellion that set the city ablaze amidst rampant police violence; and the era of Paradise Blue—1949, during the city's thriving Black business and jazz community on the brink of an urban renewal campaign that seeks to obliterate it.

Paradise Blue is the first chronologically in the historical timeline of the play cycle. I began with this play because it is the era of my grandparents. The Detroit of 1949 is not a Detroit I ever got to know. It was a Detroit with a newly arrived Black migrant population from the south. It was a Detroit ripe with promise and business ownership for Black residents. It was a Detroit that had a burgeoning auto industry that was starting to employ Black workers. And it was a Detroit that fostered jazz and bebop long before it fostered Motown.

I heard about this Detroit from my elders, but by the time I grew up, all of the businesses that they told me about were memories. The area of Paradise Valley, that was what I like to call "Detroit's Black Wall Street," had already been bulldozed and re-developed for the Chrysler I–75 Freeway that now runs over its history. When I first wrote this play, I wanted to understand how a place so sacred and so coveted by Black America could be so easily destroyed. The Black Wall Street in Tulsa, Oklahoma was out and right bombed. Detroit's Paradise Valley wasn't directly bombed, but it was quietly imploded. It was leveled through policy and urban planning and aggressively targeted gentrification.

Paradise Blue imagines this thriving community on the brink of the policy that would lead to its inevitable demise. It imagines that gentrification is something that can be stopped by a united community. It also questions what might happen to make someone want to destroy an eco system that so many others thrive in. And what if that person comes from within that eco system? What if not everyone of a village has the same experience of that village?

Paradise Blue is my attempt to look at the multiple layers of what community means. There is a surprise layer in this story that looks at the role of women in a community. How do communities treat Black women? How much could be salvaged by Black women leadership inside of communities? Where do Black women see themselves and their roles in communities, like in *Paradise Blue*, that are dominated by men?

I first premiered the play at the Williamstown Theatre Festival in 2015, and subsequently at Signature Theatre in 2018. The ending changed between the two productions, as the play has moved more definitively into telling a story of women's empowerment inside of community dynamics. Every year, the play strangely becomes more and more current. I'm not sure what that means, but life and art are always interesting mirrors to each other. Communities fighting for their own preservation may never go out of style.

The dramatic tone of the play is noir, because why not? Why can't Black stories be period and play with genre? And perhaps if we can allow ourselves to imagine Black characters inside of genres where we are otherwise found absent, we can also imagine the possibilities and limitless options that Black stories give to Black characters, and ultimately to us all.

Characters

Pumpkin, *Black woman. Late twenties. Pretty in a plain way. Simple. Sweet. Waitress, cook, and caretaker of Paradise Club. A loving thing with a soft touch. Adores poetry.*

Blue, *Black man. Early to mid-thirties. Handsome. Mysterious. Sexy. Quiet danger. Aloof. A hard shell and a hard interior. Battling many demons. A gifted trumpeteer.*

Corn, *Black man. Late forties to Early fifties. Slightly chubby (aka Cornelius). Easygoing and thoughtful. A real sweetheart with a weakness for love. The pianoman.*

P-Sam, *Black man. Mid- to late thirties. Busybody. Sweet-talker (aka Percussion Sam). Hustler. Always eager for his next gig. The percussionist.*

Silver, *Black woman. Mid- to late thirties. Mysterious. Sexy. Charming. Spicy woman. Gritty and raw in a way that men find irresistible. Has a meeeeaaaannnn walk.*

Setting

Detroit, Michigan (in a small Black community formerly known as Black Bottom, on the downtown strip known as Paradise Valley). Paradise Club. 1949.

Notes on Production

Paradise Blue had its world premiere at Williamstown Theatre Festival (Mandy Greenfield, artistic director; Stephen M. Kaus, producer) opening on July 23, 2015. The director was Ruben Santiago-Hudson, the stage manager Lloyd Davis, Jr, the set designer Neil Patel, the costume designer Clint Ramos, the lighting designer Rui Rita, the sound designer Darron West, the co-composers were Kenny Rampton and Bill Simms, Jr. The cast was as follows:

Pumpkin	Kristolyn Lloyd
Blue	Blair Underwood
Silver	De'Adre Aziza
P-Sam	André Holland
Corn	Keith Randolph Smith

Paradise Blue was subsequently produced off-Broadway in New York City by Signature Theatre (Paige Evans, artistic director, Harold Wolpert, executive director, James Houghton, founder), opening on May 14, 2018. The cast was as follows:

Pumpkin	Kristolyn Lloyd
Blue	J. Alphonse Nicholson
Silver	Simone Missick
P-Sam	Francois Battiste
Corn	Keith Randolph Smith

Paradise Blue released on Audible (Kate Navin, Artistic Producer, Audible Theatre) on March 25, 2020.

Act One

Prologue

In darkness:

A trumpet wails a painful tune. It is long and sorrowful. Almost a dirge.

At rise:

A soft light comes up on **Blue**. *He is silhouetted with his trumpet in hand. The source behind the trumpet wail. Beads of sweat dance down his face as his notes pierce the air.*

The trumpet sings as the tune becomes increasingly beautiful.

Then suddenly, a white light washes over **Blue**. *He plays a long note. It is the most beautiful note we've ever heard.*

Finally he stops. Stands there . . . dripping from sweat. Crying.

White light over him gets even brighter. He smiles—overcome with peace.

A gunshot.

Blackout.

Scene One

Lights up on an empty nightclub, This is Paradise. A sign in the window that says so is unlit.

A cardboard sign in the window says "BASSIST WANTED—ASK FOR BLUE."

A second cardboard sign in the window says "ROOMS UPSTAIRS AVAILABLE FOR RENT—ASK FOR BLUE."

Chairs are mounted on tables. A bar is stage left. Stools are mounted atop. A heap of swept trash sits in the middle of the floor with an abandoned broom nearby.

Pumpkin, *a young, pretty, simple woman in her twenties, enters from the kitchen with a dustpan in one hand. And a book of poetry in another.*

She reads with complete engagement . . . doing an odd job of trying to sweep up the trash without losing her page as she reads the following:

Pumpkin (*reciting aloud*)
    The heart of a woman goes forth with the dawn,
    As a lone bird, soft winging, so restlessly on,
    Afar o'er life's turrets and vales does it roam
    In the wake of those echoes the heart calls home

She carries the dustpan over to the trash can, and tries pitifully to balance it all. A trail of trash spills along the way.

> The heart of a woman falls back with the night,
> And enters some alien cage—

She notices the trash that she's spilled.

Ah fudge.

She doubles back and sweeps it up. Proceeds to the can again. Engulfed in the poetry.

> And enters some alien cage in its plight,
> And tries to forget it has dreamed of the stars
> While it—

More trash spilled. She scoops up the trash. Drops the book.

(*As swear words*) Mother fudge and grits!

She picks up the book. Carefully balances the trash and the book. Heads closer to the trash can.

> And tries to forget it has dreamed of the stars
> While it-breaks,
> breaks,
> breaks
> on the sheltering bar.

Finally she dumps the trash into the trash can. The book falls in as well.

Fudge grits and jam!

She digs into the large trash can to retreive the book. She wipes it free of food and other garbage nasties and flips through the pages.

My greatest apologies, missus . . . (*She reads the name on the cover.*) . . . Missus Georgia Douglas Johnson. I would never purposefully treat your beautiful words like Paradise Valley trash. No, ma'am.

Your words don't deserve none of yesterday's apple tart or steak and peas. And certainly it don't deserve none of Corn's peanut shells or Blue's broken whiskey bottles. Your words deserve to be memorized by every waking mind in Black Bottom. Yes, ma'am. Pumpkin's gonna recite your words to whoever needs some . . . elegance in their day.

The door to the club opens and **Cornelius** (*aka* **Corn**) *enters, followed by* **Percussion Sam (P-Sam)**. *P-Sam grabs the cardboard sign from the window.*

Corn   Hey there, Pumpkin. Good morning to ya.

Pumpkin   Hey there, Corn. Hey, P-Sam.

P-Sam   Where Blue?

Pumpkin   Left out this mornin'. Had to go take care of some business downtown, he say. Ya'll hungry? Got some coffee and toast in the back.

Corn   That'd be alright with me.

P-Sam *holds out the sign.*

P-Sam   When he put this up?

Pumpkin *looks at the sign.*

Pumpkin   Don't know. Musta done it just this morning. Wasn't there last night.

P-Sam   You see this, Corn? You know what this mean?

Corn   Mean "Goodbye, Joe."

P-Sam   I told you, Corn. Didn't I tell you? A little tiff. Little tiff my backside. You said it was just a little tiff and now we got to find a new bassist.

Corn   I thought it was little.

P-Sam   Ain't nothin' little when it come to Blue. Didn't I tell you? Soon as he get that bit of anger in him, somethin' little always turn into somethin' jumbo size. I told you.

Pumpkin   He done fired Joe?

Corn   Blue and Joe got into a little tiff last night—

P-Sam   Little my tailbone.

Corn   Joe wanted more off the top. Wanted Blue to start paying before we play 'steada after.

P-Sam   And what's wrong with that? Ain't nothin' wrong with wanting your money up front—

Corn   But everybody know Blue like it the way Blue like it. Blue been payin' *after* since we been playing together. You don't know cuz you ain't been playin' with him long as me. We been playin' together since he first got this place. I knew his daddy before he left it to him.

P-Sam   That don't mean a hill of beans. If Joe wanna get paid first, ain't nothin' wrong with that.

Corn   Joe don't understand 'bout the way Blue mind work. That's what I'm trying to tell you. Blue don't like nobody questioning his loyalty. Pumpkin know what I'm sayin', don't you Pumpkin?

Pumpkin   I know. Blue like things his way cuz that's the only way he understand. Stuff gotta make sense to him. (*Shift.*) I'm gonna go get your coffee and toast.

She heads into the back.

P-Sam   You know as well as I do that Joe was right. Sometimes Blue make you wait all night 'til he get the money square. By that time the woman you was leavin' with done already left with some other moe. He make you wait on his time all the time and it ain't right. Joe just speakin' his mind . . . and good for him, Corn. Good for Joe.

Corn   I'm just tellin' ya Blue got a type of organization to his mind. Joe confusing a lot of that organization. Way Blue see it, waitin' till *after* to pay us make sure we stick around to play. Make it feel like we done earned somethin' by the end of the night. That's the way his daddy taught him. He not seein' the side about it that make you lose your woman to some other cat. That's all Blue see is what he been taught. You just got to understand him, Sam.

P-Sam   I ain't got to understand nothin', Corn. Blue's spot ain't the only jazz spot in town, y'know? This is Paradise Valley. It ain't nothin' but jazz spots all over Black Bottom. And to tell you the truth, they doin' much better for business lately than this spot here.

Corn   This one of the first though. One of the original spots in Black Bottom. Called Paradise 'fore this lil' strip was even called Paradise Valley. Blue like to say Paradise Valley took its name from him.

P-Sam   See? That's what I'm talkin' about. What kinda sense do that make? Paradise Valley ain't takin' nothin' from Blue. He think he the original. He ain't nothin' but everyday ordinary. Same name is a coincidence. That's all it is.

Corn   This spot was named Paradise first though.

P-Sam   What kinda coffee you be havin' in the mornin', Corn? What Pumpkin put in that toast you be havin' everyday? Some kinda Blue-don't-do-no-wrong magic dope or somethin'?

Corn *laughs.* **Pumpkin** *enters with a tray of food.*

Pumpkin   Whipped up some eggs right quick for you too. Here you go, fellas. Something to start your mornin' off nice.

Corn *grabs a plate eagerly.* **P-Sam** *doesn't budge.*

Corn   Thank you kindly, Pumpkin. Sure is nice of you.

Pumpkin   P-Sam, ain't you hungry? The eggs is scrambled hard not soft—just like you like 'em.

P-Sam   No thank you, Pumpkin. Whatever Corn's eating, I'm gonna stay clear of.

Corn   I'll take his.

He reaches over and scrapes **P-Sam***'s plate onto his.*

Pumpkin   Did I do somethin' wrong? I thought you mighta been hungry. That's why I whipped up some eggs too.

Corn   No, Pumpkin, you did just fine. These eggs taste delicious.

P-Sam   I'm sorry, Pumpkin. I'll take that coffee though. I just need somethin' to keep me woke up. Blue got us rehearsing early and he ain't even here.

Pumpkin Should be back in a little bit. Just ran downtown for a sec. (*Beat.*) Hey there, Corn, I got a new one for you. Wanna hear it?

Corn Love to.

Pumpkin You too, P-Sam?

P-Sam Sure, Pumpkin. We got time to kill. What you got?

Pumpkin Kay. Almost got it memorized. (*Hands* **Corn** *the book.*) Hold this, Corn. In case I forget.

Corn Alright. Go'on, Pumpkin.

Pumpkin
The heart of a woman goes forth with the dawn,
As a lone bird, soft winging, so restlessly on . . .
Er . . . ummm . . .

Corn Afar?

P-Sam A who?

Pumpkin Oh okay—wait . . . don't tell me . . .
Afar o'er life's turrets and . . . vales does it roam
In the wake of those echoes the heart calls home

Corn That was good there, Pumpkin. Wasn't that good, Sam?

P-Sam That was good alright. Real smart words you got there, Pumpkin. Make it sound real pretty.

Pumpkin They not mine. Miss Georgia Douglas Johnson. They hers.

Corn What's that part she says here? About the heart of a woman goes forth with the dawn as a . . .

Pumpkin Lone bird . . .

Corn What's that mean, Pumpkin?

Pumpkin I think it means . . . well . . . that a woman is just goin' off on her lonesome . . . waitin' for somebody to love her. Somethin' like that, I think.

P-Sam Waiting for somebody to love her, hunh Pumpkin?

Pumpkin (*bashfully*) I think that's what it means . . . maybe.

Corn Well, I thank you, Pumpkin. For the good words and the good eatin'.

He slops up the rest of his food. **P-Sam** *watches* **Pumpkin** *take down chairs and prep the bar.*

He joins her.

P-Sam Lemme help you with these chairs, now.

Pumpkin Oh, it's alright, P-Sam. I can do it.

P-Sam You ain't always got to call me P-Sam, you know?

Pumpkin I like it better than sayin' Percussion Sam all the way out. P-Sam a good nickname.

P-Sam Yeah. Sure, Pumpkin. But it's you and me. It's alright if you just call me Sam. That's what anybody close to me call me.

Pumpkin I . . . feel more . . . proper . . . callin' you P-Sam.

P-Sam Proper?

Pumpkin For Blue. Don't think he'll like it much, me talkin' to you improper. For a lady.

P-Sam It ain't Blue's name. You callin' Blue, you call him whatever he say. But when you callin' my name, you can call me Sam.

Pumpkin Still . . .

She nervously mosies away from **P-Sam**. *He watches her and smiles.*

P-Sam You too sweet, Pumpkin. You got the perfect name for who you is.

The door to the club opens sharply. **Pumpkin** *jumps and moves over to the bar, wiping it down profusely.*

Blue *enters. He is a lion of a man. More in his demeanor than his stature. Thirties and smooth. He walks in and commands attention.*

Blue Where the sign go?

Corn Hey there, Blue.

Blue *sees the cardboard sign that* **P-Sam** *had—laying on the counter.*

Blue Who took down the sign?

Corn We was just lookin' at it. Thought maybe it was a mistake.

Blue Ain't no mistake.

Corn Sam was just lookin' at it.

P-Sam You fired Joe?

Blue Joe quit. I ain't fire nothin'. He quit cuz he's a fool. Good riddance to him.

Corn Quit? What for?

Blue Talkin' 'bout he want solo time. Everybody know this is Blue's Black Bottom Quartet. My club. My band. Ain't nobody gettin' solo time but me. Don't no bassist nowhere get solo time and he think he just gonna change the rules. Joe a fool. Talkin' 'bout he gonna go'on over to the Three Sixes and get picked up over there. I told him go. Three Sixes ain't better than Paradise Club. I don't care how much money they pullin' in. Money ain't quality.

P-Sam How we s'pose to play bop without bass? We can't play without Joe.

Blue We'll replace Joe. And 'til we do, I'm goin' on solo. And Corn, I'm puttin' you on too. You gonna do some old standards with Pumpkin for the intermission act.

Pumpkin Me?

Blue That's right baby. Just for intermission. You gonna be on the stage and sing for me.

Pumpkin But . . . I—

P-Sam What's that mean? Pumpkin and Corn doing standards. You doin' solos? Where's that leave me?

Blue Leave you with a roof over your head upstairs of my club free of charge. That's what it leave you. 'Less you ready to complain about that now.

P-Sam How you gonna play solo with no rhythm section? Who's gonna do your rhythm?

Blue Got a guest band coming in next Friday. Just gonna play with 'em 'til we get back swingin'.

P-Sam Guest band? You bringin' in somebody else to do percussion? What am I supposed to do if I'm not playin'? Sit on empty pockets 'til the cows come home?

Blue Didn't I say it's temporary? You do this 'til we find somebody to replace Joe. And 'til then, I ain't gonna charge you no rent. That's fair as I can think to make it. You know somebody else would do you that?

P-Sam I know somebody else woulda just let Joe have his money upfront and we wouldn't be worryin' 'bout none of this. We need to be out there lookin' for a bassist right now. Ain't one just gonna walk in here outta nowhere.

Blue Then go'on and look for one. I got other things to take care of right now.

Corn You been downtown today?

Blue That's right. Some folks downtown been comin' 'round here to do some business.

Corn Safe Eddie say they been comin' 'round by the Echo Theatre and Wilfred's Billiard Parlor too.

P-Sam Comin' 'round for what? What they comin' 'round for?

Corn Said they been talkin' about that plan. This new mayor 'bout to take office—Mayor Cobo . . . he done ran his campaign on it.

P-Sam The one where they supposed to be clearin' up the slums?

Corn Gettin' rid of the *blight* in the city. That's what he say on the radio.

P-Sam Blight? What's he meanin' by that?

Blue He means these run-down buildings over here on Hastings Street. That's what he means. And I don't blame him none. Some of these places are a real eye sore.

Make all our spots look run down. I hope he get rid of it good and send them low-class niggers back to the outskirts of the city so the rest of us can finally move on up.

Corn Them folks ain't doin' nothin' but living where they can afford. That's all. Ain't they fault some of them buildings is run down. Half of 'em don't even own them buildings. Just payin' what they can afford. Ain't they fault.

Blue Fault don't matter. Long as Black Bottom stay what it is, cramped and overcrowded—we ain't never gonna have what all them White folks got. Niggers always comin' round here askin' for hand-outs and free room and board while they get on they feet. Ain't but so much favors you can do. I rely on these bastards, I'm liable to go bankrupt.

Pumpkin I like it here in Black Bottom. Always got somewhere I can count on folks. Know Buffalo James gonna always offer me some of his corn meal if I run out here. Know Patty Poindexter gonna always give me a press 'n curl whether I got the money to pay her or gotta owe it to her the next time. These folks over here like family. Always got time to pull favors for family.

Blue Ain't nobody pullin' no more favors outta me. I been pullin' favors up to my ears and I'm goin' tone deaf.

Corn What was they tellin' you, Blue? Them folks downtown?

Blue Just come askin' about Paradise. Say the land this club is sittin' on is pretty hot. More footage than the other spots around here. City wants a piece. Maybe offerin' me a pretty penny for it.

Pumpkin You gonna sell Paradise?

Blue I ain't sayin' all that. I just say they come talkin' 'bout it. So I go hear what they got to say. That's all.

P-Sam Ain't this somethin? First you fire Joe and now you gon' put all us on the street if them downtown fellas talk to you right!

Blue Didn't I say I was hearin' what they got to say? Don't be puttin' words in my mouth, you hear me? And I done already told you—Joe quit!

P-Sam Cuz you makin' him quit!

Blue If you don't like it, nigger, then there go the door. Ain't nobody askin' you to stay 'round here.

P-Sam I just might, Blue. Don't go sayin' nothin' just to say it. I just might.

Corn Ain't no need for all that. Percussion Sam and Corn the Pianoman both a part of Blue's Black Bottom Quartet and we know that, Blue. Ain't no need for nobody else to quit.

We gonna find a bassist and be back in business. And 'til then, you go 'head and work on your solo while me and Pumpkin learn ourselves some standards.

Pumpkin But . . . I don't think—

Blue   Sheet music's upstairs. I'll get it and ya'll can practice in back while I get this spot ready for dinner tonight. Ya'll learn it and be ready to go up by next Friday. And in the meantime, Sam can go'on and find us a bassist at Garfield's Lounge he wanna be so ambitious.

P-Sam   You ain't sayin' nothin' but a word.

Blue   Alright then.

The door to the club opens. A mysterious-looking woman dressed in black enters. She wears a hat and veil. This is **Silver**.

Everyone stops and looks at her. She moves like a spider weaving a web. They watch her until she stops.

Silver   Is Blue here?

Everyone looks at **Blue**. *He looks at* **Silver** *questionably.*

Blue   I'm Blue. I know you, lady?

Silver   Naw. But your sign in the window say you got rooms for rent. That true?

Blue   Oh . . . yeah . . . yeah that's true. I got one-person rooms for rent. Not enough space for your ol' man or nothin'.

Silver   My ol' man dead. How much you charge for your rooms?

Blue   Five dollars a week. That include meals.

Silver   Five dollars a week? That ain't comparable. Place up the street got rooms for three dollars a week.

Blue   Place up the street ain't got nice hot water every day for you neither. Go'on ask folks—you think I'm lying. Lay down for a nice sleep and wake up to a roach openin' your blinds and askin' you how you like yo' grits.

Silver   Your rooms clean?

Blue   Pristine. Pumpkin see to that.

Silver   Pumpkin?

Pumpkin *stares at* **Silver** *in awe . . . and suddenly snaps out of it.*

Pumpkin   Oh yes, missus. I keep it nice and tidy for you and I starch your sheets clean. If you need anything, you can always let me know and I'll see to it for you.

Blue   Place up the street ain't got that for you. But you go'on stay up there if you think they better than what we got over here.

Silver   And what about playin' that bop? You keep late hours?

Blue   We keep as late hours as any of these other clubs in Paradise Valley. You in Black Bottom, Detroit. And this lil' strip is what we call the jazz paradise. You don't like bop or blues, you got a long way to go 'fore you find some place without it.

Silver   I ain't said I ain't like it. I know where I'm at. (*Pause.*) What if I wanna stay longer than a week?

Blue   Long as you can pay, you can stay.

Silver   Well, then . . .

She digs into her bosom and pulls out a wad of cash. Everyone watches her in astonishment.

She hands money to **Blue**.

Silver   That's thirty dollars. I want the month and then some . . .

Blue *counts the cash twice over . . . eyeing it widely.*

Blue   Go'on with her, Pumpkin. Show this woman where the room at.

Pumpkin   Alright then . . . you can follow me, missus . . . You got a name?

Silver   They call me Silver.

Pumpkin   Silver? Well, alright, follow me, Miss Silver.

Silver *follows* **Pumpkin** *out.*

P-Sam *and* **Corn** *look after them.*

P-Sam   Whooo! You see that woman?

Corn   Seen her, I did.

P-Sam   She got some kinda walk on her, ain't she?

Blue   She got some kinda money on her. You see her pull this out that fast? Somethin' ain't right about that.

Corn   What ain't right about it? She look right to me.

Blue   What a woman doin' comin' here with no ol' man? You hear that? Talkin' bout "My ol' man dead." Say it just like that, without no feelin' or nothin'. Somethin' ain't right about it.

P-Sam   She ain't got no man and she got a walk like that, she ain't gonna be in that one-person room too long.

Corn   She got some kinda sadness to her maybe.

Blue   Whatever she is, she better not bring no trouble up here in Paradise. Woman like that . . . lookin' the way she lookin' . . . all on her lonesome . . . . them kinda women ain't nothin' but trouble. You betta believe that.

P-Sam   Well, a little bit of trouble ain't never hurt nobody really. (*Shift.*) I'm gon get on. Since we ain't rehearsing no more, I'ma go try my luck with the Policy. Maybe if I bet just right, my number'll come up and I won't have to worry 'bout having no gig right now. (*Hmph.*) Joe quit . . .

He heads on out the door.

Blue Corn, that nigger gonna try me. I'm tellin' you. That P-Sam ain't worth the trust I'd give a honkie on a Tuesday.

Corn He alright, Blue. We gonna find us somebody that's gonna turn things around here. You'll see.

Blue Yeah, I'll see. (*Shift.*) Gonna get you that sheet music for Pumpkin. You got to help her sing it right.

Corn Alright, Blue. If that's what you need.

Blue That's what I need, Corn. She be scared and nervous . . . but you help her. I hear her humming and singing soft, and it sound real pretty. She got a voice in her. But you got to help it come out. You the only one can ease it out of her. You get me?

Corn Yeah I get you, Blue.

Blue Good, Corn. That's good.

He exits.

Corn (*softly*) I may be the only one who do get you. . . .

Lights shift . . .

Scene Two

In **Silver***'s room. It's rather plain. Just a twin bed. A small vanity. One tall drawer. Maybe a hanging broken framed pic. That's all, folks.*

Pumpkin *makes the bed while* **Silver** *unpacks.*

Pumpkin . . . and the meals regular—breakfast, lunch, and dinner. So you just gotta let me know if you eatin' every night or if you gettin' your meal somewhere else. Best meal is supper. I'm usually 'lowed to give three sides 'steada two. So I switch it up. Corn hash with roast beef and string beans, cabbage, and cranberry sauce . . . or sometimes we do steak and peas with mashed potato and gravy—Blue count gravy as a side on that one—and on Fridays we usually do the fish fry with some kinda potato and greens. We got hot sauce packets but we charge a penny if you want more than two. And—

Silver *stares at* **Pumpkin**.

Pumpkin Whatsthematter? Am I talkin' your ear off? Blue say I could talk a hole in your head if don't nobody tell me to hush.

Silver You do the cookin'?

Pumpkin Yes, missus. I'm a real good cook.

Silver Umph. I hate cookin'.

Pumpkin Do you?

Silver   With a passion. Can't stand the heat of nobody else's kitchen. I prefer the heat in the bedroom or some other places. But not in the kitchen. That's the wrong kinda heat for me.

Pumpkin   Oh. (*Short pause.*) Well, it's good I'll do it for you then. No worries there.

Silver *pulls out a record player and sets it atop the dresser. Pulls out a couple of records.*

Pumpkin   My goodness. You travel with that thing?

Silver   Can't be one place and my music someplace else. Go crazy otherwise . . .

She pulls out a silky nightgown and holds it up to herself in the mirror. **Pumpkin** *watches in astonishment.*

This thing . . . ain't worth the rocks in my shoes. Silk my tailbone. This some kinda imposter fabric if I ever seen it. I knew that man sold it to me was lyin', but the store lights wasn't harsh as these. I can see real good now. Cheap rayon maybe. Not no silk.

Pumpkin   I think it's pretty.

Silver   It's yours then.

She tosses it to **Pumpkin** *nonchalantly, and continues to unpack her clothes.*

Pumpkin   Oh! No—missus I couldn't—

Silver   Sho you can.

Pumpkin   But it's yours.

Silver   Not no more. Don't like the thing.

Pumpkin   But, I—

Silver   So which one of them fellas your ol' man?

Pumpkin   Oh—well, me and Blue are together—

Silver   'Course you are. He the one who runnin' everything. (*Shift.*) So them other two fellas . . . they up for grabs then?

Pumpkin   Well . . . I mean . . . I wouldn't know . . .

Silver   That mean they are. If they wasn't, you would know. Believe me that.

Pumpkin   What brings you over here to Black Bottom?

Silver   Time to pick up somewhere new. I heard of Black Bottom Detroit. 'Specially down this strip in Paradise Valley where folks got all they own business. If it's somewhere that Colored folks is doing more than sharecroppin' and reapin' White folks' harvest . . . I ought to be there. They say that here's where folks sellin' automobiles and bettin' on the Policy numbers and dancin' in the nighttime like they just as free as the Mississippi river. I'm here so I can get a taste of all that.

Pumpkin   Where you come from?

Silver   Lots of places. But Louisiana be the first.

Pumpkin   Louisiana? Place where they got all them spirits and Negroes eatin' live chickens and drinkin' they blood?

Silver *looks at* **Pumpkin** *questionably.*

Silver   You ain't never been, have you?

Pumpkin   No, miss. Never been outside Detroit.

Silver   Well, maybe you oughta leave sometime. And when you do, try out Louisiana.

Pumpkin   I love it here in Black Bottom. I don't never wanna leave.

Silver   That so? Why's that?

Pumpkin   Got roots here. And purpose.

Silver   Got family here?

Pumpkin   Made family here. Was sent here as a girl to stay with my aunt who run her own beauty parlor on Hastings St. Used to work for her and attend school over there. She passed on now, and the parlor been turned into an automobile store. But I stayed around here. With different women what used to be her customers. They took care of me. Even helped to pay for my books. And eventually I met Blue.

Silver   And the rest was history, hunh?

Pumpkin   Yes, ma'am.

Silver   Well, it's good you made you some roots here, but every woman got to pick up and leave after while. If you don't know that now, you gonna know it one day.

Pumpkin (*remembering*)
   The heart of a woman goes forth with the dawn . . .

Silver   What's that?

Pumpkin   A little bit of poetry. Just made me think of it.

Silver   You a poet? Like them fellas in Harlem?

Pumpkin   No not me. I just like it, that's all. What you said about a woman pickin' up and leavin' . . . remind me of some poetry. It say—"The heart of a woman goes forth with the dawn . . ." I suppose that's what you doin'.

Silver   Well, that's fancy of you. Recitin' poems like that from your memory. Maybe that's somethin' you can learn me how to do.

Pumpkin   Oh. (*Bashful smile.*) Sure . . .

Silver *finishes putting her clothes away. Takes off her shirt and bottoms nonchalantly—leaving her in striking undergarments. Sprays herself with perfume.* **Pumpkin** *stares at her, fascinated.*

Silver   This fella of yours . . . he be good to you?

Pumpkin   Blue. He's something special. Gifted.

Silver   That wasn't my question.

Pumpkin   I'm sorry?

Silver   I say, he be good to you? That's important to ask a woman 'bout a man. I done learned.

Pumpkin   He the best thing I've ever known.

Silver   That so?

Pumpkin   Yes, missus. Got a gentle heart and a lion's soul. Got the will to give me everything he can. But what he really got is a gift. It make it so sometimes that's all I can see. When he play, I think he's talkin' to God and together they answerin' my prayers.

Silver   Weelll . . . he must do you real good—up, down, and inside . . . way you speak on him like ecstasy.

Pumpkin   My goodness. You always speak this improper?

Silver   What's improper 'bout it? I'm just speakin' straight. Ain't that what these Detroit gangsters do? Speak straight.

Pumpkin   Why a woman need to speak like a gangster?

Silver (*seriously*)   So everybody know she ain't to be messed with.

Beat.

I can get me one of them nice hot suppers you was talkin' 'bout this evening?

Pumpkin   Oh . . . yes, missus. 'Round eight o'clock. I'll be by to deliver it to you.

Silver   That's fine by me. Now if you don't mind, I got to finish messin' with my things and get into somethin' comfortable.

Pumpkin   Oh—right.

She moves to the door with a touch of embarrassment.

If you need anything else, you just ring me and I'll take care of you. Phone booth is in the hallway out there. But I'm usually downstairs.

Silver   Be sure to.

Pumpkin *opens the door.*

Silver   And don't forget this. It's yours now.

She throws **Pumpkin** *the nightgown.*

Pumpkin—*clueless on what to do—nods and disappears behind the door.*

Silver *watches after her for a moment . . . calculatingly.*

Then she sits down at the vanity, and dolls herself up for the night.

Scene Three

Afternoon sun spills through Paradise Club. **Corn** *sits at the bar and demolishes a hearty meal.*

Pumpkin *wipes down the bar and fills the liquor stock. Occasionally, she winces from a pain in her wrist. No one notices.*

Corn   Pumpkin, you put your foot in this cornbread.

Pumpkin   Not supposed to give it to you 'til supper, but I thought maybe you could have a light taste. For listenin' to my poetry and all . . .

Corn   You keep fillin' me up with this stuff, I listen to a hundred of your poems. Hit me.

Pumpkin *eagerly rushes to the bar and picks up a book. She passes it to* **Corn**.

Pumpkin   This one she calls "My Little Dreams."

Corn   She who?

Pumpkin   Miss Georgia Douglas Johnson. My latest favorite. Goes like this . . . .
  I'm folding up my little dreams
  Within my heart tonight
  And praying I may soon forget
  The torture of their sight.
  For time's deft fingers scroll my brow
  With fell relentless art—
  I'm folding up my little dreams
  Tonight, within my heart.

Corn   What kind of fingers is that, Pumpkin? Say it scroll on the brow?

Pumpkin   Deft. Means like, you know, how somebody got good knittin' hands? Fingers got lots of skill. That's what time got. Deft fingers. And you ever known how somebody rubbin' on your head, say a woman maybe? And she maybe smooth your eyebrow some . . .

Corn   I ain't know that in a long time. Not since my Mabel passed.

Pumpkin   Well, that's what Miss Johnson means in her poetry. Time massaging her like your Mabel used to do you. She bury her dreams in her heart so she don't have to think on 'em or be sad no more. Like your Mabel.

Corn   Yeah. I buried her alright. I know what that Miss Johnson mean. Bury something deep inside so you can forget the hurt of not havin' it.

Pumpkin That's right, Corn. That's real good. You're a regular poet. An interpreter. That's what you are.

Corn Naw, Pumpkin. That's you and this stuff. I just like to listen with you cuz it's somethin' different. We got the piano. Got the trumpet. Got the percussion. Used to have the bass. Then you come with these words and bring in another kind of music.

The door to the club swings open. In walks **P-Sam**.

P-Sam Hey there, folks.

Corn Hey, Sam.

Pumpkin Afternoon, P-Sam.

P-Sam (*flirtatious*) Hey, Pumpkin pie. Got a little somethin' for me to nibble on?

Pumpkin Today we got sandwiches for lunch. Bologna and salami. I'll go make you one.

P-Sam What's that Corn was eating over here? That don't look like no crumbs from a sandwich.

Corn Yes it was, wasn't it, Pumpkin? Sandwich with the works.

Pumpkin *giggles.*

P-Sam Oh, I get it. Corn get to taste an early dinner and all I get is a measly salami sandwich.

Pumpkin I'll go put some pickles on it too . . .

P-Sam Well, la-ti-da. I'm gon' jump out my shoes cuz I get pickles.

Pumpkin *disappears to the back.*

P-Sam Say, Corn, I found us somebody.

Corn Did you?

P-Sam String-Finger Charlie over at Garfield's Lounge. Caught his set last night and it's outta sight. Talked to him—say he lookin' to leave Percy's quintet if Blue willin' to meet his fee. Percy payin' them overtime if the set runs late.

Corn Don't know if Blue gonna go for that now, Sam. You know he don't believe in overtime.

P-Sam Blue don't believe in nothin' but himself. Where I'm s'pose to play, Corn? Ain't no openings for a drummer at none of these other clubs in the valley.

Corn You a good musician, Sam. You can get your pick anywhere.

P-Sam Don't give me that, Corn. Ain't no place for a Colored man outside of Black Bottom and you know it. I been on that other stint, playin' the White man's club in Detroit and all them other cities—entering through the back door. Carryin' my card in Harlem and if I ain't got it, I ain't allowed to make no bread or play no music. Standin' on them stages and smilin' like I'm just happy to be entertainin' these no

Act One, Scene Three   33

count crackers that think of me as less than the spilled whiskey on they shoe.

Corn   We all been on that stint, Sam. One time or another. That's the cost we pay to play.

P-Sam   Tell you the truth, Corn, Blue ain't no better. He think of us just like they do. On the bottom. Only difference is he still a nigger himself, whether he like it or not, and stingy as he is, he need us. And we need each other. That's why we got to get back in business.

This the only place I can be a percussion man befo' bein' Colored. You the only one can talk to Blue, Corn.

Corn   I don't know String-Finger Charlie. How good is he?

P-Sam   Seen 'im last night do this thing ain't never seen a bassman do befo'. Tap on the strings like a hammer and make two strings play by themselves. Tellin' you—this cat's outta sight.

Corn   Maybe I'll go over to Garfield's Lounge with you tonight and see for myself.

P-Sam   You do that, Corn. And then you talk to Blue. I can't be sittin' here with no money swellin' my pockets. When a Negro man ain't got no money, it's like he smell different. Negro women sniff him miles away and turn they noses in another direction. I'm funky, Corn. It ain't right.

Corn   I'll see. That's all I can say.

P-Sam   That's all you need to say for now. (*Shift.*) How that rehearsin' with Pumpkin goin'?

Corn *looks back to see if* **Pumpkin** *is near. Coast is clear.*

Corn   Terrible.

P-Sam   She that bad?

Corn   Worse.

P-Sam   Well, I guess you can't have it all. Be all smart on them books, and sing like you know the devil up close and personal.

Corn   I don't know what to tell Blue 'bout it. He say he done heard her sing pretty but I ain't heard it yet. Ain't got the heart to make her feel bad. But she workin' and workin' and sound like she gettin' worser and worser.

P-Sam   Well, serve Blue right, then. Put her up there and see what kinda mess it is, and then maybe he'll see the light.

Corn   I hope he see befo' Friday. He say she got a voice in her somewhere. But I can't find it nowhere.

The door to Paradise Club swings open. **Blue** *walks in, zoot suit and hat. Lookin' sharp.*
Carrying his trumpet.

Corn Afternoon, Blue. You lookin' like Sunday on a Tuesday. Where you comin' from?

Blue Just out takin' care of business. Where Pumpkin?

Corn In the back fixin' P-Sam a sandwich.

Blue (*to* **P-Sam**) You pay her?

P-Sam I thought I was gettin' room and board free 'til we get more gigs?

Blue Board ain't meals.

P-Sam What's board if it ain't meals?! Include meals for everybody else.

Blue Everybody else payin'. I'm lettin' you stay up there for free. Don't mean I can afford to feed you with no money. You ain't suckin' me dry.

P-Sam How I'm supposed to bring in money when you runnin' off musicians every chance you get?

Blue Don't start with me on that, nigger. I ain't startin' in with you today.

P-Sam Listen to that. You hear that, Corn? He ain't startin' in with me. But he the one startin' everything.

Pumpkin *enters with the sandwich.*

Pumpkin Here ya go, P-Sam. I made it with pickles and hot sauce too.

Blue You charge him the penny for the hot sauce?

Pumpkin Well . . . no . . . not this time. We had a little extra so—

Blue We done been through this, Pumpkin . . . you can't keep passin' out favors like this is some kinda soup kitchen.

P-Sam You go'on, Pumpkin. You keep that sandwich, hear? I ain't got to eat nothin' from this penny-pinchin' pistol.

Pumpkin Blue, sweets, if he don't eat it it's just gonna go to waste. Might as well not let no food hit the trash. Ain't that what you told me?

Blue Give him the sandwich. But you got to pay sometime. This ain't no soup kitchen. You give niggers one and they want two. Tell 'em free room and they want free meals too.

P-Sam Sam don't need nothin' for free, hear?

Pumpkin Here you go, P-Sam. Eat up. I made it real fine. Gonna go back and get you somethin' to wash it down with too.

Pumpkin *exits into the kitchen.* **P-Sam** *picks up his sandwich and bites into it rebelliously.*

P-Sam Sam willin' to work for everything he got. Don't need no hand-outs. But you got me over here without no gig—

Blue Thought you was takin' care of that.

P-Sam I am. Ain't that right, Corn?

Corn We gonna go tonight to check out somebody s'posed to be real good.

Blue How that song comin' with you and Pumpkin?

Corn Oh it's . . . . goin' . . . special. Pumpkin's voice is . . . somethin' I can't even . . . explain . . .

Blue Good. You just gotta get her to some confidence. I can hear the music in her speak. You just gotta push it out of her. Woman like Pumpkin need a little push . . .

Corn We gonna . . . push . . . much as we can . . .

Blue That bad-luck woman been down here today?

Corn That fiiiine woman.

P-Sam Make you wanna follow wherever she lead . . .

Blue Don't go followin' her less you wanna end up in a grave somewhere.

Corn What you talkin' now, Blue?

Blue She already the talk of the town and ain't been here three days.

Corn What they sayin'?

Blue Just what I was thinkin'. Woman move up here without no man got trouble followin' her. Sittin' on a stack of money. Say she killed a man for it.

Corn Killed a man?

P-Sam I ain't heard that. But Jimmy the Greek Johnson over at the Poolhall was sayin' she done slept with over fifty men in different cities and they all disappeared.

Corn You listenin' to Jimmy the Greek? You know he ain't never told a truth in his natural life.

Blue This time I believe it. I'm tellin' you. I don't trust that woman.

P-Sam What woman do you trust?

Blue Don't start in on me, nigger.

P-Sam Say they call her a witch.

Corn Witch?

Blue A voodoo woman from Louisiana. That's what she is.

P-Sam Spiderwoman. That's what they call her. Say she been to Chicago and Minneapolis and Milwaukee too. All them places, she go walkin' like that . . . some kinda sexy spider . . . lurin' fellas into her web. And then just when you get close to her . . . she stick into you and lay her poison.

Corn (*laughing*) If ya'll don't sound like two of the silliest cats to ever play bop . . .

Blue   You laugh if you want to, Corn . . . but you be the first one to get caught in her web. Then you touch her one time and your longleg fall right off. Them Louisiana women got them spirits in them.

Silver *enters from the kitchen, unbeknownst to the men.*

P-Sam   You got to admit you curious about a lil' of it. But I like my longleg too much to take a bet on that. I rather try my luck with the Policy.

Silver   Afternoon, fellas.

The men jump. **Silver** *smiles a sexy, sinful smile. She spider-walks over to the bar and takes a seat.*

Silver   Hope I'm not interruptin' your man-talk. But I was promised me a taste of early dinner and I want to cash in.

Blue   We got sandwiches. Pumpkin be back out and take care of you.

Silver   I look like the kind of woman eat sandwiches?

Blue *glares at* **Silver**.

Blue   That's what you eatin'/ you eatin' here.

Silver (*to* **Corn**)   Say there, buttercup. You got a light?

Corn   Me?

Silver   I don't see nobody else over there lookin' cute and chubby.

Corn (*smiling*)   Well . . . I don't smoke none.

Blue *slides her some matches.*

Silver   Thanks, doll.

She lights the cigarette and takes a slow drag. They watch her silently.

You ought to have yourself a lighter. Every business owner got one of them. Personalized and inscripted. You ought to have that.

Blue   I got what I need.

Silver   That's what everybody think . . . 'til what they really need come along . . . (*Shift.*) You fellas read the paper?

Blue   You want the paper, you got to go'on over to Biddy's restaurant and spend your penny like everybody else. That don't come with the board.

Silver   Oh, I got my paper for the day. Been doin' my reading too. See what this new mayor of yours got plannin' for this Black Bottom area. Tryin' to clean it up, I see.

P-Sam   That's right, ma'am. They lookin' for folks like us to get on outta here so they can hurry up and make Detroit bright white. But we ain't goin' nowhere, so you don't worry your pretty lil' self 'bout that.

Silver Well, I just figures . . . when a city want folks to leave, they must be offerin' somethin' pretty to get rid of 'em. And you especially, sittin' on the ripest piece of somethin' over here.

Say the square footage of your land bigger 'n all the other spots in this whole Valley. This spot dead in the middle and in the best location.

Blue What of it?

Silver I just wonder what they offerin' for a place as hot as this.

Blue What's it matter to you?

Silver Don't matter nothin' yet. Could matter a whole lot if you was interested in sellin'.

Blue You think I'm gonna sell my place?

Corn Blue ain't partin' with this club. This used to be his daddy's club.

Blue Leave my daddy outta this, Corn. Miss, you can keep your side-steppin' slick talk cuz it ain't shakin' over here. Paradise Club is mine, and I ain't talkin' 'bout my plans with no simple woman.

Silver Cool down, sugar. I'm just makin' small talk.

Blue Ain't nothin' to talk about. Stuff you hearin' 'bout Paradise Club ain't nothin' but hearsay. Niggers runnin' off at the mouth cuz they ain't got nothin' better to do than worry 'bout Blue. But it ain't none of nobody's business what I do with my own spot.

Silver Sho, it is. What you do with yo' spot might be real influential to all others. Seem like what you do be everybody business. So you let me know if there's anything worth talkin' 'bout.

Blue You think you know somethin' I don't?

Silver I know 'bout how to run a club.

P-Sam Where you know all that?

Silver Come from music. My daddy was a bluesman. Grew up 'round all this type of business. And I could tell you why that Garfield's Lounge and the Three Sixes gonna keep having way more customers than over here . . . even though you got the bigger joint.

P-Sam Why's that?

Corn Sam—

Silver Chargin' too much at the door.

Blue I charge what I charge.

P-Sam What you think it oughta be?

Silver Should only be fifty cents. But you makin' it a whole seventy-five. Too high. Folks see that and don't care that you got the better trumpeteer or the best pecan pie. They feel like they bein' kept on the outskirts. All the other spots make 'em feel welcome. But here, it feel like everybody don't belong. Like even if we all the same people, only certain kinds get to come in and patron. You dividin' the people like pie. That's what make it not feel right.

Blue I ain't askin' for your business help. I been runnin' this place for five years just fine.

Silver Five years ain't nothin'. I seen goldfish last longer than five years. Five years still wet behind the ears if you ask—

Blue *bangs his hand on the bar. Everyone jumps a bit.*

Corn Blue.

Blue (*threateningly*) Watch your mouth in my spot, woman.

Corn Hey now, Blue—

Blue *walks closer to* **Silver**.

Blue Don't you think you 'bout to come in here and tell me how to run my place. You ain't been in this town five seconds and you think you know 'bout over here in Black Bottom?

Silver *remains calm. She smiles and puffs her cigarette.*

Silver I just thought you'd like to hear another idea, sugar. No need to get so uptight.

Blue You listen to me here. You come down here, you keep your mouth shut unless you wanna be out of a room. Don't think just cuz you got a stash somewhere that make you matter over here. It don't. I'll throw this money back in your face, put you out on your simple Black ass, and won't think twice about it. You understand me, woman?

Pumpkin *enters from the kitchen.*

Pumpkin Everything alright out here? Blue, sweets, you okay?

Blue *moves away from* **Silver** *and grabs his hat.*

Blue Pumpkin, come on and let's get you somethin' to wear for Friday night. Gotta find you somethin' classy for when you sing with Corn.

Pumpkin (*hesitantly*) But don't you want me to . . . finish gettin' dinner together for this evenin'? And I still gotta mop the kitchen and change the sheets upstairs—

Blue Forget about all that right now. We'll take care of that later. Just grab your coat and meet me in the back. We take the streetcar on down to J. L. Hudson's and pick you out something nice.

Pumpkin J. L. Hudson's? We goin' down Woodward?!

Blue   That's right. For my woman—only the biggest and the fanciest department store in the city. Grab your coat and come on.

P-Sam   J. L. Hudson's? They only 'low niggers to clean they floors and run they elevators. What kinda nigger you think you is to go shoppin' there?

Blue   They don't let niggers like you shop there. I ain't you.

Pumpkin   Oh, Blue! You think we can afford it?

Blue   Don't worry 'bout what we can afford, woman! Just come on and let me get you somethin'.

Pumpkin *rushes over to grab her coat from the rack. She lifts it and a pain stabs her wrist. She flinches.*

Silver *notices, as does* **Corn**.

Corn   You alright there, Pumpkin?

Pumpkin   Oh, I'm just fine. Little soreness of my wrists. Get that way sometimes when I been cleanin' a lot. Just need to soak 'em in some salts and I be fine.

Silver   Get you a box a raisins and a pint of gin.

P-Sam   Say what?

Silver   Louisiana remedy. My grandmama taught it to me. Soak the raisins in a half pint of gin and watch all the pain go away.

P-Sam   What's the other half pint of gin for?

Silver   In case of anything else you need to cure.

Blue   Pumpkin don't need none of your backwater Louisiana hoodoo. She'll be just fine.

He moves to **Pumpkin**'s *side and helps her in her coat.*

Blue   When we get back, Corn, ya'll get back to practicin'.

Corn   Sure, Blue. Whatever you say . . .

Blue *and* **Pumpkin** *exit.*

P-Sam   Say, Corn, we should head over to Garfield's 'round eight to see my man String-Finger Charlie.

Corn   I'll be ready.

Silver   Heard they serving a sweet potato pie over at that Lounge tonight that taste better than your Aunt Harriet's.

P-Sam   You want to come have a taste, baby?

Silver   That's alright, sugar. I was plannin' on stayin' on my lonesome this evening.

P-Sam Suit yourself, sweetheart. I'm gon' go put my bet in for the Policy. You got a favorite number, baby? Maybe I'll play it for you.

Silver One three one.

P-Sam One three one? How you gonna tell me something like that? One three one? You tryin' to curse me?

He heads for the door, disgruntled.

I'll see you later, Corn. (*Hmph/mumbling.*) One three one . . . crazy woman . . .

Silver *turns and smiles to* **Corn**.

Silver What's got him so uptight?

Corn You just gave him a number with thirteen in it. Nobody plays thirteen. It's an omen.

Silver Oh . . . I just gave him my old address. One three one Rue Decatur in Nawlins (*New Orleans*). Men round here just act so fussy 'bout every little thang.

Corn That's just the way these fellas are. Don't pay them no nevermind, miss. I think you were mighty nice—offerin' up your address to him like that. Let him find his own good luck.

Silver *smiles at* **Corn**. *She rises from her seat.*

Silver Say there, buttercup . . . You're a real sweet fella. I can see that from here.

Corn Thank you, miss. Name's Cornelius. But I like buttercup just the same.

Silver Well, you can call me whatever you like.

She heads for the door.

Enjoy that sweet potato pie tonight. And if it's as good as they say, you let me know, will ya?

Corn I surely will.

Silver *winks at* **Corn**, *does her spider walk, and exits.* **Corn** *sits and smiles after her.*

Scene Four

Nighttime falls on the club. Moonlight peeks through the window.

In silhouette, **Blue** *plays his trumpet. It is a beautiful and painful melody. Long, sorrowful notes.*

Soft lights illuminate the rest of the club, and reveal **Pumpkin** *putting up chairs. Somewhere in his tune, she leaves one chair down near the foot of the stage, and takes a seat. Listening.*

Blue—*in his own world*—*becomes too wrapped in his pain. Suddenly he breaks free of the tune.*

He stops and wipes his face . . . from sweat . . . or tears . . . or both . . .

Pumpkin *applauds.*

Pumpkin   That sounded real good.

Blue   Don't clap for that. Don't ever clap for that.

Pumpkin   But . . . it was good.

Blue   Mediocre. I lost my rhythm. Let it take over. Ain't never s'pose to let it take over.

Pumpkin   That ain't nothin' but the pain swoopin' in on you. That's what makes it the most beautiful, I think. The pain is the sweetest part.

Blue   It's weak. Need to practice more steada runnin' 'round this city chasin' pipe dreams.

Pumpkin   Come 'ere.

Blue *looks at* **Pumpkin**. *For the first time, we see him soften to her. For this one moment, she is in command.*

He walks over to her and kneels beside her.
Grabs her waist and holds onto her.

Pumpkin   You look tired.

Blue   I am tired, Pumpkin.

Pumpkin   You can rest now.

Blue   Ain't no rest for the weary . . . ain't that how it go?

Pumpkin   You can rest here. With me.

Blue   This is dead, Pumpkin.

Pumpkin   What's dead?

Blue   This place. Black Bottom. I'm chokin' here. I can hear it when I play my axe. Baby, I'm not right.

Pumpkin   You sound alright to me. Just achin' inside. But ain't nothin' wrong with that. Everybody got aches. Just need somethin' soft to touch it and make it better. I can do that . . . if you let me.

Blue   They're still here, Pumpkin. Them spirits.

Pumpkin   What spirits?

Blue   Spirit of my daddy. Lurkin' 'round this club. Hangin' in the walls. Hangin' in my music. Nigger won't leave me be.

Pumpkin Those just bad memories. You keep playing 'til it don't hurt no more.

Blue They more than memories, Pumpkin. They my daddy's demons comin' after me. I see myself turnin' into somethin' I don't like. Somethin' familiar, and it scares me. I got to run from 'em 'fore they kill me.

Pumpkin Run where, Blue? What you sayin'?

Blue I'm gettin' rid of this place, Pumpkin. Gonna sell it to the city. They offerin' ten thousand for this club. That's what I been doin'. Talkin' them into givin' me what I ask for.

Pumpkin Sell Paradise?!

Blue And go to Chicago. I got these fellas comin' Friday. They got a band in Chicago and they want a trumpet man. I told 'em to come hear me play so they can see I'm the one. Say they lookin' for a songbird to sing with the band sometimes. I told 'em I got the prettiest little songbird in Detroit with me. So you show 'em your pipes and get 'em to understand, Pumpkin. Get 'em to see we belong somewhere else.

Pumpkin Oh, Blue—I ain't ready. I ain't no songbird. I can't barely sing in the right key—

Blue You got the music in you. I heard it before. You singin' to yourself sometimes.

Pumpkin You hear somethin' different than what it really is. I only hummin'. Carry a tune. Maybe sound good 'til you put me in front of folks.

Blue You got to work with Corn. I seen it happen before. Take your potential and turn it into power. Then you and me can make real music together . . . in Chicago.

Pumpkin Oh, Blue. I . . . (*Pause.*) I love it here. In Black Bottom. I got folks here and they need me to take care of 'em. I don't wanna leave this and start over somewhere without 'em. Where I ain't got no people. Take a long time for folk to become family.

Blue This dead here. Don't you hear me, baby? I need you to take care of me. I'm dyin' here.

Pumpkin What about me?

An odd moment. **Blue** *looks at her curiously.*
Pumpkin *quickly realizes her mistake. Tries to fix.*

Pumpkin I mean, it ain't gonna be no better in Chicago. It's pain everywhere.

Blue Not this kinda pain, Pumpkin. (*An admission.*) I can hear her when I play, you know that? I can hear my mama cryin' sometimes and I try to drown her out. But the cryin' get louder and I can't mute it. I can't save her and she remind me over and over.

Pumpkin Oh, baby . . .

Act One, Scene Four 43

Blue   I hear Daddy too. He comin' to claim me. I ain't gonna be nothin' better and he keep reminding me too. He take my music away and all I got left is chaos.

Pumpkin   I can love all that chaos away.

Blue   Will you, baby?

Pumpkin   I will.

Blue   Then you'll come with me?

Pumpkin *retreats.*

Pumpkin   What . . . what about the band?

Blue   This band? What about it?

Pumpkin   Everybody here. What they s'pose to do without Paradise? This place our sanctuary.

Blue   Sanctuary for who? I'm tellin' you, I ain't right. The damage is in these walls. It's in this club. It's in this band. It's in this whole damn town. I don't want no parts of this no more. Detroit's gonna eat me alive. You hear me? I got to go.

Pumpkin   Blue, I'll do anything else but I don't wanna leave.

Suddenly, **Blue** *grabs hold of* **Pumpkin**'s *arms and shakes her.*

Blue   Don't say that, Pumpkin. Please don't say that / to me

Pumpkin *(frightened)*   Blue, you hurtin' / me—

Blue   You got to hear what I'm sayin' / got to understand me

Pumpkin   Please, Blue / let me loose.

Blue   I can't stay here no more—you hear? Don't make me / stay here.

Pumpkin   Blue / please.

Blue   Tell me what I want to hear / need to hear.

Pumpkin   Okay, Blue / Okay.

Blue   Tell me you gonna come.

Pumpkin   I'm gonna come.

Blue   Say you won't leave me.

Pumpkin   I won't leave you.

Blue   I need you, Pumpkin. I need you to keep quiet and don't mention this to none of the fellas 'til I got the money solid. Don't want them meddlin' and tryin' to mess stuff up. You hear me?

Pumpkin   Yes, Blue. I hear you.

Blue I need you in every way. Touch me like you say and soften the pain. Love it all away so I can be somebody better.

He releases his grip on **Pumpkin** *and drops his head into her lap.*

She kisses his forehead tenderly.

Pumpkin I will, baby. I will.

He touches him softly. Massages him with her hands. On his cheeks. On his hands. On his eyebrow.

Pumpkin
For time's deft fingers scroll my brow
With fell relentless art—
I'm folding up my little dreams
Tonight, within my heart.

Blue *looks up at her, and kisses her passionately. Harshly, even. Needfully.*

Scene Five

Corn *walks into the club, late night. Something wrapped in foil in his hands. He puts his hat on a stand. He heads to the bar, grabs a few napkins. Some silverware. Prepares the something wrapped in foil.*

P-Sam *enters the club anxiously.*

Corn Where'd you disappear to, Sam? Couldn't find you after the set. But you was right, that String-Finger Charlie was somethin' else.

P Sam Told you, didn't I? Ran off to rap with Jimmy the Greek for a minute. Had some news for me.

Corn What kinda news?

P-Sam *looks around for privacy.*

P-Sam Corn, I hit it.

Corn Hit what?

P-Sam The Policy. My number came up. Straight three in a row.

Corn Well, good for you, Sam. Got you a little bread.

P-Sam Not no little bread, Corn. A real stash. Something to spread around and get into some serious trouble with.

Corn You don't wanna be bettin' that on nothin', Sam. Just take your money and make you a little nest somewhere. Don't be like all these other fools done hit the numbers and run out with fur coats and that nonsense.

P-Sam That ain't what I'm tryin' to do, Corn. I need you to talk to Blue for me.

Corn Sam, I gotta tell ya—much as I can try to convince Blue on String-Finger Charlie, he ain't gon' be willin' to meet that fee. I can tell you that right now.

P-Sam That's what I'm sayin' now, Corn. What kinda sense do that make? When you know Blue to be all easy about this band being out of action? Somethin' ain't right about it, and I bet I know what it is.

Corn Don't go 'spreadin' stories now, Sam.

P-Sam He's gonna sell out.

Corn Blue got roots here. He ain't sellin'.

P-Sam How much that city talkin' to him for, Corn? They must be offerin' him something nice. Else, Blue got another plan. But it just don't make sense. He ain't even the slightest bit concerned 'bout nothin' but playing solo next Friday. Who you know wanna go on solo that got a quartet? 'Less they fixin' to start playin' with a new one.

Corn Sam your mind is runnin' off with your mouth. You makin' stuff up.

P-Sam I ain't makin' up nothin'. I'm piecing it all together. Jimmy the Greek called it. Said some of these rents over here is gettin' raised. And city payin' off the ones who own. If Blue sellin' out, what's that gonna mean for the rest of us, Corn? No steady bread. No place over our heads. You and me both . . . unless . . .

Corn 'Less what, Sam?

P-Sam 'Less he sell the club to me instead.

Corn Blue ain't sellin, Sam.

P-Sam Just listen here, Corn. I got me enough to make it worth thinkin' about.

Corn Blue ain't sellin'.

P-Sam That's all you can say? Blue ain't sellin'. Ain't even gonna listen to nothin' else?

Corn Blue ain't sellin', and you or nobody else is buyin'. Don't let that Jimmy the Greek get you confused, Sam. Black Bottom ain't lettin' Blue go, even if he want it to.

P-Sam How you know that, Corn?

Corn Some stuff I just know.

P-Sam Just talk to some folks around town, Corn. See if this plan to clean up the city don't mean to clean us out. Get rid of all the niggers. Just like the mayor say in his campaign—*we* the blight he talkin' 'bout.

Everybody know Blue's spot is the best spot to take. They get this, they can get everybody else too. One sell-out and it weaken the whole bunch. Unless 'steada sellin' to them, we sell to us. I wouldn't be nothin' like Blue. I'd take care of folks over here and give everybody solo time who want it—

Corn You talkin' takin' over the band too?

P-Sam I'm tellin' ya, when it's my spot, we all have a pot to piss in. I wouldn't be no cheap, hateful bastard chargin' nickels per ice cube. And I wouldn't let no crackers take from us what we done worked hard to have on our own. I ain't goin' back to playin' background for them big bands. White man say "wear this," "play this standard," "no bop." "Smile like this." "Sit like this." "Take your meal *after* these folk, nigger." I ain't doin' it, Corn.

If this spot was mine, we'd be the kings we supposed to be. I'd tell that new Mayor Cobo to go to hell he wanna take office and clean us out.

Corn That's enough, Sam. This talk you doin' gonna start a mess of hearsay and send Blue into a mighty rage.

P-Sam Corn, how long you gon' defend the devil?

Corn I ain't defending the devil. I'm trying to keep everything smooth. You don't know what I know. You don't know the limits of a man that's on his edge like I do. You ain't seen what I seen, Sam. Now I say I'll think on it. That's all I can say to you. But you got to stop this talk now.

P-Sam You think about it, Corn. And I'll zip my lips. For now.

Corn Good.

Beat.

P-Sam I'm tempted to go spend a lil' of my winnins on a fine woman tonight. Maybe try that Spiderwoman out for size.

Corn Not her. You leave her be.

P-Sam Oh don't worry 'bout me none. I ain't scared of a lil' poison.

Corn I say let her 'lone. She ain't got no interest or cause to be talking to you.

P-Sam *looks at* **Corn** *curiously.*

P-Sam What's it to you if I bother with her, Corn?

Corn *doesn't respond.* **P-Sam** *smiles knowingly.*

P-Sam (*teasing*) Oooo! You gon' git bit! She gon' put her pincers in you!

Corn Cool it out there, Sam.

P-Sam You wants to get bit—dontcha? Bet you headed there right now.

Corn I ain't talkin' on it. She's a sweet woman.

P-Sam Oh, Corn, don't go gettin' mush over this one. You walkin' a fool line. Them kinda women too much for you.

Corn I ain't askin' for your permission, Sam. I say she's sweet and I'm done with it.

P-Sam   I bet she sweet. Sweet potato pie. Just keep yo' eyes open, Corn. You can't take no more heartbreak. If she don't know that, the rest of us do. And you think about what I said . . . about Blue . . .

Corn   I'll think about it.

P-Sam   Good. I'm gon' stay outta trouble and turn in, myself. Maybe you should too, Corn.

He heads off.

(*Singing to himself.*) Sweet potato piiiieeeeee. . . . . .

Corn *grabs the something wrapped in foil and the silverware. Lights shift.*

Scene Six

Silver *sits in her room, playing a record on her record player. Charlie 'Yardbird' Parker.*

She paints her toenails calmly.

Suddenly, a knock at her bedroom door.

She raises from the vanity and opens it.

Corn *stands with a bashful smile and extends the something wrapped in foil.*

Corn   Sweet potato pie was too good to miss.

Silver *smiles slyly. Takes the pie.*

Silver   That's mighty thoughtful of you.

She cracks open the foil and smells.

Smell like all kinds of sin. Can't wait to satisfy my sweet tooth.

Corn   I hope you enjoy it well. Night, miss.

He turns to leave.

Silver   Wait a minute there, buttercup. Where you goin' so fast?

Corn   I remember you sayin' you wanted to spend the night on your lonesome. I hear a woman say she wanna be left alone, I leave her alone.

Silver   Well, that was before you brought me some sweet potato pie. It ain't no fun to taste sin all alone.

Corn   I really ought not bother you.

Silver   No bother at all, I say.

Corn *looks at* **Silver**. *She is the most intriguing beauty he's ever seen. He smiles shyly.*

Corn   I suppose . . . just 'til you finish your pie . . .

He enters the room. Stands.

Silver   Go'on have a seat now.

Corn   Ain't no seat but the bed.

Silver   My bed bugs don't bite nobody but me. Go'on sit down, sugar.

Corn *hesitates, and finally takes a seat on the edge of the bed. Uncomfortably.*

Silver *lifts her leg and finishes painting her toes as she talks.* **Corn** *notices the contour of her leg, and then tries not to. It's impossible.*

Corn   This your record player? Brought it with you?

Silver   Can't go nowhere without my music. A man I'll leave behind. But his music, I'll take forever.

Corn   This here one of my favorites. You play the right stuff.

Silver   But if you a pianoman, you must love some of the Duke, ain't that right?

Corn   Oh yeah. He's been by this club lots of times. All the greats. Mingus. Dizzy. Bird. That's somebody I got to play with 'fore I die.

Silver   Who's that?

Corn   Charlie Yardbird Parker. Make me wanna play 'til my hands fall off.

Silver   Can't have that. A pianoman's hands supposed to be the best hands in the business. Know every curve of a woman cuz the way your hands always stay curved when you play. I imagine you know how to stroke away a lot of ailment, don't you?

Corn   I suppose maybe . . .

Silver *looks at* **Corn** *and smiles. He smiles back. She stands up and spider walks over to him.*

Silver   Lemme see your hands.

She takes **Corn** *by the hands.*

Silver   Yeah . . . These look like they can play real nice . . .

Strokes his fingers.

Corn (*nervously*)   They say you been in a lot of cities.

Silver (*calmly*)   Who say that?

Corn   Folks round here.

Silver   I been in a few.

She moves closer to **Corn**. *Strokes his other hand softly.*

Corn Say you had lots of mmmm . . . mmmeen . . .

Silver Awww . . . not many men. Not too many at all. Just . . . some . . .

Corn Folks round here say things.

Silver Like what?

Corn But I don't believe none of it.

Silver What they sayin'? I'll tell you whether to believe it or not.

Her hand moves to **Corn**'s *leg. He jumps and moves over.*

Corn Just say you got secrets . . .

Silver Every woman got secrets.

Corn Say you like a spider . . . got that Louisana creole in you . . . got spirits . . .

Silver You ain't scared of no spiders is you? Big ol' strong man like you?

Corn Me?

Silver *touches his leg again. Softly. He is startled . . . but sits still. Allows it. Enjoys it.*

Corn Nooooo I like spiders, every since I was a half-pint, watch 'em weave a web . . .

Silver You ever been caught in a woman's web?

Corn Just once.

Silver And what happened?

Corn Fell in love with her. Married her. But she . . . she died.

Silver *stops stroking* **Corn**'s *leg. Looks at him compassionately. This is a real moment.*

Silver What was her name?

Corn Mabel.

Silver Was she pretty?

Corn To me, she was. Most pretty thing I ever saw.

Silver How she die?

Corn Had that TB.

Silver Shame.

Corn *looks at* **Silver** *sweetly.*

Corn You a different kind of woman.

Silver Am I?

Corn Got a bite to you. Sharp. Maybe a little bitter. But you also sweet somewhere too. I can see it in your face. Somewhere you got some sadness.

Silver We all got sadness. But I like to turn mine into fire, baby. What you do with yours?

Corn Play the piano.

Silver I'll bet you do.

She moves **Corn***'s hand to her own thigh.*

Silver You think you can play this? Find the notes right?

Corn *keeps his hand stiff.*

Corn I . . .

Silver Cuz I need you to find all the blues, and make it sound like bop. Can you do that buttercup?

Corn What about yo' pie?

Silver I got somethin' taste better'n that.

She straddles **Corn***. Puts his hands on her waist.*

Corn Whh . . . what about yo' husband? How he die?

Silver *moves* **Corn***'s hands to her breast. He gasps . . . overwhelmed by her allure.*

She smiles slyly.

Silver *(whispering)* I shot him.

Nibbles his ear. **Corn** *laughs nervously.*

Silver Kiss me, Daddy.

Corn *kisses her. Passionately.*
They fall back into the bed.

Scene Seven

Lights up on **Silver***'s room. It is daytime. The room is empty.*

A tap tap comes to her door. No answer. Tap tap again . . .

Pumpkin *(offstage)* Hello there? Missus Silver? Sheet delivery!

No answer. The door slightly opens as **Pumpkin** *peers in.*

Pumpkin Missus Silver?

Seeing that she isn't in, **Pumpkin** *enters carrying a basket of laundry.*

Pumpkin   Just gonna make up your bed for you so you have something clean to sleep on. Lord knows what kind of sinful behavior goes on in these sheets, but Pumpkin's gonna starch it all out.

She starts to re-make the bed.

She notices some of **Silver**'s *clothing lain around un-neatly. She folds and places it in drawers.*
Hums to herself. The melody has potential, slightly harmonious but meek.

Pumpkin *notices more lingerie inside the drawers and pulls out a bit. Looks at* **Silver**'s *records.*

Pumpkin (*reading aloud*)   Lester Young . . . (*She looks to the player.*) This is surely a fancy record player. Hope you don't mind if I just . . .

She puts a record on the player. "Mean to Me" by Lester Young plays.

She peeks back in the drawer and pulls out a bit of lingerie.

Uhn uhn, these things sure are . . . creative . . .

She holds the lingerie up to herself in the mirror. Enjoys it. Creates her alter ego.

Pumpkin (*putting "on"*)   Hey there, boys. I'm a spiderwoman, and don't none of ya'll come messin' with me 'less you wants to get bit. I'm a gangster woman from Louisiana, and I'll . . . I'll drink your blood with my chitlins! (*She laughs to herself. Snorts a bit.*) I'm a Black widow and if you lean too close, I'll stick you right in your Mr. Longleg and suck everything out. (*She gasps with laughter. Amazed at* her own mouth.). I'm a . . . I'm a woman. All you fellas, stop and take a look cuz a real woman done walked in the room. Not nobody to be simple and ignored. Not nobody to be proper and hushed. Not nobody to be uprooted and . . . (*Pause.*) They call me Silver.

Pumpkin *studies herself with seriousness.*
Something in this pretend world starts to feel disturbing.

She regroups and grabs the lingerie. Folds it and tries to organize the drawer.

Suddenly she spies something: gasp.
She pulls out a gun. It shines in the lights.
She freezes. Then she hastily puts the gun back and closes **Silver**'s *drawers.*

Pumpkin *grabs her laundry basket.*

Frazzled, she dashes out of the room.
The needle on the record plays on . . .
Lights fade on the room.
End of Act One.

Act Two

Scene One

Lights up on **Blue** *playing the trumpet on stage alone. The tune is beautiful but heavy. Loaded with teardrops.*

Silver *enters and watches him.*

When he finishes, she applauds. He turns to her sharply.

Silver   That's some real fine playin' you doin / over there

Blue   What you doin' down here, woman. Club is closed.

Silver   Couldn't sleep. So I figure I ought to try goin' for a little walk.

Blue   This ain't no place for you to wander. Go'on somewhere else.

Silver   Well, now, I figure I'm worth a little preview—don't you think?

Blue   I say get the hell outta here.

Silver   My my . . . sure know how to play rough there, ain't it? Don't trust a woman further than you can shove her. But I grew up in a house full of bluesmen. Brothers and a daddy. All with bigger ideas of themselves than they was ever able to be. Made 'em angry and frustrated all the time. I ain't lasted this long without knowin' how to play rough right back. (*Shift.*) Say they offerin' ten thousand to folks. You heard that?

Blue   Didn't I tell you I ain't discussing no business with you?

Silver   Well you told me, sho. But men who are contrary always got to say no at the first mention of something. If you smart, you let 'em get that outta the way before you ask for what you really want.

Blue   And what's that?

Silver   Your club.

Blue   It ain't for sell.

Silver   Everything's for sell. Business. Land. Soul. All it takes is the right price. I can match what this city think they gonna pay you, and add a lil' cherry on top.

Blue   Match it? You talkin' nonsense. It ain't none of your business what I do no way.

Silver   I just wonder what make a person wanna leave somethin' so perfect, seem like. Got Negroes over here runnin' everything and not havin' to answer to nobody but each other. You let this Black Bottom go into the wrong hands and the soul of this place ain't never gonna forgive you.

Blue   You shut up now. Talkin' outta line.

Silver *spider walks over to* **Blue** . . . *seductively.*

Silver   Can't. Not when I wants something. I got to move on it 'til I get close enough to stroke it.

Blue *grabs* **Silver** *roughly by the arm. She freezes in his grip.*

Blue   You wanna take this club out from under me? Hunh? You might got the wool pulled over these fellas, eyes, but I recognize a Black widow any way she come. You ain't gonna stick those fangs into me and control me like some prey. You ain't worth the trust I'd give the mayor or the overseer. You out to poison our plans and I ain't gon' let you. This is my Paradise. If I leave, I'm leavin' my way. You got that, woman?

Silver   I see it in you.

Blue *looks at her—baffled.*

Silver   Those demons. I see them closing in on you. Choking you, ain't they?

Blue *releases* **Silver** *and steps back. Stunned.*

Silver   My Daddy had 'em in him. Husband too. Them feelins of bein' trapped by yo' skin. Never allowed to get beyond where you at. Turns you mad. Only place you got to escape is that horn, ain't it? But horn only make it louder. Like a dope hit. Got you flyin' and dyin' all in one. I know you, cuz you and me ain't too different. You got contempt like all mens I known. I can dance with contempt and set it aside. But you . . . it rot to the core.
Turns you on yo' own kind.

Blue   Shut up.

Silver   But you ain't gonna get rid of 'em. They gon' get rid of you. Less you make amends.

Blue   I say shut up!

Silver   Set this place back in the right motion. Cuz if you don't, them demons gon' eat you alive. And when it done that to my daddy, (*digging into his soul*) he lynched himself.

Blue *grabs* **Silver** *and shakes her.*

Blue   I say shut up shut up SHUT UP GODDAMNIT!

Corn (*offstage*)   Blue?

Corn *enters the club and sees* **Blue**'*s hands on* **Silver**. **Blue** *quickly lets* **Silver** *go.*

Corn   Blue what's got you goin'?

Blue *is silent.* **Corn** *stares at* **Blue** *and* **Silver** . . . *decoding the event.*

Blue   Nothin'. Just down here practicing.

Corn Pumpkin worried 'bout you. Say you been down here for hours and won't go to bed.

Blue Ain't tired.

Corn Still, Blue. It's late enough. (*Turns to* **Silver**.) Maybe you should go'on to bed too, sweets. I'll come check on you in a few to make sure you tucked in safe and sound.

Silver *looks at* **Corn** *and then to* **Blue**. *She rubs her arm.*

Silver Alright then. (*A moment.*) Nite fellas.

She heads out of the bar.
Corn *looks at* **Blue** *sternly.*

Corn You too, Blue.

Blue Can't, Corn. I got to finish. Got to practice more. Ain't there yet.

Corn Ain't where, Blue?

Blue Just ain't there. I'm gon' stay up. I need Friday to be smooth.

Corn Blue. Pumpkin ain't gettin' no better. Might have to take her off standards. Give her somethin' else to do. I play solo.

Blue She got to practice more.

Corn Practice don't mean nothin' if the music in you too scared to get free. She tryin' her best cuz she know you want her to. But it ain't what she want.

Blue Do somethin' else then, Corn. Just make Friday night right. I can't keep on about it. I got to finish workin' here.

He walks back over to the stage with his trumpet. **Corn** *watches him.*

Corn Blue . . . you alright ain't you?

Blue *ignores this and begins to play a melody.*

Corn *hesitates for a moment, and then goes to the piano. He joins* **Blue**'s *melody. A moment of beautiful harmony.*

Quickly, the trumpet goes off tune. Music stops. **Blue** *starts again.* **Corn** *plays again. Another quick beat of harmony. Then trumpet goes off tune again. Music stops.*

Corn It'll come another day, Blue. Not tonight.

Blue Hey, Corn . . . what you see when you look at me?

Corn What you mean, Blue?

Blue Don't lie to me.

Corn I see . . . a gifted man.

Blue Am I fading? Am I . . . becoming—

Corn Love Supreme.

Blue What?

Corn That's what you trying to get to, Blue. Love Supreme. That's what he was lookin' for and never found. Your daddy. But you can, Blue. Just not tonight.

Blue *takes this in. It's sobering. He turns back to his trumpet. Can't let go the obsession.*

Blue Go'on, Corn. Leave me be.

Corn You can't force it, Blue. It got to come honest—

Blue (*sharply*) I say leave me!

Silence. **Corn** *rises from the piano.*
Blue *remains. Begins to play his tune again. Transfixed—in his own universe. Impervious to* **Corn**. *The trumpet sings an unpleasant melody.* **Corn** *watches a moment. Then he slowly heads out of the bar.*

Corn (*softly*) Night, Blue.

Lights shift.

Scene Two

Lights up on **Pumpkin** *and* **P-Sam** *at the bar. She fills him another cup. He eats toast and grits.*

P-Sam You put some cinnamon or something in these grits? They taste extra sweet this mornin', Pumpkin.

Pumpkin You don't like it?

P-Sam I ain't sayin' that. Taste a lil' different. But good.

Pumpkin I put a dash of cinnamon, and a little pinch of brown sugar.

P-Sam You ain't gonna charge me a extra nickel for that pinch, is you?

Pumpkin 'Course I ain't.

P-Sam Well, then, that's alright, Pumpkin. That's alright with me. (*Shift.*) You got some of your pretty words today? I could use somethin' soft like that this mornin'.

Pumpkin You mean it? You wanna listen?

P-Sam 'Course I wanna listen. You think I ain't got no ear like Corn? I can hear the music in them fancy words too. Try me.

Pumpkin Okay. Let's see. . . .

She grabs her book and flips through some pages. Hands it to **P-Sam**.

Pumpkin 'Kay. Hold the page right there. This one, she calls "Calling Dreams."
The right to make my dreams come true
I ask, nay, I demand of life,

P-Sam Nay? What's that word?

Pumpkin Just um . . . like "no."

P-Sam Oh alright. Go'on, Pumpkin

Pumpkin
The right to make my dreams come true
I ask, nay, I demand of life

P-Sam You already said that part Pumpkin.

Pumpkin I was just starting over.

P-Sam Oh okay then . . . you got to say that Pumpkin. I didn't know that, see?

Pumpkin I'm starting over.

P-Sam Okay. I'm ready for you.

Pumpkin
The right to make my dreams come true
I ask, nay, I demand of life
Nor shall fate's deadly contraband
Impede my steps, nor countermand.

P-Sam Say it peed on what?

Pumpkin Impede.

P-Sam That ain't what it sound like you was sayin'. It sounded sorta nasty.

Pumpkin Impede. I-M-P-E-D-E. To stop something.

P-Sam Oh yea. I see that right here. I got you now. Alright—keep goin'.

Pumpkin Sam, maybe you ought to just . . . listen. Maybe not read along.

P-Sam I can read, Pumpkin.

Pumpkin Oh, I know. But maybe the words sound better when you don't read. When you just hear me sayin' 'em to you. That's the magic in it.

P-Sam Alright then. Gimme the magic.

Pumpkin I'm gonna say it all the way through.

P-Sam I gotcha.

Pumpkin No interrupting this time.
Locked and sealed.

P-Sam *zips his lips.*

She takes a breath.

P-Sam I ain't gonna say nothin' else.

She looks at him sternly. He realizes his mistake there. Sits quietly.

Pumpkin
   The right to make my dreams come true
   I ask, nay, I demand of life
   Nor shall fate's deadly contraband
   Impede my steps, nor countermand.
   Too long my heart against the ground
   Has beat the dusty years around,
   And now, at length, I rise, I wake!
   And stride into the morning break

Pause. **P-Sam** *thinks for a sec.*

P-Sam Pumpkin, I ain't understand a word you just said. But I know one thing, it shoul' do sound like magic when you say it.

Pumpkin Thank you, Sam. Just talkin' 'bout love and dreamin'. That's all you really need to know.

P-Sam That's somethin' what makes your skin sorta blush. When you say them words.

Pumpkin I just like it.

P-Sam It like you too. (*Beat.*) That's what you should be doin', Pumpkin.

Pumpkin What's that?

P-Sam Puttin' words together. You got a nice way of doin' it. Even if it sound confusing otherwise, you got a way to make it sound like music. I can hear it in you.

Pumpkin I ain't no poet. I just like to read it, is all.

P-Sam How you know, Pumpkin? How you know what you ain't, if you ain't never tried it?

Pumpkin I don't know, I . . . You think I make it sound like music?

P-Sam Like a songbird. You could be like them Harlem cats. Puttin' them words in books. Be real classy and smart. That's what you are. Ain't Blue never told you that?

Pumpkin I'm fine just working here. Taking care of folks. I like taking care of folks. It's what I'm good at.

P-Sam Woman like you shouldn't have to take care of nobody. Man should be takin' care of you.

Pumpkin I'm okay just being here with Blue.

P-Sam But is Blue okay just being here with you?

Beat. **Pumpkin** *is affected. She shifts and starts clearing off* **P-Sam***'s plate.*

Pumpkin   Gonna take this for you now, if you're done. Get to cleanin' the dishes and finishin' the laundry.

P-Sam   Why when I get to talkin' 'bout Blue, you get to talkin' 'bout dirty laundry? Why you can't just answer me straight?

Pumpkin   I got a lot of stuff to do.

P-Sam   I see you everyday lookin' just as pretty and simple as you can be, and I think of all the things I'd like to give you. All the ways you could fit right in with what I wanna do. You a go-along-gal.

Pumpkin   A go-along gal.

P-Sam   And I like that. Don't make much fuss about nothin'. Just wanna make life easy for a man. And I can do somethin' with that.

Pumpkin   I got a life with Blue.

P-Sam   What kinda life, Pumpkin? Cleanin' his dirty drawers? You ain't got no real life with Blue. But you could have one with me.

Pumpkin   Sam, you shouldn't talk like that.

P-Sam *moves closer to* **Pumpkin***.*

P-Sam   I'm just talkin' the truth, Pumpkin.

Pumpkin   But I don't love you.

P-Sam   You'll learn to.

Pumpkin   I don't want to.

P-Sam   You need to.

Pumpkin   It ain't right.

P-Sam *is close enough on* **Pumpkin** *to feel her breath.*

P-Sam   It ain't wrong neither. It's somewhere in between.

Pumpkin   Sam, I can't.

P-Sam   Hear that, Pumpkin? You called me—Sam.

He tries to kiss her. She smacks his face.

Pumpkin   Damnit I say no!

Silver *enters the bar. Slowly.*

P-Sam *takes the hit. Backs off.*

Silver   Mornin', folks.

Pumpkin (*startled*)   Oh—mornin', missus. Was just bringing up your breakfast in a sec.

Act Two, Scene Two   59

Silver   No nevermind. I'll just have some juice right down here.

Pumpkin   Gettin' it for you right now. Bring you out another coffee too, Sam.

Silver *walks over to* **P-Sam** *and sits beside him. He slumps in his stool.*

Silver   Doll, you look like you could use a lil' sugar in your coffee this mornin'.

P-Sam   I done had enough sweet for today. (*Pause.*) I'll take somethin' spicy instead.

Silver   That right?

P-Sam   Yeah, that's right alright. (*Shift.*) Say, I hear you been askin' 'round 'bout business over here. You got ambitions for Black Bottom?

Silver   Heard that, did you?

P-Sam   I did. Notice you been talkin' with my buddy a bit. Spendin' a lot of time.

Silver   See through walls, can you?

P-Sam   I see smiles on a face ain't smiled like that in years. Only one kind of thing be responsible for that.

Silver   What of it.

P-Sam   Maybe you can put him up to somethin' for me. Somethin' what'll benefit us all. I done put the bug in his ear to talk to Blue for me, but I gots a feelin' you more persuasive than me. And maybe there's a shot you an' me can do some business together. If you fancy that.

Silver   You know, sugar . . . from what I seen—too many names on a dotted line cause too much confusion. The plans I got is for my signature only.

P-Sam *is taken aback.*

P-Sam   Oh you too good to be partners. I get it. Well, Blue ain't sellin' this club to neither one of us without some muscle behind 'im. And I tell you this, if you ain't on this with me, then you competition. We got an order to the line, sweetheart, and you play how you gotta, but be careful 'bout tryin' to take cuts. (*Shift.*) Tell Pumpkin I said no need for the coffee.
Ain't nothin' in here for me today.

He walks off.

Pumpkin *comes in from the kitchen with juice and coffee. Notices* **P-Sam** *is gone.*

Pumpkin   Where's Sam?

Silver   Say he had to go.

Pumpkin *hands* **Silver** *her juice. Looks at her uneasily.* **Silver** *watches* **Pumpkin** *knowingly.* **Pumpkin** *tries to keep herself occupied.*

Silver   Thought you might have time to teach me a bit of that fancy poetry of yours.

Pumpkin (*sharply*)   Can't. Busy. Got laundry.

Silver   Oh. Well . . . (*Pause.*) Maybe later then.

Pumpkin   Can't. Busy then too.

Silver   I see.

She is onto **Pumpkin** *as* **Pumpkin** *does a bad job of busying herself. She tries to corner* **Pumpkin**.

Silver   That's too bad. Maybe next time.

Pumpkin   Um. We'll have to see . . .

She scurries out, narrowly missing **Silver**'s *web.* **Silver** *calls after her.*

Silver   Hope your wrists are feeling better!

Silver *sits, disturbed that* **Pumpkin** *got away. She puts money on the bar and exits, unsettled . . .*

Scene Three

Dim lights up on **Blue** *and* **Pumpkin** *in the bar.* **Blue** *plays his trumpet and* **Pumpkin** *sits and listens.*

Lights up on **Silver** *and* **Corn** *in* **Silver**'s *bed. They are in the afterglow of lovemaking.*

Blue *plays softly in the bar. The two worlds exist simultaneously.*

Silver *smokes a cigarette.* **Corn** *caresses her.*

Corn   You got the prettiest skin. Like honeysmooth. Taste like it too.

He kisses her arm. She smiles at him.

And your arms. Can feel the shape of all your womanness in your arms.

Silver *blows a puff of smoke.*

Silver   Has it been that long, sugar?

Corn   Since Mabel died.

Silver   How you stay away from women so long?

Corn   Thought that part was dead. 'Til you come along and wake it up.

Silver   I got a way of wakin' up a lot of things in men. It ain't always good. (*Shift.*) Did you do what I asked you?

Corn   I ain't talk to him just yet. He on edge 'bout this gig. After the show be better.

Silver   Friday may be too late. He mighta already signed those papers by then.

Act Two, Scene Three 61

Corn I got to give him his chance to find what he lookin' for. Then I'll know what to do. Don't worry 'bout him sellin'.

Silver I know when a man is close to breakin', and I see that in your buddy.

Corn What you askin' ain't easy.

Silver But it's necessary.

Corn There's more to it than just sellin'. I knowed Blue a long time. Knew his daddy, name was Clyde Sr. What Blue don't tell nobody is he Clyde Jr. But better not call him that. He liable to pull his knife on you. Clyde Sr. gave me a shot. Let me play with the house band to keep from runnin' the streets. He made a legacy of Paradise Club, and Blue been trying to hold it together, but lately . . .

Silver Daddy got a cloud over him, don't he?

Blue's *tune in the bar changes. A melody of difficulty. Grows increasingly heavy.*

Corn Blue's daddy had that thing where his mind wasn't always right. Sometimes be talkin' to himself or to somebody who wun'nt there. But the man could play a trumpet like he was touched by God. And Blue got that same gift in him. But it come with a whole lot of extra.

Ate his daddy alive 'til he killed Blue's mama when Blue was a young man. Said he saw the devil trying to take her, and he was tryin' to / save her.

Silver My / God. . . .

Corn So he strangled her to death. Blue seen the whole thing. And his daddy wind up in the crazy house. That where he died.

Silver That kinda dead weight make a man dangerous. It can turn on you.

Corn Blue ain't a bad man. He just wanna be mighty but the world keep him small. Cost of bein' Colored and gifted. Brilliant and second class. Make you insane.

Silver He's divin' deeper than most. Don't you see that much?

Corn But I know what he needs.

Silver What's that.

Corn Love Supreme. That's what we call it when you hit that perfect note that cleans your sins. Like white light bathin' him with mercy. It's that part in the music that speak directly to God, and make you ready to play with the angels.

Silver When you got demons that deep, they don't redeem you. They kill you to the soul. It's time for him to move on 'fore that happen.

Corn What you want to run a club for, hunh? You stay here with me, and I'll make sure you don't need nothin' else.

Silver You talk like this gonna be somethin' permanent.

Corn Isn't it?

Silver *looks at* **Corn** *questionably.*

Silver Doll, listen here, I done learned from enough men not to settle my bags in anybody's heart too long. Cuz it start off good, but sooner or later I ain't gonna be able to fill all your needs. And then it's gonna be heartbreak city. I spare myself and you the pain.

Corn What make you think I need anything else but this?

Silver Men always do. And I can't give it baby.

Corn Why can't you?

Silver Cuz I'm broke. And ain't no fixin' me.

Corn I like broke.

Silver Not like this.

Corn How you know?

Silver Cuz I'm cursed.

Corn What you mean?

Silver Childless. Can't have 'em. Body just cursed.

Blue's *melody changes. More aggressive rhythm.*

Corn *looks at* **Silver**. *Touches her stomach. She moves his hand.*

Silver Ain't nothin' but dead in there, baby. Don't no life happen here. Couldn't give none to my husband and he hated me for it. Cursed me to hell. And almost sent me straight there, too. But I got out of that. I'm here and I'm fightin' for my piece at life. What's a woman if she ain't bearin' fruit? Ain't no other place for her in this world 'less she runnin' her own business. Got to find another way to be fruitful. I ain't gonna be nothin' frail to get preyed on. I'm gon' do the preying if it's any to be done. And this Paradise Club is ripe for the taking. So come on, baby. Tell me you gonna talk to him, so I can be something more than just childless.

Corn And then what happens to this? Us here?

Silver You gon' be the headliner, baby. I'll see to that.

Corn I wanna be the headliner right here.

He touches her heart.

Break the curse. I can do that for you, if you let me.

Silver *touches* **Corn**'s *hand. Then his face.*

Silver You must really like the taste of pain, don't you?

He answers her with a kiss.
Blue's *horn leaps in volume.*

Silver *and* **Corn** *fall back into the bed as lights crossfade to* **Pumpkin** *and* **Blue**.

Blue's *final note shifts. Moves from passionate to broken. He pushes again. It becomes piercing.*

Pumpkin *drops her teacup. It shatters.* **Blue**'s *note pierces. Pierces. Pierces.*

She rushes over to him as he blows his trumpet. She tries to stop him but he keeps on. The note pierces.

Pumpkin (*screaming*)   Blue!

She extends her arm and he pushes it away.

Pumpkin (*screaming over the notes*)   Blue, baby! Please!

He pierces more. In a trance almost. A battle between him and his trumpet. Fighting something in the notes.

Pumpkin *tries to grab hold of him and tug at his arm. His trumpet falls.*

Blue   Nooooooooooooooooo!

He shakes her and pushes her violently. She flies into the tables and onto the ground.

Blue   Let her go—motherfucker! Let her go!

He picks up a chair and throws it recklessly. Then he falls to the ground and wails.

Pumpkin *lays still. Alive and alert but frightened.*

Blue (*muttering*)   I couldn't-could-couldn't stop stop stop it . . . couldn't-save-save-her-couldn't-fight-back-fight-back-fight him him him-couldn't-didn't-do-nothing nothing nothing

Pumpkin (*softly*)   Blue . . .

Blue   Killed . . . killed-her-killed-her her her I-did-I-did—was me me me

Pumpkin   Wasn't you . . .

Blue   Was me me me . . . I'm gone . . . gone . . . gone . . .

Pumpkin   Blue, it's alright . . .

Blue   I'm gone . . . gone . . . dead . . . dead . . . dead . . .

Pumpkin   You alive, Blue, baby. You here with me. With Pumpkin.

Blue   Pumpkin?

He stops. Looks at **Pumpkin** *. . . like a stranger. As if it's his first time seeing her.*

Blue   Pumpkin, I'm dead. I'm not here. They got me, Pumpkin. Stole my soul. I scream to 'em and they scream back. Won't let me forget. Won't silence. I can't hear the notes in the scale. I'm outside myself watchin', but I can't get in. It took me, Pumpkin. The madness took me.

Pumpkin *slowly goes over to* **Blue**. *She kneels beside him. He looks at her. A looming feeling.*

Blue   You gonna leave me, Pumpkin.

Pumpkin   What, Blue? Why would you think—

Blue   You love this place more than you love me and I ain't gonna be able to stop you. I ain't gonna have nothin' left. I'm gonna die here, Pumpkin. If I don't get out soon, I'm gonna die.

Pumpkin   If we leave here, Blue, you really think the hurtin' a stop? I mean, all of it?

Blue   It got to, Pumpkin.

Pumpkin   Even . . . with me?

Blue   It just got to.

Pumpkin *considers.*

Pumpkin   Okay, Blue. I ain't gonna let Black Bottom hurt you no more.

Blue *grabs* **Pumpkin** *and falls in her lap.* **Pumpkin** *holds him strangely. Unsettled . . .*

Scene Four

Lights up on **Silver**'*s room. Evening light spills through the windows.*

Silver *listens to Dizzy and Bird on the record player.*

A soft tap at the door.

Pumpkin (*offstage*)   Missus, I got your supper with me. Just gonna leave it for you out here.

Silver *goes to the door and opens it.*

Silver   Come on in here, honey. Let me talk to you for a sec.

Pumpkin   I got a lot of other deliveries to make. And the kitchen is a mess—

Silver   Only for a sec? Could use a lil' girl talk—

Pumpkin   I still gotta go straighten the bar, and then meet with Corn so I can get ready—

Silver   I know you been through my things.

Pumpkin *freezes for a second, and then quickly enters the room—closing the door behind her.*

Pumpkin   It was only an accident—

Silver   'Course it was.

Pumpkin   I didn't mean to be inconsiderate. I just came to change the sheets—

Silver   And listen to a little Lester Young and sort through my drawers.

Pumpkin   I didn't—

Silver   Relax, honey. No need to worry so. I ain't mad at you.

Pumpkin   It was a terrible mistake and I swear I won't do it again.

Silver   You see somethin' you like? Want it for yaself?

Pumpkin   Oh no, missus. No, I don't want to bother in anymore of your things.

Silver   You sho?

Pumpkin   Yes, ma'am.

Silver   Cuz I figure you musta got a lil' curious—bout somethin'. And I can take all that curiosity away right now.

Pumpkin   No, I'm fine. Really.

Silver   Just let you have a lil' look—see.

She pulls out a gun. It shines in the lights. **Pumpkin** *gasps.*

Silver   This what you so 'fraid of? This lil' bitty thing?

Pumpkin (*nervously*)   I . . . I don't need to see that, missus. It's your . . . private—

Silver   Ain't too private no more. Or is it? You tell me.

Pumpkin   I ain't . . . told nobody . . .

Silver   No? Not even yo' man?

Pumpkin   No . . . nobody . . .

Silver   Huh . . . (*Pause.*) Well, that's good, then. Men find out a woman got a gun, they ready to lock her in a dungeon and throw away the key.

Pumpkin   Why you . . . why you have it?

Silver   For protection.

Pumpkin   Protection from who?

Silver   Anybody. Everybody. You think a woman can move on her lonesome from town to town without the know-how to put a bullet in somebody's head?

Pumpkin   That ain't for a lady to do.

Silver   Says who?

Pumpkin   That's why a woman ain't supposed to be on her lonesome. Travel with a man by your side and he be all the protection you need.

Silver   That so? That what your man do for you? Make you feel protected and safe?

Pumpkin   'Course he does.

Silver   That why you got those bruises on your arm?

Pumpkin *falls silent.*

Silver   Seem to me like you ain't no safer than me on my lonesome. In fact, I'll say I'm the better of us two. Cuz I know how to shoot straight and aim direct. And I ain't shy when I got this in my hand, neither. Ain't no wallflower. I'm front and center on the floor. And I ain't afraid to use it. That's where people get you. They see you got it but don't 'spect you to use it. But once somebody see yo' gun, they done seen all your cards right there on the table. So you either fold, or you take the win. And me, I always take the win.

Pumpkin   What happened to yo' husband?

Silver   That's a tale for another day.

Pumpkin   Why you move here on your lonesome?

Silver   I told you, he died.

Pumpkin   How he die?

Silver   Bullet in the head.

She looks at **Pumpkin**—*who has now scrunched herself up in a corner.*

Silver   Now, gal, why you so far over there? What you so 'fraid of? Ain't you never held one of these before?

Pumpkin *is still.*

Silver   Well, goodness, come on. Let me be your first.

Pumpkin *is still.* **Silver** *laughs.*

Silver   You think I'm gon' shoot you? (*Laughing.*) Don't you think I woulda done that by now?

Pumpkin   I really ... should be ... going now ...

Silver   Alright now, that's enough.

She walks over to **Pumpkin** *and grabs her hand.*

Silver   You can't be a prissy lil' thing all yo' life. Sometimes you got to learn some other tricks. Grab it.

Pumpkin   No, missus, I can't—

Silver   I say grab it!

Pumpkin *takes the gun timidly. Holds it like it smells.*

Silver   It ain't dirty drawers. You got to hold it. Give it a grip.

Pumpkin   I don't want to.

Silver   Here. Like this.

She moves behind **Pumpkin**. *Puts her hands over* **Pumpkin**'s *hands.*

Silver   You got to hold it firm. It's a delicate egg. Too tight make it bust. Not tight enough and it slip right out your hands. Got it?

Pumpkin *nods. She holds the gun.*

Silver   Now you don't wanna put your finger by that trigger too soon. Hold it up here.

She moves **Pumpkin**'s *finger.*

Silver   You do it too early, and you liable to blow somebody's brains out just for sayin' good morning.

Pumpkin   My arm feels heavy.

Silver   You ain't used to it, that's all. When you get used to carrying it, won't feel like nothin' but another piece of you. Your best friend.

Pumpkin   This ain't got nothin' in it, has it?

Silver   You think I'm fool enough to give you a loaded gun?

Pumpkin   My arm's gettin' tired.

Silver   Hold it straight. Support it with your other hand. On the bottom. Like this.

She places **Pumpkin**'s *hands properly.*

Pumpkin   I'm breathin' funny.

Silver   That ain't nothin' but power and nerves runnin' through your blood. Mixin' all together. Feel almost thrillin'. Like holdin' a man's Mr. Happy in your hand.

Pumpkin   You speak so dirty!

Silver   Feels good. Try it.

Pumpkin   I can't.

Silver   Just say somethin'.

Pumpkin   Like what?

Silver   Anything that comes out. You can say what you want with a gun in your hand.

Pumpkin   I don't know what to say.

Silver   Tell somebody to move out your way.

Pumpkin   Move outta my way.

Silver   Even with that gun you ain't scarin' nobody. Say it like you mean it.

Pumpkin   Move outta my way!

Silver   Good. Now tell 'em they better not mess with you or you'll shoot their balls right off 'em.

Pumpkin   I can't say that.

Silver   Say it now! Go'on!

Pumpkin   Don't you mess me with me or I'll shoot you right in your—

Silver   Balls.

Pumpkin   So nasty.

Silver   Say it.

Pumpkin   I can't!

Silver   Balls! Go'on. I'll shoot you in your—

Pumpkin   It's too nasty—

Silver   Scream it! I'll shoot you in your—

Pumpkin   Balls! Balls balls balls! In your balls!

Silver *bursts out laughing.* **Pumpkin** *laughs too. They crack up for a moment.*

Silver   My goodness! You got a dirty mouth.

Pumpkin   I sound silly.

She sets the gun down.

Silver   Sound silly at first. But the more you believe it, the more everybody else will too. Take time, but you soon learn.

Pumpkin   I don't need to learn. I'm not gonna be like you. Not movin' from town to town lettin' anybody in my bed who fits the season. Can't make no home that way.

Silver   You can't make a home your way neither.

She grabs **Pumpkin***'s wrist and* **Pumpkin** *flinches.*

Silver   How many times he put his hands on you today?

Pumpkin   I need to get goin'—

Silver   Is it everyday? Or just whenever he got troubles?

Pumpkin   That's none of your / concern, missus

Silver   Don't matter whether or not it's my concern. I know what I see. And I tell you one thing, gal. You in a heap of trouble if you think you 'bout to make a life with this man. A man with demons ain't gonna see you as nothin' but a gateway to hell. Whenever them spirits come callin', he got to fight anybody they tell him to. And if you in his way, then he gonna fight you.

Pumpkin Blue got troubles, yes. But every man got troubles. We take it and we ease it much as possible. That's what a woman do. Black Bottom is the source of most of it. Soon a change gon' come and make things better for 'im.

Silver Waitin' on a man to change is like waitin' on the seventh sign. When it comes, it's gonna bring a whole lotta destruction with it. I wouldn't wait for that if I was you.

Pumpkin He's a good man. I know you don't see that, but he is. Use to court me at the Main Library on Woodward. Love goin' there to study when I was schoolin'. The architecture . . . those majestic steps. Blue come to walk me home everyday after I finish my reading. Wait for me on those steps like I was royalty. He be there with his trumpet in his hand and play for me when I walk out the door. That's when I first seen it. This man has a gift. The kind that make you feel like somebody just to be close to it. Sometimes his lovin' hurts, true. But when it feels good, it feel like Heaven. Even if just half good, that's better than nothin'

Silver A gift is good. But a gift can blind you. Don't get no man's gift confused with that man in the flesh.

Pumpkin You don't know him.

Silver I know men.

Pumpkin Blue ain't all men.

Silver He's a man. Men is men.

Pumpkin Things'll change soon.

Silver You be dead 'fore they do.

Pumpkin I can't move like you. It ain't me. I like soft words and taking care of folks. You got your way to make it through and I got mine. I know how to make a man feel safe and that's my trade. I'm a go-along gal.

Silver That ain't you. That's just the makeup you wear. You a thinkin' woman with her own words. But you play these mens just the same as me. Make 'em feel safe so they make you feel safe. But, doll, ain't none of us really safe. No matter what they tell you.

Pumpkin Blue just ailing right now. Ain't we all?

Silver You want to keep ailin' with him? Or you want it to stop? Tell me now. True.

Pumpkin I . . .
I want it to stop.

Silver Then make it.

Pumpkin How?

Silver *moves calmly.*

Silver Get you a revolver.

Pumpkin What?

Silver Or you can borrow mine.

Pumpkin What you mean?

Silver Woman got to put her foot down sometimes. Or it ain't never gonna stop. Sometimes, only thing can make it stop is a bullet.

Pumpkin *looks at* **Silver**—*stunned.*

Pumpkin You're not serious.

Silver I'm bein' straight.

Pumpkin I would never . . .

Silver Keep it in your stocking. Under your pillow. In your boudoir. Wherever you can get to it.

Pumpkin I would never do that.

Silver Or carry it in your purse—

Pumpkin I say I would NEVER!

Silver You don't know what you would do 'til it's just you, him and the devil. Trust me, gal. You don't know.

Pumpkin Where would I even . . .
. . .
. . .
No. No, I don't want to think about this. You a filthy dirty Creole woman and everything they say about you is true. You just tryin' to poison me.

She walks to the door and opens it. She stops and turns back to **Silver**.

Pumpkin Yo' husband . . . How he die?

Silver *pulls a cigarette from her bosom and lights it.*

Pumpkin You a sick woman.

Silver Any man put his hands on a woman is asking to be shot. Straight between the eyes. And if you know what's good for you, you betta get your gun.

Pumpkin—*caught between stunned and intrigue*—*storms out of the room.*

Silver *takes a long . . . long . . . long . . . drag . . .*

Scene Five

A horn plays in the distance. It is **Blue**. *He stands in silhouette, similar to the beginning of the play. He struggles through his horn and slowly starts to find the notes. It is not perfect, but there is something on track about it.*

Something promising.

Lights come up on Paradise Club. The floors and bartop glisten. The place looks pristine and ready for opening.

Corn *sits at the piano playing a soft tune.*

Pumpkin, *dressed simply, recites a poem . . . It is almost musical. She begins meekly at first, but then, as if the truth of the words overwhelm her, she increasingly gains vocal power. She is half-reciting/half-singing. She sounds amazing.*

As **Corn** *plays underneath her, they become perfectly harmonious.*

Pumpkin
  I want to reach you softly
  Touch you where you ail
  Lift you in your sadness
  Winds beneath your sail

  I want to reach you purely
  In truth and love sublime
  I become the sun
  Come cascade in my shine

  I want to reach you deeply
  My palm upon your core
  Releasing every darkness
  Until you ache no more . . .

Corn *stops. Beams at her.*

Corn   That was good, Pumpkin.

Pumpkin   Think so?

Corn   That's the music in you. You found it. That those Miss Johnson woman's words open you like that?

Pumpkin   Not this time, Corn. (*A small admission.*) My own.

Corn   You wrote that one yourself, Pumpkin?!

Pumpkin   Think it'll be okay for this evenin' 'stead of the standards?

Corn   I believe it's worth the try.

Silver *enters the bar.* **Pumpkin** *spots her.*

Pumpkin   Well then . . . I better go get dressed 'fore we open.

She walks past **Silver** *briskly.* **Silver** *eyes her carefully. Then turns to* **Corn**.

Silver   Your playin' sound real good, sweets. You 'bout ready for this evenin?

Corn   About. Got to finish suitin' up, but I feel like Pumpkin gonna be alright—

Silver   That's not what I mean. You know what I'm talking about.

Pause.

72   Paradise Blue

Corn   Like I told you: Tonight. After. Not before. Too much going on before.

Silver   We better hope after ain't too late.

Corn   You think about what I said too? 'Bout you and me?

Silver   I did.

Corn   So is that a yes?

Silver   Well . . . (*sincerely*) it ain't a no.

P-Sam *enters the club loudly. A hint of intoxication in his walk. He approaches the bar.*

P-Sam   Well . . . look at this place. Look like a real happenin' spot tonight, don't it?

Corn   Hey there, Sam. You alright?

P-Sam   Is I'm alright? Ain't that the question of the motherfuckin' year. Is I'm alright? Let's see there, Corn. I ain't got no gig. I ain't got no woman. And I'm drunk on some three-penny wine from Alfie's Liquor Sto'. What you think, Corn? That sound alright?

Corn   Sam, you ain't lookin' good.

P-Sam   Well, nigger, you ain't lookin' good neither. You lookin' like a backstabbing fink if I ever saw one.

Silver   Maybe I should freshen up for the show.

P-Sam   Freshen up good, baby. Cuz Sammy know all about yo' tricks. Go'on put on some of that rose smellin' perfume and them sugar tastin' drawers that got my buddy here all dumb struck.

Corn *squares off to* **P-Sam**.

Corn   Sam, watch your mouth there.

Silver *holds out her hand to stop* **Corn**.

Silver   It's okay, sweets. We'll finish this later.

She exits. **P-Sam** *looks after her with contempt, and then turns back to* **Corn**.

P-Sam   Was she worth it, Corn? Was the cootie worth it?

Corn   What you talkin' 'bout, Sam?

P-Sam   Nigger, don't be tryin' to play dumb on me. I ain't no clown.

Corn   I never say you was a clown—

P-Sam   You double-crossed me damnit!

Corn   Wait a minute, Sam. What you mean?

P-Sam   You know what I mean. That spiderwoman got your nostrils stretched so tall they blockin' yo' eyesight! You cuttin' side deals on me with her, ain't that it?

Corn I just told her like I told you. I'm gon' talk to Blue and see if he'll listen to what you have to say. Both of you.

P-Sam No leanin' him no particular way?

Corn That's it, Sam.

P-Sam Corn, you a lyin' monkey. I ain't never thought I'd see the day when you look me straight in the eye and lie. But you done messed up now. Ain't keep yo' eyes on the prize. And that nigger sold it! Just like I say!

Corn Sold what, Sam? Paradise? Nawww . . . that can't be. Blue ain't leavin' this spot—

P-Sam That's bullshit, Corn! He done already left it! Ask these other clubs-they all seen it. Blue's name on the list of sellers. Gave his word and the handshake and signin' this club over on Monday. Monday! And along with him goes Percy at Garfield's Lounge, and Harold from Three Sixes. Even the Norwood Hotel gettin' bought out with this new plan. It's just like I was tellin' you. You get one—you get 'em all. And Blue done started a train wreck we coulda stopped if you'da been keepin' your ear to the ground steada up in some crazy woman's cooter.

Corn Hold on, Sam. Monday ain't here yet. That mean he ain't signed it. A list ain't nothin' but a promise. We don't know the final plan less we hear it from Blue hisself.

P-Sam Listen at you—hear it from Blue. You gon' trust Blue over half of Black Bottom?

Corn If what they say is true, I got to hear it from Blue's mouth. See it in his eyes. Then I'll know what I know.

P-Sam Then let's get it from his mouth then! Call him right now. Blue! Blue! Bring your sell-out tail down here, nigger!

Corn Sam!

Pumpkin *enters. She is dressed in a stunning red gown with red painted lips, and a rose in her hair. She is breathtaking.*

Pumpkin Sam? What's the matter down here?

P-Sam Pumpkin, this ain't none of your—

P-Sam *sees* **Pumpkin** *for the first time fully. He is caught off guard.*

P-Sam Concern . . .

Corn It's alright, Pumpkin. Sam just a little drunk.

P-Sam (*to* **Pumpkin**) You look . . . good . . .

Pumpkin Thank you, Sam.

Corn Pumpkin, where's Blue?

Pumpkin Gettin' his suit on. Upstairs. Should be down in a sec.

Corn I'm gonna go get him and we'll settle this once and for all.

He heads off. **P-Sam** *stares at* **Pumpkin**—*mesmerized.*

P-Sam Pumpkin, I ain't never seen you so . . . done up.

Pumpkin Tonight is special, Blue say. Had to look classy.

P-Sam You look too classy for Blue. Hell, too classy for every fella in Black Bottom. You deserve the top of the line. Somewhere you can write your poems and won't have to clean one dirty dish. Get you a maid to do that.

Pumpkin I don't need none of that, Sam. I'm fine right here.

P-Sam Why you fine like this, Pumpkin? Just tell me and I'll let you be. Why you won't even let me pretend to give you nothin' better?

Pumpkin I don't know, Sam. I don't know why I can't love you. I think you so sweet sometimes. I like to laugh with you. And I do wonder what it'll be like if I closed my eyes and just let you in. I listen to the way you drum and it sound so scattered and rough. Somehow, it works for that bop sound. But for my ear, it just don't sound like a trumpet. When I hear that horn, I get lost in its pain and its beauty. It speak to me different. I just don't know how to change what my ear is favorable to.

P-Sam I sho wish I did, Pumpkin. I wish I knew how to turn you to my kinda sound.

Pumpkin *looks at* **P-Sam** *sincerely.*

Pumpkin You a good man, Sam.

P-Sam It sound so right when you call me that.

Pumpkin *touches* **P-Sam**'s *face gently. He softens to her touch. She smiles.*

Blue *walks in with* **Corn** *at his heels.*

Storms over to **Pumpkin** *and grabs her roughly by the arm.*

Blue What kinda game you playin' at? You tryin' to make a fool outta me?

Pumpkin No no . . . Blue, I—

P-Sam Let her be!

He grabs **Blue**'s *arm and turns him around.* **Blue** *snatches his arm back.*

Blue What the hell you want here, nigger.

P-Sam I wanna hear you tell it, that's what. Tell Corn and everybody up in here how you sold us out.

Blue I ain't got to tell nobody nothin'.

P-Sam You gon' say it, goddamnit. You gonna tell everybody how you put Paradise Club on the list to be sold for ten thousand dollars. Gonna sign it over on Monday. You tell Corn right now, nigger!

Blue I ain't tellin' you jack.

Corn Blue, tell him you ain't sellin'.

Blue I ain't got to tell him a motherfuckin' thing, Corn. Nigger come up in here like I owe him somethin'. I don't owe nobody nothin', you hear me? I do what I wanna do cuz it's my place! Ain't nobody got to live with my madness but me, you hear me?

P-Sam You? You you you you YOU! Everything always about YOU! But this ain't just your club. You might be the one to own it, but you ain't the one to make it. We all make this Paradise. You wouldn't have nothin' to stand on all this time if it wun'nt for me, Corn, and Joe backing you up and makin' you sound good.

Blue Makin' me sound good?

P-Sam You wouldn't have no club if it wun'nt for Pumpkin keepin' this place pristine—

Blue You keep Pumpkin outta yo' mouth, nigger.

P-Sam This ain't just your club. This club belong to everybody who done had a piece in keepin' it alive. And you damn straight you owe us, nigger. You owe every moe in Black Bottom! We the backbone of this place. And if you ain't had us, you ain't had nothin' but bricks.

Blue You can have all that and leave me my bricks. This place Paradise to you but it ain't to me. You don't know what this is to me. You and all these bloodsuckers comin' round—nothin' but a bunch of worthless niggers scrapin' the bottom of the barrel and livin' on pipe dreams. You can die here, nigger. But I ain't.

P-Sam Worthless?!

Blue That's what I said.

P-Sam I'll show you worthless, motherfucker.

He lunges into **Blue**. *They tussle.*

Corn Sam!

Pumpkin Blue!

P-Sam and Blue *are at each other's throats.*

Corn *tries to pull them apart, and gets knocked back.*

Silver *enters and jumps back with a start, as the men come charging her way.*

Finally **P-Sam** *pens* **Blue** *and starts choking him.* **Pumpkin** *runs off stage.* **Corn** *rushes over to* **P-Sam**. **Blue** *struggles.*

Corn Sam, no! Let him go, Sam. Let him go.

P-Sam I should kill you, you-out motherfucker!

Corn No, Sam. Let him go.

Corn *tries to pull* **P-Sam** *off of* **Blue**. **Blue** *gasps and catches his breath.* **Corn** *grabs* **P-Sam**.

P-Sam   Get off me, Corn! Let me go!

Finally **Corn** *releases* **P-Sam**, *who tries to catch his breath.* **Blue** *rises quickly and charges over to* **P-Sam**. *Grabbing him from behind into a headlock.*

Blue *pulls out a knife.*

Corn   Blue . . .

P-Sam *struggles in* **Blue**'s *grip.*

Blue   Who you gonna kill, nigger?

Corn   Blue don't . . .

Silver *moves behind the bar. Searches for some kind of weapon.*

Blue   You wanna kill me, nigger? Hunh? Then do it. Do it right now.

P-Sam *struggles in* **Blue**'s *grip with more urgency. Gasping.*

Pumpkin *runs onto stage with the revolver in her hand.*

Gunshot.

Everyone halts. **P-Sam** *falls from* **Blue**'s *clutch . . . alive and gasping.*

Pumpkin *holds her hand high in the air. The gun smokes.*

Everyone stares at her—stunned.

Pumpkin   Next one won't be no warning.

Corn *moves toward* **Pumpkin**, *slowly.*

Corn   Pumpkin . . . gimme that now . . . gimme that gun . . .

Pumpkin *aims the gun at* **Blue**.

Pumpkin   The devil is in you. I can . . . I can see it now. I see it.

Blue *stares at* **Pumpkin** *like a stranger. A betrayer.*

Corn   Come now, Pumpkin. Go'on gimme that . . .

Pumpkin (*to* **Silver**)   I want it to stop.

Silver (*cautiously*)   Okay . . .

Pumpkin   All the ailin', you hear me? Every last part of it. I want it to stop.

Corn   It's gonna stop, Pumpkin. We all gonna be okay, now. Just let it be . . .

He reaches out to **Pumpkin**. *She turns the gun on him.*

Pumpkin   No!

Corn   Okay. It's okay, Pumpkin. Gimme that gun . . .

Pumpkin   I say no! No more.

She waves the gun from **Corn** *to* **Blue**.

Pumpkin   I'm not leaving. Every part of this place is who I am. It's killin' you but it's keepin' the rest of us alive. I can't let you take me from here, Blue. You just ain't right. It don't matter where you go. I can see it. You already gone.

Corn   Blue, grab your trumpet.

Blue   Say what?

Corn   Go'on that stage. Play your axe. Get ready for tonight.

Blue   I ain't—

Corn   You do it now, Blue. That's what we need right now. We need a soothin'. Ain't that right, Pumpkin?

Blue   Corn, you talkin' crazy.

Corn   Do it, Blue. This the moment. You got to play for your soul now.

Blue *looks at* **Corn**. *Then to* **Pumpkin**—*who keeps the gun aimed straight.*

Corn   Play like you gonna kill all them demons and open up the gates of Heaven in your song. Play your axe.

Blue *slowly walks to the stage. Questioning each step. Unsure whether to follow . . . but something in him does.* **Pumpkin** *follows his path with the gun. Hands steady.*

Blue *reaches out to his horn. He plays a note at first. Stops.*

Blue   I'm losing it.

Corn   Nah you ain't. I see it in your eyes, Blue. This the moment. It's gon' come right and perfect. You just got to keep playin'. Love Supreme.

He considers. Tries again. Begins a tune. Soft at first. Then increasingly beautiful.
The trumpet sings.
Then suddenly, a white light washes over **Blue** *as he plays.*

Everyone stares at **Blue**—*transfixed and mesmerized.*

Pumpkin *is caught in the music. It is her prayer.*
She lowers the gun slowly—hypnotized.

Blue *plays a long-lasting note. The most beautiful note we've ever heard.*

Then finally, he stops. He is sweating. He is crying. His body shaking with pain and guilt and sorrow.

White light over him gets even brighter.

Corn *nears* **Pumpkin**. *Eyeing her lowered arm and gun in hand.*

Corn See, Blue? You found it. That moment of perfect harmony. We your witnesses. Seen it all. And it's time for the madness to stop now. End on a good note.

Blue *wipe his tears. He smiles. Peacefully.*

Corn Ain't that right, Pumpkin?

He looks at **Pumpkin**. *Nods at her knowingly. Steps aside from her.* **Pumpkin** *is clear, confident, resolved.*

Pumpkin That's right. For everybody. No more hurtin'.

She raises the gun at **Blue**. *Gunshot.*

Blackout. End of play.

Cost of Living

Martyna Majok

Introduction

"When you're writing, you're trying to find out something which you don't know. The whole language of writing for me is finding out what you don't want to know, what you don't want to find out. But something forces you to anyway."
                                                                                                James Baldwin

"Write about what you don't know about what you know."
                                                                                                Eudora Welty

Cost of Living was born from a place of grief and loss. From a yearning and hope for something that transcends our finite bodies and limited time and geography. For something that remains alive with those we leave behind.

I wrote Eddie's monologue on one blizzard of a Saturday night in what was turning out to be a year of many "breaks." I had been going from sublet to couch to sublet, as I struggled to make enough money to afford to rent a place of my own. (It would be 13 moves total in one year, which included one apartment with a bed bug infestation.) I was just about to head out the door to work, on that January Saturday night, when I got a call from my boss at a restaurant in the LES. He thought I'd stolen $100 from the register. I hadn't, I told him. Though I wish I'd had cuz I was fired for it all the same.

It had just begun snowing outside the windows of my sublet apartment in Brooklyn as I hung up the phone. Now there was just quiet and stillness. No rush to get to the train, no noise of life and people, no place I had to be. I'd need to find more work tomorrow. But tonight, I would sit down with myself and find out what was there.

What came flooding in was thoughts of Paweł Majok. He was soul-achingly dear to me, the closest I ever came to a father, and he had recently and unexpectedly passed away. I didn't have the money to fly to Poland to be at his funeral with the rest of my family. But, probably even more than that, I was afraid to go. I was afraid for it to be real, afraid that I would have to say goodbye. I'd never felt further away, in every sense of the phrase. I found myself wishing I could see his ghost, longing for some kind of magic, for some kind of sign, of something beyond. And it was Eddie Torres' voice that came to sit with me on that snowy night.

The rest of the characters would arrive incrementally over that year of continued breaks. They're composites of people I know or have been and aspects of what I was feeling at that time. I had been wondering about care. About the nature of helping others and being helped. About need and survival. I was thinking of the survivors in and around my life. About personal, national, and global grief. I tried to build a home for four people in *Cost of Living* where they could feel held by each other—and where I could feel held.

If you had told that freshly unemployed writer alone in her sublet what the future held for this play, she would not have believed you. I'm eternally grateful to Mandy Greenfield for opening the door to that future, for trusting and believing so fiercely in me and this play. And to everyone at the Williamstown Theatre Festival who gave so generously of their life and time on this earth to help tell its story. My gratitude to you, forever.

Characters

Eddie, *late forties, male.*
Ani, *early forties, female, pronounced "Ah-nee."*
Jess, *mid-twenties, female.*
John, *mid-twenties, male.*

Setting

The urban east of America. Jersey.
The near present.

The Prologue, Scenes Seven, Eight, and Nine occur on the same Friday night in December, a week before Christmas. The rest of the play spans September through December.

Notes

Dialogistics

Slashes // indicate overlap.
Ellipses . . . are active silences.
[Square brackets] are words intended but unspoken.
(Non-italicized parenthesis) within dialogue are meant to be spoken.

A note on John's language

John has a speech pattern that manifests itself in a kind of halted way of speaking. This is due to the vocal tension of his cerebral palsy. The breaks and spacing in his lines are meant to simulate that halting rather than to indicate any sort of poetic recitation.

Some notes on performance

Self-pity has little currency in these characters' worlds. Humor, however, has much.

For the Jersey mouth, the word "fuckin" is often used as a comma, or as a vocalized pause, akin to the word "like." ["I can't like, decide, y'know." = "I can't fuckin, decide, y'know."] It's a word with extra purpose. It's not necessarily *just* a container for anger.

A note on casting

Please cast disabled actors in the roles of John and Ani.

Please assemble a cast that looks like North Jersey and its beautiful diversity. In the Prologue, Ani's full name can be Ania Łucja Skowrońska-Torres or Ani Luz Hernandez-Torres or Ani Li-Torres or Ānanda Singh-Torres, amongst many options. Ani's full name should be chosen to suit the actress playing her. Also, in the prologue, *Na zdrowie* can be replaced with *Salud*, or یف صحتک:, or 건배, etc., to suit the actress playing

Ani. In Scene Eight, the phone call should be translated into a non-English language to suit the actress playing Jess.

Notes on Production

Cost of Living had its world premiere at Williamstown Theatre Festival (Mandy Greenfield, artistic director; Michael Sag, general manager) opening on June 30, 2016. The director was Jo Bonney, the stage manager was David Lurie, the set designer was Wilson Chin, the costume designer was Jessica Pabst, the lighting designer was Jeff Croiter, the sound designer was Ben Truppin-Brown, original music by Justine Bowe. The cast was as follows:

Jess	Rebecca Naomi Jones
John	Gregg Mozgala
Ani	Katy Sullivan
Eddie	Wendell Pierce

The play subsequently opened at Manhattan Theatre Club (Lynne Meadow, artistic director, Barry Grove, executive producer) on June 7, 2017. The cast was s follows:

Jess	Jolly Abraham
John	Gregg Mozgala
Ani	Katy Sullivan
Eddie	Victor Williams

The play won the Pulitzer Prize for Drama in 2018.

for Paweł Majok

"And I believe I can do this in an ordinary kitchen with an ordinary woman and five eggs . . . She and I and the kitchen have become extraordinary; we are not simply eating; we are pausing in the [lonely] march [of living] to perform an act together, we are in love; and the meal offered and received is a sacrament which says: I know you will die; I am sharing food with you; it is all I can do, and it is everything."

—Andre Dubus, *Broken Vessels*

"There's something about taking the cart back instead of leaving it in the parking lot. It's significant. Because somebody has to take them in. And if you know that, and you do it for that one guy, you do something else. You join the world. You move out of your isolation and become universal."

—Andre Dubus, *Dancing After Hours*

"Czemu tak się rozsypujemy? Człowiek to głupio skonstruowany."
"Why do we crumble like this? People are stupidly engineered."

—Paweł Majok

Prologue

An empty space. An empty stage. That is, a bar in December.
Specifically, St. Mazie's bar in post-Bloomberg Williamsburg, Brooklyn.
One might call it a hipster bar.

A man. **Eddie Torres**. *An unemployed truck driver. He looks out of place here.*
Eddie *is a man who understands that self-pity and moping are privileges for people who, in their lives, have friends and family who unconditionally love them and will listen to their shit. Anything he tells you, he hopes will be entertaining or funny or interesting because he knows you're not obligated to stay and listen to him. When he slips into sadness, he bounces back fast. He would have made a great uncle.*

He nurses a glass of seltzer.

Eddie The shit that happens is not to be understood.

That's from the Bible.

The shit that happens to you is Not To Be Understood.

So, see, this fucked me up a little when one day comes this call from Columbia Presbyterian. Is this Mister Torres? There's been a complication. I'm forty-nine and I've done nothin but love the fuck outta this woman for two decades and a year almost. Nothin. Who deserves that?

And a week from her birthday. Seven days.

We were gonna go to Maine. For her birthday.
See the trees.

I leave the lights on now, every room.
Smoke signal: I'm still here.

Holidays are hard.
Christmas next week—that's gonna be hard.

But listen to me holy shit the GLOOM. Get a drink. On me. Made a promise to myself. A penalty. I start talkin gloom, I get it in the WALLET. Lemme buy you a drink. What do you want? Order what you want, I'm payin. This place is my fuckin SWEAR jar.

Order what you want. Go ahead.

Me myself personally, I'm off it. That first day you wake up to find you are *not* in a pool of some kinda liquid, my friend? Vomit, say, or piss? That day? That day is a beautiful fuckin gift upon yer life, man. You are grateful for that day. And you are ready.

That day's the day it's all gonna change.

Signs are real.

This I know cuz I used to drive trucks. Cross-country. Loved it. Loved every aspect of the job. The scenery. Every aspect. The fuckin *scenery*. Utah? Jesus H, man. Utah's gorgeous and no one even knows!

But then I got popped for a DUI. In a car. Blocks from home.
Lost my CDL.
Shit's Creek.
So I got the memories. And some unemployment.

That life is good for people. I was thankful for every day they ain't invented yet the trucker-robots. That life is good. The road. Sky. The scenery.
Except the loneliness.
Except in the case of all the, y'know, loneliness.
This was what my wife was good for.
Not that this was the only thing.
But everyone what's married there's, y'know, the *fuuuuck* days. Like, *fuuuuck* what did I do. What did I actually fuckin do here.
Cuz, y'know, you married a *person*. And a person's gonna be a person even if they're married.
That's a lesson. That's a lesson for yer LIFE right there.

But still I
I still

still loved her.

She would text me. On the road.
At night. In motels.
Which, alone, can be, can drum up certain feelings.
This is why there's Bibles in motels.
We're all of us, in motels, on the road to somewhere we ain't at yet and that makes us feel feelings.
Roads are dark and America's long.

And I mean this wasn't *poetry*, these texts.
This wasn't like, y'know . . . (*tries to remember a verse of a poem, can't*) . . . poetry.

"Thinkin Of You."

"How's Things."

"Yer check came today."

"Off to bed."

"Goodnight."

That little buzz in my pocket or on the nightstand, that's the rope gets tossed down to you at the bottom of that well. When the thoughts come. Y'know. The Thoughts. That loneliness. The texts, they're like, climb on up outta there, y'know. Get up outta those thoughts, y'know, cuz "Thinkin Of You."

Truckers got wild imaginations.

Lots of time to think.
Just not much time to do much with all we been thinkin except what don't take time at all.
And what's cheap.
(*Toasts.*) *Salud.*
(*Remembers, re-toasts.*) *Na zdrowie.*[*] She taught me that.

Sips his drink.

And sleep. And we sleep.
If we can.

So I started textin her.
After she passed.
Like every few days.
"Thinkin Of You."

"Off to bed."

"Hope yer well."

. . .

"Miss you."

I'd lie a little too.

"Job hunt's goin good."

And joke.

"My love to Jesus."

"Slip in a good word."

. . .

"What are you wearing."

It was nice.
To talk.
To think of her, I mean.
It was just a nice thing that happened.

I owe you another, by the way. For the gloom.

Tries to change the subject/mood.

So I was hopin that, for like community service, they'd gimme a gig that was around people. Like bringin food to old people or like bein in plays. Walkin puppies, somethin like that. Brushin cats. But I'm painting fences in Livingston.

Humane Society's full up.

---

[*] Pronounced *[naz drove-yeah]*. See note on casting.

So now my phone's got all this paint and shit on it now, on the cover. "Thinkin of you."

. . . .

I prolly shouldn't be here. At uh, at St. Mazie's here. In uh, in Williamsburg here. All you young people here. With yer fashions. With yer . . . Pabst.

Prolly shouldn't be here.

Sips his drink.

This is seltzer, this.

For now.

It's maybe not good for me, right now, to be here.
Too close, y'know how sometimes you get so close? You just get a little too close? Moths, man. Like a moth. I know I shouldn't be here but I'm, tonight I'm, I'm comin home from paintin fences, right? Take the train. Bus. Walk. I'm home. Shower. Eat. Like usual now. Alone. And I'm sittin in my house, my apartment, my home, and I'm lookin at the boxes. All the boxes. Of her stuff. And I'm thinkin how this was her mug. Her bowl she liked. The chair. And I'm tempted. Not gonna lie. I'm tempted as all fuckin fuck. Not even 7 yet. Places will be open. Stores. And, even if they're not, then bars. I can do whatever I want. I remember I can do what I want cuz why not, actually. Actually, why the fuck not.

And that's when the phone buzzes.
On the table.

I didn't scream.

But shit I jumped.

. . .

"Thinkin of you too."

. . .

I may or may not have pissed myself at that moment.

It's my wife.

It's comin from my wife.

Her number.

Her number

My wife!

Fuckin, fuckin Ani! Ania Łucja Skowrońska-Torres*! My wife!

And then I realize
I realize her number they gave away her number.

---

  * See note on casting.

She's officially gone.

. . .

And I'm straight up tempted right then.
Why not.
It's not even 7.
Why not.

Buzz.

Thing buzzes again.

"Where are you?"

I wonder how long this person's got my messages for. I wonder if I should be embarrassed. I sent her a picture one time. (Not that kinda picture, buddy:) Of a fence I painted.
I don't remember everything I said.

Buzz.

"I'm at St. Mazie's."

This is not my wife this is not my wife I know cuz *cmon* this is not my wife I wanna make that clear to you that I don't think this.

But

In that moment?

In that moment, I was comforted to know she's with the good guys. With St. Mazie. And that heaven is Catholic.

Buzz.

"It's a bar."

Buzz.

"In BK."

Looks confused.

The fuck is—?

Buzz.

"Brooklyn."
Thank you.

Buzz.

Makes a judgmental face for Williamsburg.

"Williamsburg."

Buzz.

92   Cost of Living

"You?"

. . .

Buzz.

. . .

"You?"

. . .

It's 7 o'clock in Bayonne. The snow just started fallin.

And I wonder what to do.
This is not my wife this is not Ani my wife.

But

But honestly, I dunno what else to do.
Except I *do*, I do know what else to do.
I always know what else I COULD do.
But maybe
maybe something . . .
the shit that happens is not to be understood
and so maybe I should get some fuckin pants on and GO.

I'm in a cab (okay my car don't tell nobody).
I'm on the PATH.
I'm on the L. (The L!)
I'm here.

I'm here.

He takes in the Williamsburg bar.

And nobody looks like my wife.

Or at me.

Except you.

Yer
Yer real nice.
Yer a real nice guy, man.
I ain't been buzzed yet, texted, since, so. So maybe whoever it, y'know, she's gone.

Man. A ghost ever stood YOU up, man?

Shit listen to me. The GLOOM. That's number three. Yer killin me here. Get a drink. On me. No no no don't even think about passin, man. I owe you.
My treat.

He tries to catch a bartender, who ignores him, passes him by. He looks back at his guest.

Y'know what though? Whoever it is, was, Miss Mazie Saint Mazie or whatever this place is, fuckin, I hope she's havin a good night. I say that genuinely, man. Even though she stood me up. The punk. I'm playin. I hope she found someone here and ended up she's havin a real good night right now. Whatever that means to her. I hope she found someone to share the night with. That's important. Seemed like she really needed someone to talk to.
It's important.

Go ahead, man. Drink's on me. Made a promise to myself. A penalty. You get just one more drink for all I put you through. Go ahead, I'm payin.

. . .

Please?

Scene One

Early September.
It's raining outside.

An accessible apartment in Princeton. A well-kept and rich one.

Jess *stands alone, a bit nervous. But hiding it. She wears a soaked hoodie and jeans/ sweats. First-generation child of an immigrant. Does not come from wealth, nor does she try to seem it. Has a hard time keeping her feelings and opinions to herself. Which has gotten her in trouble. Still, she can't help it. Or doesn't want to. She will put up a fight when she needs—and sometimes even when she doesn't or perhaps shouldn't. Can take care of herself. Though perhaps wishes this were not always the case.*

It's been a while. And she feels very foreign here.

Jess Nice apartment.

No response. She waits.
She judges his nice apartment.

Should I be—?

John (*from off*) Hold on.

Jess Cuz I could—*[tidy or]*

John (*from off, "stop talking"*) Can't hear you.

Jess Is there somethin you want me to do?, while yer—

Flush, offstage.

Cuz I would never take advantage of the hourly rate, if I were hired. Not, y'know, doin anything while yer—in there.

John *enters in a wheelchair.*

He is beautiful.

John *has cerebral palsy.*
A kind of halted way of speaking.
Otherwise, he is determinedly polished.
Comes from wealth and wears it, undeniably.

Jess *had prepared for this. Had prepared to look unfazed.*
But she is. She is fazed.
And he is beautiful.

He looks her over a while before speaking.

John Do you have a problem being alone?

. . .

Jess No.

John You would get to think a lot. Waiting's part of the job.

Jess Sorry, I never worked with the, differently abled—

John Don't do that.

Jess What?

John Don't call it that.

Jess Why, I—

John Don't call it differently abled.

Jess Shit is that not the right term?

John It's fucking retarded.

. . .

Jess So what do I, how do I, *refer* to you?

John Are you planning on talking about me?

Jess No.

John Why not?
I'm very interesting.

. . .

Jess (*re: bathroom*) So after you, y'know, then would I have to . . .?

John Why do you want this job?

Jess I thought, the experience and I—, it'd be a very Meaningful Experience—

John Why do you want—

Jess The money.

John Good.

Jess And I'd be good at it. I'm responsible.

John Oh good. So you wouldn't lose me.
Have you ever washed someone before?

Jess Yeah.

John You have?

Jess Yeah.

John (*dubious assessment*)

Jess (*not meek, but clearly not a story she cares to share*) You need me to like, describe it?

John How much can you lift? Think you can lift me?

145 pounds.

Wet.

Jess I can lift you.

John You don't need to bench-press me. You would help lift me out of my chair, and onto my shower seat. Then you wash me. Every morning. My hair. Teeth. Trim my whiskers, on occasion.
You'd keep me handsome.

John *reaches a shaky hand out to* **Jess**. *She hands him her resume. He takes it, with two hands, and unfolds it—possibly partly with his mouth—and smoothes it out on his thighs. Looks at it. Judges.*

Jess Whatever I haven't done, I'd figure it out.

John And this is all present employment?

Jess Yeah.

John A lot of present employment.

Jess (*a quiet dig*) Fer some people. Yeah.

John These are late bars?

Jess What?

John (*impatient*) These are late bars, bars that stay open late, that you // work at?

Jess Depends but. Yeah. Yes. They're open late.
(*Suddenly realizing.*) I understood you It wasn't cuz I couldn't The way you How you Your um—Yeah they're open late.

John *looks back down at the resume.*

Jess I'd set an alarm.

John You went here?

Jess Where?

John To school. Here.

Jess Yeah.
I went here. Few years ago. Fer undergrad.

Why wouldn't I.

John So why are you still here? In September. At the start of the school year. If you graduated.

Jess Fer this job.

John Interview.

Jess Fer this job interview.

John Curious.

Jess What.

John That you're here for *this* kind of job.
If you graduated from // Prince—

Jess I graduated.
With honors.

John It doesn't say on the—What // did you study—?

Jess I'm just lookin for a side job. Somethin extra. For on the side.

John In addition to all the—// cocktail wait—?

Jess It's a loud as fuck alarm.

. . .

And you?, yer here for . . . (*Trying to guess his age.*) . . . // college?

John PhD.
Graduate School.
For Political Science. Just moved here.
From *Cambridge.*

He waits for her to be impressed. She's giving him nothing. On purpose.

Near Boston.

Nothing.

. . . Massachu—

Jess Harvard.

John Since you mention it.

He judges the resume. **Jess** *gets nervous.*

Jess   Listen whatever I haven't done, I'd figure it out—

John   How much life have you lived?

Jess   I'm . . . twenty-five—

John   Numbers don't interest me. How much life have you seen?
Not everyone can do this work.

Jess   Why? You make shit hard fer people?

John   This "shit" can, by nature, be hard. Not everyone can cut it. I don't hire from agencies; so some applicants think they can do it and then it turns out they can't.

Jess   How come you don't hire from agencies?

John   I don't have to.

Jess   Why not.

John   I have money. I can basically do anything I want except the things I can't.

Jess   What's wrong with agencies?

John   They don't appreciate my lawsuits.
If their people mess up, I can sue them so agencies limit aides to just doing the basics.

Jess   . . . What kinda stuff goes beyond the basics?

John   You ask a lot of // questions.

Jess   What might you be havin me do that's not the basics?

John   Various things. // I don't have a—

Jess   But what would I—

John   If you don't interrupt me—because, you see, it can take me a minute—if you don't interrupt me, you'll get all the information you need.

Jess   Sorry.

John   Forgiven. I don't have a list but things come up. You do whatever I need, within reason. You *would*, I mean, if you were hired.
You'll have to pardon my, well, suspicion but you're not what usually applies for this job.

Jess   And "what" usually applies?

John   Oh you know.

Jess (*she does*)   No. Please tell me.

John   I need someone who can really do this work so if you're not willing to—
I'm sorry but—

Jess   A lot.

John What?

Jess Of life.
Is how much I've lived.
So when a man tells me I'd hafta do some Various Things for him for money, I gotta push that man for a little clarity.

John Okay.
Well, when a woman says she went to Prince—

Jess Cuz she did. She did. She says it, she writes it in her resume, cuz she did. She went to school, she's lived a lot of life—before and after school—and she could do this. I could do this. If yer surprised I'd be applyin for a job like this, while workin a buncha jobs like those (*re: resume*), after goin to a place like this (*re: school*), then sorry, bro—

John John.

Jess If a man like you—

John // Like what.

Jess —livin how you do—

John And how's that?

Jess If you don't understand why where I went to school, *that* I went to school, doesn't mean shit for some people—then I dunno what yer payin for in there.

John I'm fully funded // actually—

Jess But I am not yer professor. Yer professor gets health insurance.

John Not necessarily—

Jess I'd do whatever, okay?, whatever you needed.
I'd do whatever.
John.
Within reason.
Sorry—sorry I interrupted you.

John *looks at her.*

Jess Please.

John *looks back down at the resume.*

It might look at first like defeat.
Perhaps **Jess** *turns toward the door.*

He looks back up.

John Jess.

Jess Yeah?

John -ica?

Jess Just Jess.

John Early riser, *Jess*?

Jess Can be.

John 6 a.m.?

Jess (*lying*) . . . yup.

John Well, then

He extends his hand out to her.
A moment.
She watches it shake.

Then she shakes his hand.

Here we go.

Scene Two

Early September.
It's raining outside.

A different accessible apartment. In Jersey City, NJ. A largely empty one, in transition and under-loved.

A woman enters. **Ani**.
She is in a wheelchair. Severe incomplete spinal cord injury.
Quadriplegic. Though some of the fingers of one hand are partially functioning.
Ani *is a woman whose world has not extended very far beyond North Jersey and just you try to say something to her and watch what happens. She has her own ways and she is fine with those ways and those that do not agree don't need to stick around—as many haven't. She can seem brusque or intense to some people. A cat that resists being pet. Until it wants to be.*

Eddie *enters with her, holding an umbrella over her. Then remembers the umbrella:*

Eddie Oh shit.
Bad luck.

He closes the umbrella. Sets it aside.
Their interactions used to have ease. **Eddie** *muscles it now.*

So this is yer new . . .

He is surprised at the place. Takes it in.

Ani.

You need to get some color in here. (*The worst:*) This beige? No. Feel like I'm walkin into a paper bag. You could get some kinda yellow in here. Some baby blue, some yellow. Good for emotions. I read that. It's therapy. Colors work on yer feelings.

Blue's for stress, like—relief. Red's for passion. And yellow I dunno but it's *yellow*. Ask yer nurses. Watch. They'll tell you. Shit's science.

Ani (*bone dry*)   I thought I'd try yoga.
Fer my emotions.

Eddie   . . . Can you // do—?

Ani   NO.

Eddie   Okay.

He looks around for something helpful to do.

Ani   What're you doin // here—?

Eddie (*looking for tasks*)   OkayOkayOkay. Pillow! Got yer pillow here.

He tries to put it somewhere behind her head or back. Sees she's strapped in all over . . .

I'ma just fluff THAT.

. . . fluffs and sets the pillow aside.

Okay. Blanket. Just blanket you with THAT.

He tucks a blanket around her chair.

You lose weight?

. . .

I will punch myself later for that. On yer behalf.

Or—Y'know what:

He takes her paralyzed arm.
She's confused at what's going on at first but has no control over it.
Oh no. Is he really doing this?
He is. He's really doing this. She can't believe he's doing this.

He punches himself with her paralyzed hand.

She doesn't look happy.

He sees her face, not looking happy.

And he awkwardly puts her hand back down by her side.

Ani   The fuck is wrong // with you?

Eddie   I don't know.

Ani   Strap it back in!

Eddie   Sorry sorry.

He straps her wrist back on the arm of the chair.

Ani Flatten it out.

Eddie What?

Ani My fingers, you gotta—Flatten // out my—Or I'll lose those too.

Eddie Right.

He returns her hand to pre-fist position, flattening her fingers on the palm pad of her chair.

There you go.
You good?

Ani Don't I look it?
What the fuck are you // doin here—?

Eddie The bed's the wrong way.

Ani What?

Eddie Yer bed's faced away from the window.

Ani Leave it.

Eddie Lemme move the bed.

Ani Leave it.

Eddie Lemme just do this real // quick.

Ani (*finality*) NO, EDDIE.
Just—// leave it.

Eddie Sorry. I do that.

Ani Okay?

Eddie Okay.

Ani Okay?

Eddie *Okay.*
Damn.

Ani But thank you.

Eddie (*sass*) You *would be* welcome.

Ani Why were you just standin outside my place // in the rain like some—?

Eddie I'm just sayin you could get yerself some light. Ani. By the window. Light's good. Keeps you happy. Serotonin. Vitamins. There is vitamins in the sun that's only in the sun that—and we need it. So listen, it gets cloudy or rainy or some shit like this again 'n see if they'll get you a box.
One a those boxes with the light comin from it.
Get one 'n put it by yer face.
It's for serotonin.

It's supposed to shoot like, serotonin at yer face.
When there's none outside.

It's prob'ly covered in yer plan.
'N if not, you lemme know.

Ani I'm still on yer plan.

Eddie Right.

Ani So you'll know.
You'll know if I need a box.
To keep me happy.

Eddie True.

Ani We can figure all that out, the insurance, soon's the papers—

Eddie We don't gotta // talk about that right now.

Ani I'm just sayin that for now I'm on yer plan. Til the papers.

Eddie We can hold off on the papers. I'm sayin if you need. Fer the insurance. They're just papers.

Ani They're a lot more than that.

. . .

Why are you here?

Eddie You look into that stuff I sent you?

Ani What stuff?

Eddie I emailed you! Good stuff. Cuz those guys you go to?, they can move yer arms fer you, y'know, stretch you out or whatever they do on like the *physical* level, but there's other kinds of therapies you can do. They're prob'ly just givin you the basics over there.

Ani So I should paint my fuckin walls is what yer sayin.
Then I'm cured.

Eddie Listen I have seen Miraculous Shit on YouTube. Actually, on the whole Internet. It's good to have in yer back pocket, y'know, cuz insurance, my insurance, won't always . . . y'know.

Ani You tryin to get rid of me?

Eddie What?

Ani Off yer insurance? // Fast as you can? That's why yer here?

Eddie What?, no! I'm—no, man! All I'm sayin's maybe colors! Yellows. Blues. That's all I'm sayin. I dunno if you knew about em so I'm, now you know about em. (*Like he's not allowed to say it.*) I . . . I've been thinkin about you.

Ani   When?

Eddie   What?

Ani   Was it when I went unconscious from the sepsis? Was it then? When I woke up from the surgery. The second surgery. Or when they said I need one more. Maybe it was May. The day I learned to move a finger. Or was it just September. When I find you standin at my door. When exactly, Eddie, in the last six months since I saw you after the accident, did you think to think of me?

. . .

Eddie   I wasn't sure you wanted to see me.

Ani   What in the world would give you that idea.

. . .

. . .

Eddie   There's also this thing I read says certain smells, right, // could—

Ani   I know.

Eddie   You don't even know what I was gonna say.

Ani   That shit's not real.

Eddie   What shit.

Ani   Colors. Smells. All that. Not real.

Eddie   I dunno, I seen on YouTube—

Ani   Okay well my nurse is comin by at 7—

Eddie   Oh cool good *cool*. So *she* // can tell you—

Ani   So you can go. You can go.
Thanks fer . . . settin me up.
I'm all set up now.
All set.

Eddie   Yer welcome.

Ani   Bye.

Eddie   Except . . .

Ani   What?

Eddie   I texted you . . . about . . .

Ani   What?

Eddie   There's just one // thing—

Ani   WHAT?

Eddie Except I gotta get my stuff?
I still gotta get some more of my stuff?

. . .

I texted? Last week. You, yer nurse, musta accidentally packed some of *my* stuff. I texted you about me comin by at some point to get my stuff. I called too. You ain't answer so—

Ani So get yer stuff.

Eddie But I—okay—this is funny—so I kinda left forgot my, the, suitcases . . . at—

Ani I don't have any suitcases.

Eddie So some are comin by.

Ani Some . . . suitcases are comin by?

Eddie In a few.

Ani Just . . . rollin by?

Eddie In a car.

Ani She can't come in here.

. . .

Eddie You want me just to wait outside?

Ani Yes I do.

Eddie (*"yer right"*) Okay.
. . .
. . .
In the rain?

Ani Do what you want.

Eddie But like but what would you *prefer*?

Ani Do what you want.

Eddie Okay.

Ani Fuckin, *prefer*.

Eddie I'll wait right here then.

Ani Then wait here.

Eddie Okay.

He waits.

Want me to put on some music?

Ani What is wrong with you?

Eddie No, not like—not like . . . *[sexy]* . . . *music*. Like . . . fer therapy. // I read—

Ani No.

Eddie Okay but yer not supposed to do like, homework or somethin, some kinda physical therapy homework? After yer appointments?

Ani You didn't read about it? On the whole Internet?

Eddie How can I help? Ani. While I'm here, how can I help?

Ani You don't gotta help me with shit. We're separated. Congratulations on yer suitcases.

. . .

Eddie I'll wait outside.

Ani *watches—or senses—him walk toward the door.*

Ani Sometimes they give you . . . physical therapy homework.

Eddie *turns back.*

Eddie Like what?

Ani (*bone dry*) Like "Try to move."
They do say I should listen to music.

Eddie See, I was tryin to tell you about that. And you'll do that?

Ani It's not—

Eddie Do that. It works. I dunno how—they don't explain in the video—// but just *listen* to it—

Ani I'm about to say some shit to you, Eddie, 'n I want you to hear it, okay?, so here's a Notice, an Advanced fuckin, that I'm about to say some shit I want you to hear. Okay?
You listening?

Eddie . . . yeah.

Ani Don't interrupt me.

Eddie Yeah okay go.

Ani I'm sad 'n I'm gonna—   **Eddie** You want the music?

Let's try that again.

Ani I'm sad 'n I'm gonna—I'M SAD.   **Eddie** You don't want the music?

Ani 'N pissed. 'N I'm gonna be sad, pissed 'n sad, fer however long I'm pissed 'n sad, 'n that's fine. I feel like feelin whatever I feel right now. In my paper bag. 'N that's fine.

There's no recovery from this.

My spinal cord's shattered. This: Is it.
I know you know that so please just . . . don't. Okay?

I can mail you yer shit.
I mean not *me*. I can't, fuckin—But somehow I, yer shit will be mailed. The nurse can mail em.
I'll consider that box fer my face.

She sees **Eddie** *on his phone.*

Ani   Are you // listening?

Suddenly, music.
Eddie *plays some music off his phone.*
Upbeat. And way too loud.

Eddie   How can you be sad with THIS?!

He dances.

He's having a great time.

He tries to involve her and then eventually he realizes how shitty that makes him that he's dancing and she can't.

And he stops.
The music still plays.

Eddie   I can paint the walls // fer you.

Ani   Turn it off.

Eddie   It's therapy, it can—

Ani   It's not. That's not therapy. Turn it off.

He turns it off.

. . .

You still can't dance.

. . .

. . .

. . .

Eddie   Look who's talkin.

. . .

. . .

. . .

They look at each other.
And crack.

Laughter.
We can see why they were once good together.

There's a moment where they stop laughing.
And recognize that. And maybe this is both a good and bad thing.
Ani puts down her abrasion for a moment.

Ani   The way the therapist explained it music if you really wanna know

Eddie   I'm listening.

She has had no one with which to share new information.
It's a vulnerable act. And he is listening.

Ani   ... is when music plays, the body goes lookin for the things it's missing. The broken things. The shit that's disconnected. And it tries to bring everything back together. Like it used to be. Back in order. Order like ... music.
(*A dig, before he can contest her.*) Classical shit.

The PT's helped me to (*she indicates she's moving her finger*) a little, and just on that hand, but the music's supposed to ...

You listen and ...

She moves the fingers of one hand as if playing piano.

yer body tries to imitate the ... sense that music makes // which is why—

Beep-beep.
Car horn outside.

There she is. The end of all that.

Can I just—can I just mail the stuff, Eddie?

Eddie   That's expensive.

Ani   I'd rather mail it.

Eddie   I'll just go get the bags // and—

Ani   I got an emergency button on this thing. I'll press the shit out of it I swear.

Eddie   Who do you [*think I am?*], cmon. You don't gotta threaten me // like I'm some kinda, fuckin—

Ani   I'm askin you then, then I'm askin you: Can I mail yer stuff.
Say yes.

He hovers by the door.

Eddie   I'll send you the list. A list. Of my stuff.

Ani   Is she livin with you?
... In our ...? In ... Bayonne?

Eddie   No.

Ani Will she?

. . .

Eddie (*caught*)   . . . it's just cheaper fer us both to, instead of—

Ani (*"no more"*)   Okay.

Eddie I can't pay fer a place on my own and help you at the same time.

Ani I'll pay it back.

Eddie (*not unkindly*)   Yeah but
but I'm payin it now.

. . .

Ani She's patient.

Eddie What?

Ani Only beeped once.

Eddie I should head out.

Ani Yeah.
Maybe you should.

Eddie Ani—

He decides not to say whatever he was gonna say.

Don't worry about the stuff. Fuck the stuff, it's not important.

Ani Which stuff?

Eddie It's nothin I can't live without.

He wonders if this is goodbye for a while.

Bye, Ani.

He hovers by the door, sees if she'll look at him.
She doesn't.
And exits.
Ani, *alone.*
Silence.
She takes in that she's alone.

. . .

. . .

She closes her eyes.
A finger moves.
The fingers of one hand move.
As if playing piano. Or trying to.
She plays an invisible piano with a few of her fingers on one hand.

. . .

We watch her in silence.
. . .
Then, car engine.
A car drives away.
She opens her eyes.
No one.

Scene Three

September. Early morning.

John's *apartment.*
Jess's *first day at work.*

Jess *prepares to shave* **John**'s *face.*

Jess   You tell me if I fuck up.

John   If you fuck up, you'll know.

Jess *moves the razor to his face.*
About to do it but—

John   Don't fuck up.

About to do it but—

Tired?

Jess   There's a knife in my hand.

(*A breath, gets ready.*) Okay.

She shaves him.
When the razor is far from his face—

John   Was it a long night?
At the bar?

She shaves him. Hesitantly.

Jess   Yup.

John   Me too. Long night.
Had a paper to write.
Tired?

Jess (*lying*)   Nope.

John   I am.

Jess   It's not the same.

John   What.

110   Cost of Living

Jess (*re: shaving*)   It's hard to do this when yer talkin.

John   I'm not contagious.

Jess   What? I know.

John   So come closer.

She does.

"The better to see you with, my dear."

Jess   . . . What?

John   Nothing.

She shaves him.

I hired an English major who doesn't talk.

Jess   Who said I was an—

John   Why else not list your major? On your resume.
Art history.

Jess   No.

John   Ceramics.

Jess   No.

John   Then tell me something about yourself.

Jess   So you can make fun of me?

John   No.
Depends.
Tell me something.

Jess   I can tell you I ain't cut you yet. I can tell you that.

John   You're about to see a lot of me. To know a lot of me.
You will take off my clothes and I will have nowhere to hide.
I don't really have a choice in that.

Jess   You had the choice to hire me.

John   And my choices don't stop there.
Every morning you walk in here, I have a choice about that.

It would be nice to know who is taking off my clothes.

Jess   You want a story?

John   Or a vase. If that's how you express.

Jess   I work at a bar. I drive there. In a car. Then I drive away.
I work at another bar. Take the train there, then I take the train back.
I work at bars. What do you want me to say? I went to college. This one. And I work

at a bar.
Bars.
The End.

John I'm just trying to talk.

Jess Well, I'm not my favorite thing to talk about.

John Why not—

Jess You gonna tell me to smile fer you next?

John No—

Jess Smile, sweetheart.

John // No—

Jess (*wipes his face with a towel*) I think yer good. No blood.

Jess *moves away from* **John**.
Perhaps **John** *sits there a moment.*
Alone. For just a moment.

John (*kindly, one more try*) Where are you from?

Jess Okay, what's next? Shower. Right. I shower you next.

No response.

(*Takes it upon herself to try to manipulate his chair.*) Okay, let's go—

John *moves himself away from her.*

John You want to just get it over with?

Jess . . . What?

John You don't like to talk about yourself—Or to me—And you're clearly—So let's just get this all out of the way.
The last thing I want to be reminded of every morning, first thing in the—is how uncomfortable my body // makes—

Jess I am not uncomfortable.

John Really?
Because I am.

John (*cont'd*) The knees and elbows can't stop drawing // towards each other. I fight to keep them apart. The joints feel like magnets—Try it.

Jess I am not uncomfortable with yer—I feel perfectly—Did I mess anything up?, Cuz I don't think I messed anything up.

Jess Try what.

John What it would feel like.
Your knees and elbows—

Jess Like pretend to be—Are you askin me to make fun of you?

John You are making fun of me by thinking you'd be making fun of me. It's part of the job.

Jess The job's to shave you, shower you, brush yer teeth, to // get yer—

John To take care of my body. Right. To understand me and the needs of my body. That's your job.

Jess And how's imitating you gonna help me shave yer face?

John I'm not asking you to—
Okay.
Okay.
Maybe this Maybe you Maybe this just isn't working // out.

Jess No, okay—Fuck—Look, I just started—

John If you treat me like a job—

Jess You *are* my job.

John Like I'm not even—

Jess You'd fire me cuz I don't wanna, what, mock you?

John No, // I'm not asking you to—

Jess Cuz I didn't entertain you // on command?

John No, just—

Jess I am not uncomfortable—

John (*the frustrated end of his rope*)   Then why can't we have a human conversation.
This was a mistake.

Jess Most people assume my name's Jessica.
It's not.

My mother came to the country with no English, very little, and she's in this hospital in Newark—it's not there anymore this is clearly like a few years—and the nurse hands me to my mom for the first time. She was here alone. No family. And the nurse asks my mom like, what'll you call her? And my mom just looks at her. She said that's the moment it hit her, how alone she is. How little English. How everything now it's hers. Her shoulders. And she thought the nurse said—When my mom was asked a question, she'd usually either just say yes or no or okay like judgin on if it was a man or a woman she was answerin, or if they looked nice, I mean most times people just asked her like, do you want a bag or are you okay and so she says yes or no or I'm okay. And so my mom, when the nurse asked my name, she I think she meant to say yes but, in her, y'know, her accent . . .

So my name's Jess.

Just Jess.

They were nice enough to put two s's.

. . .

John   You tell everyone that story? That's your story, right?, that you tell everyone?

Jess   Y'know what how bout I just finish the job and you can judge me on that. So shower. // I'll shower you now.

John   I didn't mean to judge you—

*Jess reaches carelessly for **John**'s shirt, as if to undress him.*
*The surprising, forceful contact causes **John** to spasm and splay.*
***Jess** pulls away, instinct.*
***John** risks falling out of the chair but catches himself.*
***Jess** freezes, doesn't know what to do.*

*Throughout the following, **John** recovers.*
*At some point **Jess** assists him in a small way.*

John   My body—
if you get too close, too fast—

My body over-protects itself.

Anytime I reach beyond myself, it's violence.
You reach and you shake and it always feels beyond you.
So you have to throw yourself—your arms, your hands—at what you want.

He grabs her arm.
Holds her.

Have you ever been hit?

. . .

Have you ever been—

Jess   Why.

John   That's what it's like. Under my skin. From underneath my skin. Like people hitting me from beneath my skin.

He lets her go.

And that's what you'll be working with. Every morning. Is touching, shaving, undressing, washing and clothing—that.
That's what I'm like.

They stand apart a moment.

Jess   That the story *you* tell everyone?

John   No, actually.
No one ever asks.

Jess Well, I clearly wasn't gonna.

John And I don't like to talk about it.

Jess Why did you?

John Because I never did.

You're the first, my first I ever hired on my own.
Since I started living on my own.

I never . . .

Something feels unsatisfactory to him.
He goes back to logistics.

There's an after-shave lotion you can use.

Jess What else you never done?

John What?

Jess You said you never . . . so . . .
What else, John, have you never done?

Something new is beginning.

Tell me something about yourself.

Scene Four

October.
Evening. **Ani***'s apartment.*

Ani Hell no.

Eddie But I know you, yer body—

Ani More reason fer no. You knew how fuckin amazing it *was*.

Eddie I need the money.

Ani Why? Fer her?

Eddie No. Fer like, in general.
Cmon, you'd rather have a stranger, some kinda—stranger comin in to take care of you? You don't know people, Ani.

Ani I knew *you* 'n see what happened?

Eddie Y'know it's really hard to talk to you when all you got is trumps on me.

Ani I'm not hiring you.

Eddie Discrimination.

Ani Fine. Cuff me.

Eddie You wouldn't hafta pay me as much as someone else.

Ani How's what's-her-fuck feel about this?

Eddie Great.

Ani She has no idea.

Eddie No, we definitely communicated about it. You really got a button?

Ani What? // Yes I do.

Eddie An emergency button, you got one? Then press it.

Ani No.

Eddie Press it.

Ani No.

Eddie Press it.

Ani No!

Eddie Press it if you don't want me here.
Press it.

Ani I really gotta say, Eddie, that I never got as huge an urge to get the fuck outta this chair as when I saw yer fuckin face. Since I seen you last month? The weaponry that's been dancin in my dreams, the violence that I would like to do to you is so—creative that that's when I feel like I could just vault outta my body. Outta this chair. Those moments are my most alive.

Eddie So hire me.

. . .

You been thinkin about me?

Ani What?

Eddie Since "last month."

Perhaps he sings/dances a bit, as in their first scene.

Ani Get the fuck outta my house.

Eddie Ani, whatever I don't understand now about . . ., I will. I learn fast.
Just gimme a week. Just gimme a trial run fer like, a week.

Ani Yer here cuz you feel like a fuck.

Eddie I always felt like a fuck. I'm just variations of that feeling from day to day.

Ani And when you quit feelin like the lowest of a fuck, however or whoever makes you feel even half a rung higher, then you'll leave. I know you.

Eddie   You know that One Time that happened.

Ani   Yer *livin* with her in our place in Bayonne, that's more than once.

Eddie   We were separating. At the time, the first time, you 'n I were—We're //
separated!

Ani   Right. I know you.

Eddie   That's right. That's right you do know me. You know me as a man who's been twelve years sober. A man who's been twenty—almost one—years faithful. I wasn't some perfect // fuckin y'know, but—

Ani   Yup.

Eddie   But I was pretty good, Ani. You can't deny the numbers. Twelve. Twenty almost one.
Not spotless, especially with the—But pretty good. Shit, compared to—

Ani   What.
Me?

Eddie   To before.

Compared to *me* before. Twelve years ago 'n then the nine before that? Compared to that, I done pretty good. That part I don't need you to confirm fer me. I know that. I know I got far. I know that in like, myself. That I come a long way. With that shit?, with me before?, a *week* is far.
(*A quiet truth.*) Proud of that. So.
I've taken care of you before. When you were goin through // yer own—

Ani   (*not proud of this, stop talking*)   Okay.

Eddie   Not tryin to hold that over you. I know what that is, to hafta be taken care of. I'm just sayin . . . you seen my work.

Ani   Yer what?

Eddie   You woke up the next day. You ain't die. So I guess that's my like, work sample. Yer my work sample.

Ani   I was blacked out fer most of yer work sample.

Eddie   Like I said, you ain't die.

Look, how much money you actually have to spend? How much would this cost you to get someone—?

Ani   I get checks. And I've applied for // some things.

Eddie   And all the hidden costs? I got a nice fat report from the Internet about *that*.

Ani   I'd rather find some way to pay someone than just hang on yer insurance forever like a fuckin, or onto you—

Scene Four

Eddie How? // How would you—?

Ani I dunno, man, but I'd rather do that!

Eddie And go a few days without bathing? Having brushed teeth? Eating?

Ani I'd rather find someone I can trust—

Eddie Like yer nurse tonight?

Ani This is one time This is one time this is happened She had her schedule wrong probably she probably had her schedule wrong.

Eddie Just this one time, she fucked up. This the only time?

Ani Just this time.

Eddie And yer okay with that? Yer okay with that? You'd trust her again? To show up? To do what she's gotta do?

Ani . . .

Eddie Just once.
Like me.

Ani What do you think's gonna happen you come take care of me a few hours a day? Huh? You brush my teeth a couple mornings, dump my bedpan a few times and BOOM, consc*[ience]*—fuck-shit, clap yer hands when I say Boom.

Eddie What?   **Ani** You dump my bedpan and BOOM—clap yer hands.

Eddie Like, // applause—?

Ani CLAP. Like one clap.
And BOOM, clap yer—CLAP YER—

He claps.

Not yet! Aaaand BOOM—

He claps.

Aaaand BOOM.

He claps on "boom".

And BOOM—

He claps on "boom".

And BOOM—

He claps on "boom".

And BOOM (*he claps*) and BOOM (*he claps*) and BOOM (*he claps*)—You dump my bedpan a few times and BOOM (*he claps*)—conscience cleared?

. . .

Eddie . . . This what you did with yer nurse? Maybe this is why she ditched you.

Ani Yer not doin penance on me.

Eddie Yer right cuz yer not my fault. This wasn't my fault.
You right now?, The way you are? (*He claps.*) Not my fault.
Look I know you won't forgive me fer the—I know that. Even though we were separated.
Technically. Which, I mean maybe you'll forgive // me but—Okay.

Ani Nope.

Eddie All I can hope for then, I guess, is some kinda shift. Not forgiveness I guess but. I dunno.
I can just hope fer something like that.
But I didn't do this to you. So.
So, no, I don't owe you penance for that.

I'd be doin a service. Fer free. Or at a real cheap rate, if you need that to make it feel . . . whatever.
And temporary.

Ani . . .

Eddie . . .

Ani You know what we talk about? My nurse 'n me? What we talked about? Nothin usually. She'd ask me how I'm doin, how this 'n that feels. Any problems? Physical problems? The weather. Straightforward shit like that. She tells me the weather all over America. We sympathize over snow in Chicago. We shake our heads at the humidity in Atlanta. We sigh about Minnesota. That must be awful, we say. That must be so awful fer people. Wherever she's got family, I know about it. I know about what their days must be cuz she tells me their weather.
I fuckin love that bitch.

Eddie . . . it's still raining outside but it's supposed to // clear up tomorrow.

Ani And it's nice—It is sometimes real nice to just think about someone's weather.
To feel bad fer their snow.
To forget I used to live a different way.
To forget what other people gotta do for me that I can't anymore.
That I did this to myself.

Eddie You didn't—
It was an acci*[dent]*—Bad luck.
I'm sorry.
I'll never bring that up again.

Ani We got too many trumps on each other. Decades of em.
I can see why you'da gone to her. It's nice to talk about other things . . . the weather . . . sometimes.

. . .

Okay, I'm done. No more of that talk.
New apartment. New body. New life. Old nurse.

Eddie   Could I just try?

Ani   Why?

Eddie   Cuz you don't have much of a choice in it.

Ani   . . . Why don't I?

Eddie   Cuz I already told em I'd take care of things.

Ani   I do have a button.

Eddie   Okay. And it went right to me.
I'm yer emergency contact.
I'm still yer emergency contact.
So when it turned out yer nurse couldn't come tonight, they called me.
I said I'd go over 'n check on you.
I said I would
'n I'm here.

Ani   . . . I can change those forms.

Eddie   'N who would you put? Who do we know in our lives who'd come? Who's got the money or the . . . *[responsibility]* . . . who you think could do this?

. . .

Can I—please—try to help you this week?
I've got a week before I hafta head out again for a drive. Seven days.
Seven.
Just the nights.
Seven nights, starting tonight.

Ani   Why?

Eddie   If I fuck up, I'm gone. They're findin you someone new anyways but fer now—

Ani   But—why, Eddie?

Eddie   Cuz I'd like to see you.

. . .

Seven nights.

. . .

Ania*?

---

*   See note on casting.

…

Something shifts for **Ani**.
She sees her lot.

…

Ani   My birthday.

It's my birthday next month. Three weeks.

I forgot.

…

…

I'll be forty-two.

…

Eddie (*as though he is the present*)   Happy birthday, baby.

Scene Five

December.
John's *apartment.*

Jess *showers* **John**.
We watch the entire act.
It takes as long as it needs.

Jess *wheels* **John** *into the shower.*
She helps lift him from his wheelchair onto his shower seat.

How this happens: **John** *embraces* **Jess**, *who he uses as support.* **Jess** *holds onto* **John** *as he pushes himself up and pivots on his toes from the wheelchair to the shower seat.*
She undresses him completely.
She runs the water.
Tests it on herself.
Tests it on his arm.
He nods if it's okay.
She washes his hair.
She soaps his body and rinses it off.

Jess *picks up a conversation she began earlier.*
There is more ease between the two now.

Jess   I mean I don't love these women either—sometimes they're worse than the but I'm not givin the girl tequila when she's that fuckin *done*, y'know.

John   Naturally.

Jess Especially when she ain't order it. I mean I'll take a man's money whatever but No Rapes On My Watch. This girl's on the couches we got, in the back, right, half dressed, half asleep (and this place is not, y'know, it's *loud*), and this guy to me he's like, YO cmere. Like 'Ey-oh!, OVER HERE. And he's one of those, y'know, with the button dooooown—

John Right.

Jess jeeeeans

John (*judgment*) God.

Jess with the hair, y'know what I'm sayin?

John Oh yes.

Jess And orange. He tans. Bro, it's fuckin December. And he's like This girl needs a *shot*. So I'm like Listen Chief I think she's *good*. And he's like Listen bitch—

John Uh-oh.

Jess Who's got the money, he says, and who the fuck are you?

John Wow.

Jess And he throws this balled-up dollar in my face.

John Some people.

Jess Bouncer palmed his greasy head 'n threw his douche ass out.

John Good.

Jess Right in the snow. Man, fuck rich people. No offense but, heads on sticks. France should happen here.

A moment of silent showering.

I don't understand why people here gotta judge you by yer job. I'm not my job.

John People have to judge you by something.

Jess Except no the fucks don't.

John How else will they know if they're winning or not?

Jess I don't judge people.

John (*makes a judgmental noise*)

Jess I make a sincere effort not to judge people.

John Well, I hope you never drown.

Jess I hope you never drown too, John.

John Because if it's you and Michael Phelps and I swimming in the Hamptons and you get a cramp? And you call on me because you're not judgmental? I think you'd probably die.

. . .
I judged you.

Jess   How'd you judge me?
Here, you want yer—(*wash cloth*)

John   Yes please, here—

Jess   Got it?

John   Got it, thanks.

Jess puts into John's hand a soaped-up wash cloth.
He uses this to wash his genitals.
Jess turns away so he can have privacy.
It's not awkward. Routine.

Jess   How'd you judge me?

John   Well.
I think.
I judged you well, I think.
You haven't lost me.

He drops the cloth on the shower floor—he's done with it.
She rinses him.

Jess   You don't gimme the chance to lose you.
You barely leave.

John   I leave.

Jess   To class, maybe.

John   I don't *just* go to class.

Jess   I never see you go out.

John   Big campus.

Jess   The neighborhood, even. This area. When I leave, after I'm done here every morning, you usually just—hang.

John   I don't like to be rushed.

Jess   Never see you, all I'm sayin.

John   Well
I never see you.

Jess   When would you be seein me? I don't live here.
I don't even come around here except fer you.

John   I—
I never see you, except when you're working, is all I'm saying.

Jess   I don't go out much.

John   At all.

Jess   It's cold.

John   Not all the—

Jess   Lately, yeah! Lately it's been cold as—And, man, anyways, you go out, you spend money. Coffee. Fuckin, ham sandwich. All that's money.

John   So you, what, stay home? Read? The cereal box I guess because books are "money."

. . .

Jess   I work.

John   Okay but
You can't It's not possible to work all the—

Jess   You can. People can. They do.

John   That doesn't seem like a life.

The silence of task-doing.

Jess   I sleep.
For fun.

She has laid a towel on the wheelchair.
She lifts him from his shower seat and helps situate him onto his wheelchair.
Dries his body.

John   Why—For what are you working so much?

. . .

Jess   Everything.

She puts on his pants. Shoes.

(*To herself.*) Who's got the money, he says, and who the fuck are you.

John   Don't worry about that—

Jess   He's right though.

John   No he's a—

Jess   It does matter who you are.
And what you have.
It matters.

. . .

John   Well
I think as long as you—

Jess   —work hard?

She works.

Those guys I serve at the bar? They make more in an hour—with a finger—than I make in a week with my whole entire body.

It matters who you are. Family. Connections. If there's gonna be a net when you fall.
Cuz everybody falls.

I'm the first one born in this country. And I'm the only one left—
I was supposed to be the one to—

I was supposed to be the net.

John   Is there something going on?

Jess   I'm just exhausted.

John   What's going on?

She looks at him.

She considers for a moment whether to tell him what's going on. Decides against it.

Jess   Polo or V-neck?

John   Crew, please.
The olive one.

Jess *retrieves a shirt.*

Jess   Nice. Is this another new one?

John   I may have even *gone out* for it.

She dresses him.

Jess   So how'd you judge // me?

John   What about merit?

Jess   . . . What about it?

John   Aside from family and—
Doesn't merit count for something?

Jess   Depends.
On who's the judge.

John   Well, you're not not-privileged either.

Jess *was about to contradict him.*
Then realizes what he's referring to.

Jess   No.
No, I'm not not-privileged either.

John   And you're not completely alone.

Jess *doesn't reply.*

John   You've got me in any case.

Jess   My employer.

John   Your . . . well . . .

Jess   What? You pay me.

John   Yes but.

But

I'm here.

. . .

(*Re: attractiveness.*) And also you're . . .
I mean in terms of "things you've got going for you."
You're also. . .

Jess   What.

John   Cmon.

Jess   What.

John   You know.

Jess   No, what.

. . .

John   Can you um can you fix my—

Jess   Yeah.

She adjusts his clothes. She is close to him.

John   You um . . .

Jess   Yeah?

John   You smell good.

Jess *and* **John** *feel how close they are to each other.*

Jess   Perfume.
Samples.

I take em from magazines.

John   It's nice.

Jess   It's prob'ly yer soap. On me.

She moves away to return to work.

So how did you judge // me—?

John   Your body.

This catches **Jess**.

John   For one.

Was that a compliment? Flirtation?

Whether you can lift me.

. . .

Jess   Okay.
And?

John   And how you move.

Jess   And how's that?

John   Why don't you go out?

Jess   Much

John   At all. Why not? Someone like you?

. . .

Jess (*a dare; she knows what he means*)   Someone like what, John.

John (*knows she knows what he means*)   And because you went to school here. Was another way I judged you.
It means you're not a dumbass.

Jess   Yer not gonna say it?

John   Fuck nope, Jess.
Quite right.
Fuck nope.

Jess *should have finished dressing* **John** *by now. She takes in her work.*

John   How do I look?

Jess   Good.

John   Good.

. . .

Good.

Jess (*preparing to leave, putting on a winter coat*)   Okay, well if—

John   Are you around tonight?

Jess   Am I, around?

John   This— . . . ?

Jess   Friday night?

John   Would you want to come over?

Jess   "Come over"?

John   At 7?

Jess   You don't usually ask me to come by at night.

John   I know.

Jess   And on a Friday night.

John   I know it's late // notice—

Jess (*finality*)   Yes. Yeah. I would. I wanna come over. Tonight.

. . .

John   Yeah?   **Jess**   Wait.

Jess   Lemme um, lemme just call 'n see if I can—

John   Right.
No of course. // Right.

Jess   No y'know what Fuck it.

John   No, don't // do that.

Jess   Someone'll cover. I'm sure. Fuck it. Yes.

She's convincing no one.

John   Are you // sure?

Jess (*rapid-fire*)   It's just—Friday night, I make the most on—and they're hard to, y'know, cuz you gotta work *up* to—They start you on Mondays Tuesdays shit days til you—Fridays are—And they don't always give em back if—Which is fucked—And there won't be as much—cuz, December now—And Fridays are—no yeah—yeah no—But everyone wants—But no yeah no someone'll want that. Someone'll take that. Someone'll jump on a Friday shift.
I'll see you at 7.

John   . . . Are you // sure?

Jess   Yes.

John   Yeah?

. . .

Jess   Yeah.
Love to.
I'd love to come over. Tonight.

Yes.

John Good.

Jess Good.

John Cool.

She wipes some saliva that has collected on his mouth, perhaps with a little extra care and sensuality.

Jess Cool.

John Tonight.

Jess Yeah okay.

She looks at him. A spark in her.

Tonight.

And she exits the bathroom.
With some sass in her step.

Scene Six

October. **Ani**'s *apartment.*
Ani *is being sponged in a bath by* **Eddie**.

A radio on.
It plays quietly in the background.

We watch them a while.

Ani I fuckin hate this.

Eddie I know you do.

Ani Cuz it woulda been good to feel this before. To have had you do this kinda stuff with me before.

It's nice.

You fuckin prick.

A moment of washing.

You coulda done this when it // mattered—

Eddie How's the water?

Ani Good.
I'm tired of yellin at you.

Eddie Me too. Of you yellin at me.

Ani I've thrown every awful string a words I could think of at you these past few days 'n I'm a very creative // person but yer still here.

Eddie That's true you had some good lines.

Ani You come back.
I thought you'da gone but yer here.
I don't trust that. There's something about that I don't trust.

Eddie Say the word 'n I'll go.

. . .

Ani Yeah I don't trust that. You'll be back.

A moment of washing.

How's the water feel?

Eddie Hm?

Ani To you?, how's it feel?

Eddie Oh shit is it too cold? Shit sorry. // Sorry sorry.

Ani No no no. It's good for me.
I'm askin fer you. How's it feel to you?
Yer hands are in it too.
I just don't want it to be too cold fer you either. Also.
I also want it to be nice fer you.

You prick.

Eddie That's nice of you.

Ani It is, prick. I know.

Eddie (*re: the water*)
It's great.
Thank you.
It's great fer me.

His hands reach into the tub.
Between her legs.

They stay there a minute. Frozen.
Or pull away.

. . .

Ani You *can*.

Eddie What?

A look.

Oh.

130   Cost of Living

Oh.

Ani   You may have um noticed when you were—

Eddie   // uh huh

Ani   undressing me // that—

Eddie   Yeah.

She pauses for him to get it.
He is getting something completely different.

I don't think I should, Ani. It might complicate // things—

Ani   No so I started bleeding, it's my //—this morning—

Eddie   Oh!
Right.

Ani   See this is why I wanted a lady to do this.

Eddie   No no I can, it's not // weird. I can—

Ani   I'm not askin you to . . . inside, I'm—Jesus—It's not any sorta wild—action that I'd need ya to do here. I just I know you usually avoid that area. In general. Lately. (*Sudden embarrassment.*) Jesus Christ.

Eddie   It's fine.

Ani   Just since yer cleaning, // y'know, *around* that area—

Eddie   It's okay.
It's fine it's fine.

. . .

It's fine.

Like this?

. . .

. . .

Ani   Yeah.

Eddie   It's fine.

. . .

Ani   I can't feel much.

Of anything. There.
I just want you to know in case yer like . . . feelin weird.

Eddie   I'm not.
I don't feel weird.
Totally normal.

Ani I'm not sayin I don't. Or I won't. I could.

I feel that . . . kind of feeling.

It's just not on that part of my body.

. . .

Eddie Where is it?

. . .

Ani It's somewhere else.

. . .

The sound of hands in water.

. . .

Ani I imagine things.
It's all imagining now. I imagine things.

Eddie What things?

Ani Nice things.

In case you were wondering.

That's what I do these days.
My mind is a great lover.

She re-thinks.

It's a good lover.

It's my memory I worry about. My mind's limited. I can only really imagine . . . variations of what already happened in my life. But in like, slightly different ways. So my imagination's got all this . . . grime that won't come off it from my memories.

Eddie's *hands in the water are doing something to* **Ani** *that she has loved for years.*

We should not know this has been happening until we hear how he talks to her—

Eddie You can't feel this?

What I'm doin right now?

. . .

You can't feel that?

. . .

. . .

. . .

Ani No.

Eddie *stops.*
And he continues washing.

A song of slow piano from the radio. Perhaps Satie.

Eddie   You listenin to this song?

Ani   Hm?, what?
Yeah.
Yeah it's nice don't change it.

Eddie   You wanna learn to play it?

Ani   Hilarious.

Eddie   No I mean I can't play it either. Not like, traditionally.
Always wanted to learn though. Anything. Any kinda instrument.
The sax. // Or, y'know, or maybe the piano.

Ani   God, not the fuckin *sax*. Oh yeah piano, okay.

Eddie   Think it woulda been cool to learn.

Ani   Well.
You still could.

Eddie   Used to pretend I could. My folks, they got me this little keyboard for Christmas once. Li'l Casio. They thought I'd be a champ at it. Long fingers, y'know. And I wanted to learn, Tried but. Nothing. And it killed me cuz I mean they *bought* it—with money they ain't really have, y'know. They bought it without realizin how much lessons cost and that school don't give em.
So I'd pretend to be able to play.
There was this control on it where you could still play it but no sound had to come out. So I'd imagine what it'd sound like. To play. If I could.
I'd put the radio on. Find the station where they play piano. And I'd act like I was playin that.
Beautiful stuff. I'd act like that was me playin that.

. . .

(*Re: radio.*) It's a good song.

Ani   You never told me.

Eddie   Hm?

Ani   You never told me that.

They listen.

Then, **Eddie** *takes one of* **Ani**'s *arms, and drapes it along the bathtub edge.*

Ani   What're you doin?

Eddie *rests one hand on her arm, then the other and he begins to "play"* **Ani**'s *arms like a piano.*

He mimes the music that's playing on the radio.

*It should look like the music is coming from **Ani**'s body.*

He's good.
He knows the song.
His fingers are beautifully accurate with the piano music.
It lasts long enough to move something in the two.

Eddie   Always wish I could.

He plays.

You feel that?

. . .

. . .

. . .

Ani   Yeah.

. . .

He stops playing. And returns her arm to the water.

. . .

Eddie   What do you wanna do fer yer birthday?
Weather's supposed to be nice next month.

Ani   It'll be November. In New Jersey.
And you can't tell weather that far in advance.

Eddie   We can plan on it bein nice. 'N if it's not, then we'll roll with it.

Ani   "We"?

Eddie   What would you wanna do?

Ani   You won't be here.

Eddie   Why not?

Ani   You got yer drive.

Eddie   What if I took off?

Ani   'N what if you paid yer bills?
Don't take off work.

Eddie   Listen, woman, I'm gonna do what I'm gonna do.

Ani (*not unkindly*)   Don't promise me things, Eddie.

. . .

Eddie What would you wanna do?

Ani *looks at him suspiciously.*

Ani Mm. You wouldn't like it.

Eddie It's not about me.

Ani Maine.
I wanna go to Maine.
Fer my birthday.

. . .

. . .

Eddie It's cold up there // right?

Ani See?

Eddie And it rains a lot and it's all like, fancy boats 'n shit? // Lobsters.

Ani Yer thinkin of Seattle.

Eddie They got fancy boats there too, right?

Ani Maybe. Never been. That's why I wanna go.

Eddie Okay yeah but Maine? That's like—Canada. Why you wanna go to Maine?

Ani I saw this picture once on Janey's desk—some trip she took with her kids after the divorce. To Maine. // The—

Eddie Like, a photo? You wanna go to Canada cuz of a—?, shit, I'll show you some photos of Cancún, you'll change yer mind about, fuckin, Canada.

Ani The frame was made outta wood but like, real wood. It was just four little twigs tied together but somehow it looked nicer than if someone tried to fix it into wood. And Janey's got a hat on—cuz it's so *sunny* in Maine—so you can't see her eyes but you can see her mouth which looked . . .
It's her in a field and she's holdin a stick like a cane. It's just her . . . by herself . . . and she's . . . fine.
And there's a lot of green.

Eddie Is that . . .? Is that where you were goin? That night?

Ani That's what they told me later. When the ambulance found me, they said that's what I said.
I wasn't. But.
But maybe I would've. If I'd kept drivin.

I'd hafta change a bunch of doctor's appointments if I went anywhere fer my birthday.

Eddie Yeah but. Yer birthday!

Ani Yeah but I don't wanna fuck around. With appointments. And it costs a lot to . . . do anything. Fer me to do anything.

Don't take off work.

Eddie I tore up the papers.

Ani What?

Eddie Or I will.
I will. When I get home.
The divorce papers.

Ani Don't talk about papers right now.

Eddie Okay.

Ani Papers were trees.

A moment of not talking.

Eddie Can you smoke in here?

Ani I can do anything I want in here.

Eddie *lights a cigarette.*
He alternates puffs between them, using his hands.
One for him. One for her. For him. For her.
They don't need language for this.
He knows she'd want some.

The following is quiet and simple.
They know each other better than anyone.

She leave you?

Eddie What?

Ani Did she leave you?

Eddie No.

Not yet.

But the . . . clouds are there.

Ani People are hard.

They smoke.

What are you gonna do?

. . .

. . .

Eddie Is there a world, Ani, where . . . where you and—?

Ani No.

. . .

. . .

We should think he understands. And drops it. But—

Eddie Why not?

Ani (*not antagonistically, just clear-eyed*) If I give you reasons, Eddie, you'll just—talk. It's not a game where you gather up all yer points fer this 'n pit em against all my points fer that 'n who's right 'n who's wrong. It's not like that anymore. If you wanna help me, you can help me. You helped me.
But if you ever came back, . . . like, Came Back . . . I'd need to know it was fer me. Not fer . . . anything else.

(*A rare glimpse into her longing.*) If I weren't like this right now, would you be here?

. . .

Eddie Yeah.
Yes.

. . .

Ani That's not a thing I'll ever know.
Everything's started over fer me—

Eddie It doesn't have to though.

Ani If everything was perfect in yer life, no holes you had to fill, you wouldn't be here.

Eddie That's not how people work. People don't go after people *unless* they fuckin need em. And everyone fuckin—needs em, someone. That's what life is, what yer life, my life . . . is. Okay?

That's how people work. In life.

Where's yer ashtray?

Ani They prob'ly didn't pack it. Fer fuckin, my own fuckin good 'n shit, the fucks. Check the kitchen though.

Eddie Be back. Don't go anywhere.

He gets up to exit the bathroom.

Ani Hey.

He stops.

Eddie What's up?

Ani It's been nice to get to know you.
Again.

Scene Six

This week.

Eddie You too.

Ani You prick.

Eddie Maybe you'll take me to Maine one day.

Ani Yeah.
Maybe.
Maybe I'll see you there one day.

Eddie Or you'll take me. I wiped yer fuckin ass this week—

Ani Oh my // God.

Eddie Fer *free*. You owe me fuckin—Canada.

Ani Go to the fuckin kitchen.

He smiles at her.
She smiles at him.
The pricks.

Eddie Be back.

Eddie *leaves the room.*
Ani *alone.*
She sits with herself in the tub.

Ani (*to offstage* **Eddie**) I think I'm gonna go back to work. In a few months. See Janey. Everyone. What do you think? Think I'll do that. I'd like to.

She awaits a response.

Eddie?

He can't hear her.

She stares out. Sits with herself in the tub.
She starts to wonder where he is.

Tries to turn her head.

Ani Eddie? Did you hear—

Suddenly, she slips down into the tub.
Not intentional.
Becomes submerged.

We hear yelling from under water.

From off, we hear rummaging in the kitchen.

Eventually, **Eddie** *returns, holding a plate for an ashtray.*
He drops the plate and reaches into the tub to retrieve **Ani**. *She gasps for air.*

138   Cost of Living

He holds her against him.

She gasps.

Ani   You can't leave me in the—
You can't leave me in—

Eddie   I'm sorry.

Ani   You can't—
You can't—
You—

Eddie   I'm sorry.

She gasps.

Ani   Don't go.

He holds her to him.

Scene Seven

Friday evening.
John's *apartment.*

Nice lighting.
Music plays.

Jess *enters. She carries a black plastic shopping bag. Sets it down.*
She shakes snow off of her. Takes off her coat.
She's dressed up. DTF. Lookin good. Feelin good.
She takes in the music and mood-lighting. Impressive.

She adjusts her dress. Tights. Hair.
Pulls a magazine sample of perfume from her bag and applies it to her chest and maybe under her arms.
She looks back to see if he might be coming and then she also applies some between her thighs.

She poses, ready.

Jess   John?

Flush, offstage.

John (*off*)   You're early.

John *enters.*
He turns off the music with a remote.

You're dressed so—

Jess   Yeah.

John Nice.

Jess It's true.

John You look nice.

Jess Well, you only see me in the mornings so—

John I need a shower, though, and // you're all—

Jess Oh. A—?
(*Intrigued.*) Yeah?
Yeah okay.

John Could we maybe start with a shower?

Jess I can get into that.

John I know this is a bit different from our usual—

Jess Uh-huh.

John And then maybe a shave.
An extra good shave.

Jess I can do that.

John I thought if it was too early, like early in the week or this morning, if you shaved me too early, I'd be prickly.

Jess Cuz yer a fuckin gentleman like that.

John And you're good at it.
And . . .

Jess Uh-huh . . .

John And I'm nervous.

Jess You don't hafta be nervous.

John And excited!

Jess Well it's good to talk before.

John I used to consider hookers.

Jess Yeah but maybe let's not talk about that.

John Yes that's not a very manly conversation. I used to think when I spoke of hookers it would be manly.

Jess Don't talk about hookers.

John But I just wouldn't know where to start looking for—see, another unmanly, I simply shouldn't ever talk about hookers.

Jess No.

140   Cost of Living

John   But if we don't talk about how far we've come, Jess, not doing certain things, how will anyone know how far we've come?

Jess   What do you wanna do first?

John   Brag.

Jess   Well how bout I could shave you first.

John   Good plan.

Jess   Then shower.

John   Yes.

Jess   So the cream, the—

John   Right. I see where you're going with that.

Jess   —the shaving cream would get washed right off yer body. In the shower.

John   Do we have time for both?

Jess   Fuck yes.

John   I'm meeting her at 8.

. . .

Jess   Wait.

John (*in his own world*)   Mm. What time is Maybe I should skip one. If I had to skip one, shower or shave: which?

Jess   For a . . .

John   First date!

Jess   With a . . .

Jess   Hooker?   **John**   Graduate student!

John   Madelyn.
From *Oxford*.
From *actual* Oxford.
PhD with a focus in *Hume*, the minx.
I'm meeting her at 8. Just like her figure.
How does one even do this.
When someone's so (*unsaid: wonderful*)—
There's just something so (*unsaid: wonderful*) about her.

Amidst this, while **John** *is oblivious,* **Jess** *takes from her plastic bag a bottle of wine.*
Opens it. A twist off. Pours a glass.

John   What is this?

Jess   Pinot.

She puts a straw in his glass.

John   Good idea.

He drinks from the straw. And wonders.

Oh Jess.
Jess Jess.
How does one do it?

She drinks from the bottle.

Jess (*as if to herself*)   Shave and a shower.

John   Shave and a shower, yes.
Please.
Thank you.

Jess   What time you gonna be done?

John   What?

Jess   With yer date.

John   Well, that depends. *Late*, I hope.
Oh, but you don't have to wait up.
You can go after this. And I can pay you for the whole—

Jess   But like two hours? Four? Dinner and a movie? Four hours? Five?

John   Oh. I'm not // sure—

Jess   Could I stay here?

. . .

John   In my apartment?

Jess   Just while yer gone.
I'd like to stay here.

John   . . . Why?

Jess   I won't fuck with yer shit. Promise.

John   But . . . without me here?

Jess   I just want one night.
I just want something that's mine fer one night.
Even if it's yours.

Say yes.

John   But—

Jess   Because I took off work.
On the night I make most my money fer the week. To live.
So I could be here.

With you.

John *sees her dress.*
The wine.
Her face.

John   Oh.

Jess   No one's gonna be here, right? This place will just be here. Warm 'n empty. With no one in it while yer gone.

John   Yeah but—

Jess   Say yes.

John   . . .

Jess   . . .

John   I don't really . . .
I
I'm sorry but I don't feel comfortable. You here.
Without me.

Jess   Why.

John   I just—

Jess   Why.

John   You've taken some stuff // before—

Jess   What stuff.

John   It doesn't—

Jess   What.

John   Soap.

I know you took, which—It's fine.
It's just (*unsaid: soap*)—But—
I would rather be here.
Whenever you are.

That's all.

Jess   I can give it back.

John   It's fine.

. . .

Why'd you take it?

. . .

Jess   I can give it back.

John   Could we just
Let's just
Shave and a shower.

And I'll pay you overtime, since you're over time.

Okay?

Jess   Shave and a shower.
Okay.
Yeah.

John   Thanks.

An awkwardness and strangeness hangs between them. Something's changed for good.

Hey at least you'll get to go home early.
For a change.

Jess   Right.

John *exits toward the bathroom.*

. . .

Jess *stands a moment . . .*

Jess   Right.

. . . then runs out of the apartment, her coat in her arms.

Scene Eight

Jess *has just run out of* **John***'s apartment, humiliated and lost.*
It snows around her.
She takes out her cell and makes a call.

The disappointment of an answering machine.
Raw need floods a non-English language.

Jess (*italics not in parenthesis indicate words spoken in another language*)   I was really hoping you'd pick up. *I miss you. So much. I wish I could talk to you.* (Re: illness.) *I wish you were still you.*
I love you.

I'm sorry. I just—I miss you. *I'm sorry. I'm sorry.*
I'm sorry.

Bye, *Mommy.*

She hangs up.

144   Cost of Living

She looks up and watches the snow falling out the sky.

Snow.
Wind.
Night.

She exits.

Scene Nine, or Epilogue

Eddie's *apartment.*
Boxes inside. Snow outside.
Later that night.
Something feels different.

Eddie *enters, goes to a box. Rummages through it.*

Eddie (*to someone offstage*)   It's somewhere in here sorry. Sorry I know it's in here somewhere.

He rummages.

You wanna come in? Warm up a bit while I—

He rummages. Sees this person has not budged.

Or—okay. Or keep enjoyin the view.
Of Bayonne.

Jess *walks into the doorframe, careful, alert, suspicious. And on the defensive. She wears a coat. Beneath it, the dress she wore to* **John**'s *tonight over the warmest sweatpants and winter boots she owns. She does not fully enter yet.*

Eddie You can see pretty much the whole rest of the apartment from where yer standin. So that's the tour.
But you can also come in.
If you want.

Jess   Where is she?

Eddie   Oh.
She kinda comes 'n goes—

Jess   Yer wife kinda comes 'n goes?

Eddie   We're uh
We're separating so she—

Jess   You said you 'n yer wife live here. That's why // I was even willing to come near here.

Eddie   We do. We did.

Jess   So where is she? She gonna be hidin in the closet? In one a these boxes?

Scene Nine, or Epilogue

Somebody gonna jump out these boxes and like, take my organs—(*Re: door.*) Keep it open.

You really got a wife?

He shows her a picture from his wallet.

Could be yer sister.

Eddie It's not.
And anyway, even if it was, wouldn't it calm you down you just met a dude carries around pictures of his—adopted—sister?

Jess Just sayin, not really a lady's touch in here.

Eddie Well, neither is that car you were sleepin in. Miss Lady.

You checkin to see if I had money?

Jess What?

Eddie In my wallet.

Jess No. What? // No, man—

Eddie See, this is why people don't help people.

Jess (*turning to exit*)   This was a stupid idea—

Eddie Just drink some tea at least!
If yer just gonna go back 'n fuckin, sleep in yer car all night—then come in a minute, have some tea.

She stops. Snow falls around her in the door frame.

It's awful outside. And you, out there, in yer icebox of a car.
I woulda invited you in no matter who you were. A man or a—

Jess Right.

Eddie I woulda.
1 a.m. on a Friday night, you don't know who could be out there.

Jess I've been doin this a few weeks now, I can handle myself.

Eddie A few weeks?, you been sleepin in yer—?

Jess I usually have heat goin. But the battery died.
Where's the—

Eddie Found it.

He finds a blanket in one of the boxes. **Ani**'s *blanket.*
He hesitates then hands it to **Jess**.

Jess Thank you. This is really gonna be—Thanks—helpful. Out there.

She is about to leave—

Eddie If you could just—leave it by the door? In the morning? Or whenever yer done // with—

Jess Yeah, okay.

Eddie Appreciate it.

Sentimental.

Jess *is about to leave—then remembers where she's come from and where she's going. Pauses.*

Jess I'm just gonna warm up for a minute.

Eddie Okay.

Jess That's all.
Then I'm gone.

. . .

Eddie I got pizza should still be good. I can heat it.
(*Carefully.*) I won't . . . I won't give you money. But I'll feed you.

I knew a lady, not far from here, she died in her car doin what yer doin. She'd keep her car runnin while she was sleepin in it and a gas can in the back in case she ran outta—And one night it tipped over. A lady. Young. Thirty-two or something, thirty-three. They found her in the morning. Suffocated. The fumes.
A stupid thing. Small, stupid things.
A gas can.
And then she—wasn't.

I saw you in yer car and I—I dunno, you never know, y'know?

Jess *hasn't moved.*
Snow around her.

Eddie I got pizza. If you want it.

Jess What kind?

Eddie Plain.

Jess It's good?

Eddie From last night.

You gonna come in?

. . .

Jess I dunno get the pizza.

. . .

Eddie You gonna steal my shit? While I heat this slice?

Jess What shit am I gonna steal? 'N put where?

Scene Nine, or Epilogue

. . .

. . .

Eddie Don't steal my shit.

He exits, to heat a slice. We hear a microwave in the darkness of the apartment.

Jess stands—looking around—but always near the door.

Eddie returns. The microwave hums in the distance.

Jess I work.

Eddie Okay.

Jess I'm not some kinda—just sleepin in a car, okay? // I work.

Eddie Okay.

Jess Til 4 a.m. some nights.
At bars, so don't get any ideas.
I woulda usually been workin tonight. Fer most of the night.
I—I wasn't tonight. But I usually woulda.

The microwave beeps.

I'm not some fuckin—just sleeps in a car. I went to school. I work.

Eddie You wanna come inside?

Jess I am inside.

Eddie More inside?

Jess I'm good here.

Eddie Okay but the snow is—

Jess Oh.

Eddie I mean, I don't have any nice stuff or anything, *rugs*, that I'm like, worried about here but—snow's fallin inside.
I don't want you to trip.

Jess I'm careful.

Eddie Okay.

She still stands by the door.
Then, she takes one step closer in.
And closes the door slightly—still keeping it open. Ready.

Want me to take yer // coat?

Jess I don't walk into houses, I want you to know that, I also don't just walk into houses.

Eddie Yeah of course—

Jess I'm careful. I sleep during the day—usually—cuz I'm so careful. I arranged my life so I work at night—till // 4 a.m. some nights—

Eddie Till 4 a.m. yeah that's late.

Jess Don't make fuckin fun of me, you ever work all fuckin night?

Eddie Yeah. Yes. I have.
Lots of times actually.
Too many.

Jess . . . Okay.
Okay so you know.

I sleep at different points in the day, at some point in the day. People leave me alone, mostly. They see someone asleep in their car but it's in the day, the early day, and they kinda leave you alone. Mostly.

Eddie It's cold though.

Jess Yeah.
Yeah I haven't figured that all out yet. This season.
It is.
It's cold.

She sees the past few months of her life in her mind. Tries to pretend they aren't there.

It's really fuckin cold.

The microwave beeps again. A reminder.

It's little breaks, y'know? Car. The car. Health stuff, some problems—that cleans you out fast. Bad luck. Mistakes. Some mistakes. Was hoppin on couches fer awhile but that gets old quick—bein the one that always needs something. I got old.

Eddie Where's yer . . . ?

Jess I don't have family here, not anymore, in the country.
She got sick 'n went back.
We couldn't afford—Not here.
I've been sendin money but it's—you know—

Eddie Yeah.

Jess Not enough.   **Eddie** Never enough.

Jess So I'm sleepin in her car.
I can send more that way.

We used to live not far from here. So that's where I park.

Eddie By my place.

Jess Yeah.

Eddie So we're neighbors.

. . .

She died.

Jess   Yeah I know, the woman in the car—

Eddie   No. My wife. She died. Last month.
Please don't go.
Or you can go. If you want. But don't. Please.
We can have an arrangement. You can crash every once in a while.
Or
Or you can live here.

We can split the place. This place. I'll pay more. I don't have much, y'know, money but. I'm outta work now but I'll get employed again. I just—I need someone here. I just need someone here. With me.
I'm sorry yer a woman.
Not *that* yer a woman but I know that makes this all a little weird.
I keep the lights on now. Every room. All the time.
I would pay fer those! You wouldn't hafta pay fer those.
It's . . . it's just um . . . being alone . . . here is . . .
I don't know what to do—

The microwave beeps.

Jess   The pizza's . . .

Eddie   Yeah.
Yeah okay.

This feels to him like a defeat.

But he will still get the slices. He exits.

Jess *looks around.*
She closes the door.
It's instantly warmer.

She considers.

Eddie *returns with two slices of pizza on paper towels.*

Eddie (*re: paper towels*)   Plates were dirty. Didn't wanna make you wait.

She sees him. Sees something in him.

He sees something too.
In this moment, he doesn't think he'll ever see this person again.
You want it, um, to-go? In a bag?

Jess   How much is rent?

Eddie   Twelve! We can pro-rata it!

Jess   Don't get too excited.

Eddie (*he is*) I'm not!

Jess Yer not excited I could be livin with you?

Eddie I am. I // "would."

Jess Don't get excited. I'm just askin.

Eddie I'm not a weird person either.

Jess Cool I trust you now.

Eddie I don't even go to bars. Not usually. Or stay out late.

Jess But you were tonight.

Eddie But I'm usually not. I'm usually not so I wouldn't have usually even seen you out there, that late, in yer car. This was an unusual thing I did tonight. I was goin to meet someone.
I got stood up actually.
By a—

I was on my way home. And I found you.

Jess Oh you didn't "find" me.

Eddie Okay.

Jess You saw me.
I *let* you see me.

I was just askin. About the rent. Just—to ask.

Eddie Sit. Eat.

Jess I'll stand.

Eddie Okay.

He holds out her slice.

Jess Take a bite of my pizza.

He does.
Ta da. Still alive.
Then he gives her the slice.
She holds it, unsure whether to eat it.
Or to stay.

Eddie The poison's gonna take at least an hour so we got some time still to conversate.

She stares at him.
He laughs.
He laughs at his own joke.
Maybe he laughs too loud and too long.

Maybe he becomes devastated at thinking about death, even joking about it, at this moment in his life.
Maybe he thought he was okay sooner than he really is.
Something happens to a very lonely man here.

I'm not a weird person.

Jess   I think I'm gonna go.

Eddie   Do you have tea? Fer the car?

Jess   I don't have any way to make hot water.

Eddie   I'll give you some. Please don't go.

She puts down the slice somewhere.

Take the slice.

Jess   That's okay.

Eddie   What's yer name?

Jess *(exiting)*   I'm sorry.

Eddie   What's yer number?

Jess   No.

Eddie *(approaching her)*   Area code? Did you get a new number recently? What's yer area code?

Jess   I have mace in my bag!

He freezes. Hands up.

Eddie   . . . Thank you fer tellin me. Instead of just—

Jess   You don't seem like—
It's just unfortunate that some people have already lived a lot of life before they meet other people.
I'm sorry.

She goes to the door.

Eddie   Just—okay—be careful though, okay?
Stupid things. It can be a small, stupid thing. A blood clot while I was gone on a drive. A tiny vein. And then she wasn't.

Jess *(about your wife)*   I'm sorry.
(About leaving.) But . . . I'm sorry.

Eddie   Just—be careful.
And—and make sure someone's watchin you, I guess, in y'know . . . in some kinda way.

Jess   973.

Eddie What?

Jess Is my area code. 973.

. . .

Eddie Oh.
Okay.
(*Disappointed.*) She was 201.

Jess Thanks fer . . . trying.

Eddie Thanks fer . . . yeah . . . you too.

Jess *exits.*

Eddie *takes off his coat.*
It slumps or hangs somewhere.

He stands alone in his space a moment.

He goes to the pizza she left.
And he holds it in his hands.

. . .

Then, his phone buzzes from somewhere within his coat.

He stops.
He turns towards it.
Stands.

. . .

He fears going to his phone.

. . .

Then, the doorknob turns.
He jumps back.
Snow.
Wind.

Eddie Come in.

Snow.

Then, **Jess** *enters.*

She has a thermos with her.
She stands with the snow around her.

Jess I brought coffee. But it's old.

Eddie I have pizza.
But it's cold.

You wanna come in?

She takes off her hat.
And takes one step inside.
Toward **Eddie**.

He takes one step toward her.

Two people stand together in a fading light.

End of play.

Actually

Anna Ziegler

Introduction

The afternoon of the day when my play *Actually* opened at the Williamstown Theatre Festival, I fractured my ankle while walking across the grass from my dorm to the theater. I literally broke a leg on opening night! In theory of course this is good luck, but I was also left in a walking boot for the larger part of the autumn to come (an autumn that also included the play's New York City premiere at the Manhattan Theatre Club). My injury was nothing at all like the events depicted in *Actually*, but it also bore shades of them. Of that gossamer-thin line between good and bad. In the play, two college freshmen spend a night together that eventually lands them in the middle of a Title IX hearing, one student having accused the other of assault. They spend the course of the play telling the audience about their lives, describing what brought them to that moment, and that bed. Why they were drawn to each other and what might have led them to misread certain signals. The goal of the play is to make it increasingly difficult to stand in judgment of either person and so bombards the audience with information about each on the theory that the more you know about someone the harder it is to place blame, or want to. It's a play about the complexity of life, and of justice. In some ways, it's become even more relevant since I started writing it in 2015. We are now living in a world where it seems that everyone stands in judgment of everyone else, always. And we very rarely hear the whole story.

I believe this complexity is at least in part what drew the indomitable Mandy Greenfield to the play when she selected it for the festival in the summer of 2017. It was the spirit in which she guided our discussions of the play, both one-on-one and with the director Lileana Blain-Cruz and the actors Joshua Boone and Alexandra Socha. She inspired all of us to make the production as nuanced as possible, and we had long conversations about how to get the balance right in a story that intentionally walks a tightrope. She shepherded and believed in a play that risked being divisive but aimed to unite. I was grateful for that support, and I still am.

The two characters in the play, Tom and Amber, are flawed individuals, as are we all. They are real people capable of all that humans are capable of—obfuscating, deceiving themselves, not understanding, not wanting to be impolite or to embarrass themselves, of letting need or insecurity take precedence over empathy. The play asks that you consider whether "good" people can make bad mistakes—or worse. And in so doing it tests our empathy, our ability to acknowledge ambiguity and our capacity to forgive, qualities I prize in other people and that many of the plays I most admire aim to examine. Still, for the sake of the world, I hope the play will become less relevant in the years to come.

Characters

Amber, *early to mid-twenties, high-strung, talkative, charmingly neurotic. She does not present as insecure. She is Jewish.*

Tom, *early to mid-twenties, appealing and confident with some swagger that conceals a deeper vulnerability. He is African-American.*

Notes on Production

Actually was a co-world premiere by Williamstown Theatre Festival and Geffen Playhouse which opened at Williamstown Theatre Festival (Mandy Greenfield, artistic director) on August 12, 2017. The director was Lileana Blain-Cruz, the stage manager was Dane Urban, the set designer was Adam Rigg, the costume designer was Paloma Young, the lighting designer was Ben Stanton, the sound designer was Jane Shaw. The cast was as follows:

Tom   Joshua Boone
Amber   Alexandra Socha

Actually was subsequently produced in New York City by Manhattan Theatre Club (Lynne Meadow, artistic director, Barry Grove, executive producer) opening on October 31, 2017. The cast was as follows:

Tom   Joshua Boone
Amber   Alexandra Socha

The play was developed/written in part at the Sallie B. Goodman Retreat at McCarter Theatre.

*Lights up on a college party. Princeton. Two students, freshmen—***Amber** *and* **Tom**—*are outside on the quad. A first date. Sort of. They're drinking. A lot.*

Amber So I was reading tonight in our psych book about the pratfall effect, and it's actually really interesting: it's about how a person's attractiveness increases or decreases after he or she makes a mistake. So a highly competent person, like, say, a celebrity, would be *more* likable after committing a blunder, while the opposite would be true if—

Tom God, do you ever stop talking?

Amber What?

Tom (*with a small smile*) Just stop talking.

Amber Okay.

Tom I'm gonna kiss you now.

Amber Oh.
Okay.

They do. **Amber***'s not sure what to do with her hand so it hovers awkwardly over* **Tom***'s shoulder, not touching it.*

Amber Let's play a game. Let's play Two Truths and a Lie.

Tom (*emphatic*) Um. No.

Amber Come on.

Tom Okay. I have two truths for you . . . I hate games and I hate that game.

Amber But you'll play it.

Tom And why would I do that?

Amber (*forcing herself out of her comfort zone*) If you wanna sleep with me tonight, for one thing.

Tom (*without missing a beat*) Who goes first?

A sharp shift in tone. **Amber** *and* **Tom** *abruptly turn to face the audience.*

Amber So.

Tom In some ways I've been on trial my entire life.

Amber It wasn't an actual trial. It was a hearing but it felt like a trial. We sat across from each other. At these long wooden tables. I felt like I was a character in *The Crucible*. Maybe because our "trial" was in a classroom where I'd happened to read *The Crucible* earlier that semester.

Tom We sat across from each other.

Amber The room was very cold. I had to wear *two* layers. The cardigan I carry with me because I am *always* cold but also my jacket. *Inside.*

Tom I couldn't believe how cold this girl got. She'd have goose bumps like sitting outside on a 75-degree day.

An abrupt shift back to each other, and into the scene.

Amber Okay my first truth is: I thought I'd fall in love on my first day of college.

Tom (*that's weird*) First day?

Amber (*she speaks very fast*) Well, my parents did. My dad was my mom's professor in a class called History of the American South and she liked his accent and in a sort of twisted way that he was old enough to be her father and I guess he liked being able to lord it over her and probably her looks—my mom was very attractive back then—because then they were together.

Tom That was allowed back then?

Amber You don't even know if anything I just said was true.

Tom Okay. Fair point.

Amber Second one: I have never excelled at any sport.

Tom But you're on the squash team.

Amber Third one: I have no feelings for you whatsoever.

Tom *stares at her.*

Amber So now you guess.

Tom No, I know. I'm thinking.

Amber Lay out your thought process.

Tom Well, I'm an arrogant bastard so I think you do like me . . . And that shit about your parents is either too detailed to be a lie or so detailed it's the obvious lie.

Amber Hm. Interesting.

Tom You're on a team here so I think you've excelled at sports. And I'm way confident you're into me—

Amber So you've said.

Tom But—I'll go with the lie is about your parents.

Amber The lie was not about my parents.

Tom Then you're no good at sports.

Amber I'm no good at sports.

Tom How the hell did you get on the squash team?

Amber *Anyone* can get on the squash team.

Tom Is that right.

Amber I mean, you don't have to be great. You can be good, or just okay. It's a great way to help you get into college.

Just like being Black.

Tom (*incredulous and amused*) Um. You know you can't say that. Right?

Amber But it's not a micro-aggression or anything.

Tom Cause it's like a *macro*-aggression.

Amber (*unapologetic, matter-of-fact*) Come on. Everyone has things that help them get in. I'm not saying either of us is remotely unqualified to be here.

Tom (*in disbelief*) Wow. Okay.

Amber No, I'm sure you're super-smart. You had to beat out a shit ton of other Black kids to get in. I just had to beat out some other mediocre squash players.

Tom You think my only competition was other Black kids?

Amber Mainly, yeah. We all fill some stupid niche, which reduces us to something much less than what we are, but that's the way it goes. Has it been very hard for you, being Black?

Tom (*laughing*) God, you really are, like . . . a piece of work.

Amber But has it?

Another sharp turn out to the audience.

Amber See it became, almost immediately, "the matter of Anthony dash Cohen." (*Bashfully*.) Which I couldn't help thinking looked like what our last name would be if we got married . . .

Tom I get an email from the Office of the Vice Provost of Institutional Equity and Diversity. It's from some dude named Leslie. He made it clear that he was a dude by saying, "Because the name can be ambiguous I want to make you aware that I am a man." I'm told to come into the office at my very earliest convenience.

Amber What happened was I told Heather who told our RA Olivia who told whoever she told.

Tom I honestly thought maybe this was about my being an asshole for not joining the Black Student Union.

Amber But I didn't know Heather would tell anyone. She just came into my room and was like, "Amber. People are saying you were *topless* at Cap last night. What the fuck. Were you super-wasted?" And I'm like, "That's the least of it. I mean, Thomas Anthony practically raped me." . . . And she looked at me with these wide eyes, like she was kind of seeing me for the first time . . . and I knew immediately that I'd said something I couldn't take back.

Tom So I'm sitting across from Leslie, and the guy has an enormous beard. Part of me wonders if maybe there *is* a woman behind there.

Amber And so I tell her what happened. Or what I can remember. But I don't tell Heather everything. I mean, why should *Heather* know everything?

Tom And he's like, "I assume you know why you're here" and I'm like, "Enlighten me, Leslie" not realizing I shouldn't be, like, a dick right now. And he squints his eyes at me like he can't believe what he's hearing.

Okay, so even though my mom was always like, "Don't give anyone any reason to write you off" I'm still not great at gauging when I really should be polite. Like in 11th grade I once said to the school psychologist: "Who's *your* shrink, shrink?" I mean, I had this one weird thing and my high school sent me into therapy. What's that all about?

Amber So I just say to Heather that things went pretty far and she's like but that's not rape and I'm like I know that, Heather. What might have maybe constituted something approaching sex without my one hundred percent consent was that he got a tiny bit rough with me and at first I was into it but then I wasn't into it anymore and I stood up and was like, "Actually, um" but he pulled me back and kept going. And then she says, all horrified, "And all you said was 'actually'?" and I'm like yeah. And she's like, "But that's not no" and I'm like I know that, Heather—I am aware that two different words in the English language are not the same word . . . Also, I was just so so drunk.

Abrupt shift back to the scene.

Tom Okay, so I guess I'll say . . . in the spirit of truth . . .

Amber Or maybe a lie.

Tom If I can, one day I'd like to play piano professionally. Like in a symphony. Or jazz piano. Or, like, the orchestra pit of *Hamilton* / or something.

Amber Oh God I love that show.

Tom (*impressed*) You saw it?

Amber No!

Tom Okay . . . The second one is . . . my mom is the love of my life.

Amber Aw. That's sweet. That better not be a lie or you're kind of deranged.

Tom The third one is . . .

Beat.

I feel most out of place when people would assume I feel most comfortable.

Amber Like when?

Tom You don't even know if that one's true.

Amber (*kind, knowing*) I know it's true . . . The question is which of the other two is the lie.

Tom Oh fuck.

Amber   What.

Tom   I fucked it up.

Amber   You forgot to lie.

Tom   I straight up told you I hate games.

Amber   Wanna do it over?

Tom   I'm just too honest. What can I say?

Amber (*gentle*)   Then tell me some other things that are true.

Beat. They turn to the audience.

Tom   I was playing the piano in one of the music rooms during a free period.

And this teacher Emily Mackey, who couldn't be more than five feet tall, and who teaches percussion (*which is like "percussion"—who even takes that?*), she walks in and asks if I'd mind if she listened to me play.

I was like sure, be my guest, and I just kept playing. And yeah, maybe I stepped it up a little because I had an audience. And maybe it wasn't totally lost on me that Ms. Mackey looked about eighteen and also that she was a type I hadn't tried before—you know: boy body, flat-chested, short hair.

Amber   But, like, who is Heather to judge because she's probably always had great sex. I bet even her first time was amazing, with, like, candles, and some guy who *worshipped* her because she probably gives head like a porn star, and I'm sure she lost her virginity in, like, 9th grade so she never had to be embarrassed, in high school, that she hadn't done it.

Tom   So when she stood up and was like leaning on the piano while I played, I might've gotten pretty fancy with my fingers, just sort of dancing them over the keys.

I don't mean to come off, like . . . but at the time I felt I knew a coupla things. One was that I was decent-looking. Or maybe a little better than that. And the other was that I was a damn good piano player.

And she's sort of swaying. Ms. Mackey. I'm playing Bartok's third piano concerto, which is kind of a weird one, sort of all over the place, and not always the most, like, melodious, but she's *into* it.

And then, at the end of the first movement, she sits on the bench next to me so our legs are touching. And it's this fucking electric electricity and I don't know what to do about it. So I look her in the eyes and wait a second to be sure I'm reading everything right before I kiss her.

Amber   Whereas I was always really scared of *everything* about it. Like when I was little I remember wondering, like how you possibly get yourself into the situation where sex would actually occur. It all seemed so impossible to me, and embarrassing. And then, when you're older, you start thinking about how to *avoid* sex—because it's actually right there in front of you from 7th grade on, and that's, like, terrifying. But no one *admits* that. No one admits that if you hook up with a guy but you don't go as far as he'd like, or if you go *too* far, like my friend Rachel did, then you end up on a private blog that does *not* stay private, which you definitely don't wanna be on except if you're not it means no one has noticed that you even exist.

Tom   So . . . the funny or maybe sad thing about Bartok's third piano concerto is that he died before he finished it. He was writing it for his wife's birthday; he was gonna surprise her and I guess he did—but not in the way he was going for.

And the funny or maybe sad thing about that afternoon when I was playing it is that Mr. Damion, the chair of the music department at Carpenter, this total walking prick—I mean, the guy literally looks like a penis—well, he walked right into the room, and there I am, on top of the tiny percussion teacher, playing her like a fucking symphony.

And . . . um.

The least funny thing about what happens next is that she says I came onto her. And also, that I was aggressive or something.

Amber   At some point later it occurs to you that maybe sex should actually be a *pleasant* experience. But how to make that happen is a whole other thing. I mean, how can you control what kind of sex you're about to have? You usually don't know until you're in it. Or maybe not even til after it's over. Like days or weeks or even *years* in the past. Which is what I try to tell Heather, but she's very definite about things, so she's just like: if he raped you, he raped you, okay? And I'm like, "Okay!"

Tom   I mean, credit to my mom, because she didn't believe it for a second . . . Said it was racism. Plain and simple. And, you know . . . maybe it was.
Maybe it was.

Ms. Mackey got fired, so I guess that's . . . But then everyone asks why she's gone so by December of my junior year, I'm the guy who fucked this sweet little teacher literally and figuratively, even though we didn't actually fuck, and I have to see this shrink because what if I'm like totally depraved, which seemed like such a joke.

Amber and Tom   But now

Amber   I realize it's my default state. This zone of wanting something and not wanting it at the same time. And, like, what happened with Zach was a big example of that.

Tom   Leslie looks at me and says, "This is about you and Amber Cohen. I believe you two are acquainted." And then there's this silence while my brain computes that. Me and Amber Cohen. And my first thought is she did something weird, like maybe she's in trouble for doing something really fucking weird, but then I look at his face and I can tell it's not that.

Amber   Zach's my friend Rachel's brother, this totally white bread frat guy type, not the brightest bulb but *cute*, you know? And I liked him probably in large part because he never seemed to know who I was, even though I was over at Rachel's all the time and always tried to look nice for him but also not like I was *trying* to look nice because you can't seem to be trying to look nice when you're going over to your friend's house to do Latin homework.

Tom And he starts talking about "Title IX" and how it's his responsibility to oversee all investigations of conduct that might have violated the policy. And he's speaking really carefully and not making eye contact and it's making me feel like I did when I was going out with this girl Alexa at Carpenter who was actually a sort of minor celebrity—like she had this blog that I never read but white people like Lena Dunham were all excited about it or something? I didn't care; she was hot and we'd go to her apartment after school and no one was ever home and then one afternoon I was sitting around in my *underwear* and her mother just, like, walks in and Alexa is all, "Oh this is Tom; I told you about Tom, didn't I?" which she clearly hadn't, and the mother acts as though she's so excited to see me there, which she clearly isn't, and the whole thing is so uncomfortable and I sort of knew that if I'd been a different guy she would have sent me home on the spot but instead there I was having *dinner* with them and being talked to like *I* was the celebrity, like they'd be so disappointed when I'd finally have to leave.

Amber I was a senior in high school and I'd just gotten into college. Like, *that day*, I mean.

I'd come home from school and I was scrolling through this really dumb email where you have to rank like the five best books you've ever read and then send it onto the second person on the list and I was trying to decide whether to make my number one, like, *Gone Girl* or *The Iliad*, when I see I have a new email and the subject line is "Welcome to . . ." but you can't see the whole thing, so I open it and it's Princeton.

Tom I'm like, what policy, Leslie? I honestly don't know what he's . . . But then he says "sexual misconduct." . . . And he says it strangely loud, like he's embarrassed, which embarrasses *me*. See, I've never had any clue what to do with someone who's trying to hide how they feel . . . probably because *I* am always trying to hide how I feel.

Amber Which is . . . I mean, I was *not* expecting to get in. I really wasn't, even though being a mediocre squash player can help a lot because colleges need to fill their teams, and there just aren't enough really excellent squash players. But still I didn't expect anything that good to happen to me. I was always kind of not the best at anything, you know?

Like, I was never the *prettiest* girl. Not, like, ugly. I mean, I *can* actually look in the mirror and see a person who's kind of attractive, looking back at me. I don't know. My mom told me once I was "pretty enough" which one hundred percent of shrinks would probably agree explains everything.

Tom So I'm just like . . . what? And he says it even louder, even though the problem wasn't that I didn't hear him.

Amber The day I got into Princeton was the second night of Passover and Rachel had invited me to her family's seder. But I mean, who does the *whole* service on the *second* night? And not only that but her dad asks everyone at the seder to discuss things, like why is it worse to be indifferent than stupid? In reference to the four sons. And why do we say next year in Jerusalem?

And before I know what I'm doing I'm looking right at Zach and saying something about Jews and longing, and I know my face is very very red and kind of splotchy. Which is what happens when I'm embarrassed, so the whole world can see exactly how I'm feeling at all times.

Tom   So, just to be clear . . . Amber says I violated the policy? And he says yes, she has lodged a complaint. And I'm like, "But that girl is seriously into me" and he gives me this look like I'm deluded. (*A realization.*) Which I guess I am.

Amber   After the seder, we're all just hanging out, and Zach wants to watch hockey because the Rangers are having an okay season so they're "worth watching," but, you know, they lose. In like overtime.

And Zach is not happy. I guess he's one of those beleaguered fans who takes everything really hard, and he's like, "I'm gonna have a fucking drink" which makes it sound like he hadn't *already* been drinking all night long, but now he switches to beer, even though it has barley or wheat in it or whatever and isn't something you're supposed to have during Passover. But he's just like, "Fuck it. The Rangers weren't supposed to lose during Passover either." Which doesn't make any sense.

Tom   I ask him: what exactly does she say I did? And what you can see of Leslie behind that beard turns this bright shade of red and he's like, "She says you raped her, Thomas" . . . and I can't help it but I start to cry.

Amber   Rachel had fallen asleep on the couch, and Zach asked if I wanted to see this app on his phone that's like an updated version of Angry Birds Star Wars, but really he just wanted me to come sit next to him because once I was there he kind of touched my wrist and I froze and of course he knew. I mean, really he'd probably known

Amber and Tom   For years

Tom   my dad was a star. A math wiz, a point guard, a model son. But by the end of high school he was drinking, and getting into fights, and he never made it to college, which haunted him forever. And here *I* am, at *Princeton,* sitting across from Leslie, who asks what questions I have about the rape I may or may not have committed within the first two months of school. And then there they are too, creeping into the corners of your mind: those men swaying in the trees, because they're always there.

Amber   And he stands and kind of pulls me up with him, and we go to his room and he's kinda stumbly drunk and I am completely sober and we fall onto the bed and he is not exactly gentle with me but I don't really mind; the next day I get a UTI and it hurts so bad, but I don't know that right now and eventually he takes his fingers out of me and squeezes one of my boobs really hard, and I moan a little because I think that's what people do but he puts his finger to his mouth like I've made this faux pas by making a sound, a gesture I remember at least subconsciously because now I am always silent during sex, always always, like you practically don't know I'm there, and then he climbs on top of me and sticks it in. And the whole time, which isn't a long time, I keep thinking, "I got into college today" which, in conjunction with what's happening right now, makes me feel like a . . . yeah, like a different person, I guess. And when he's done he grunts a little, like this sound is just getting pushed out of him and it's not exactly a happy sound, but still I feel weirdly privileged—and in all honesty, grown up—to know what Zach Lieberman sounds like when he comes.

Tom And I just blurt out: I'm innocent until proven guilty, right? And Leslie looks kind of apologetic and then, really gently, is like: yes and no . . . In the coming weeks, before the hearing, there will absolutely be a comprehensive investigation . . . but also you should know that college campuses are not the criminal justice system. There's no judge or jury. A panel of three "neutral" appointees will interview you and Amber and any witnesses to try to get a full picture of what happened and then we will "convene" altogether and discuss. And I'm like, "Thanks, Leslie" and he's like, "Of course, Tom" so, like, I guess he thought I was being sincere.

Amber It snowballed. I'm suddenly the most interesting person Heather has ever met and she wants to be with me all the time. She even waits in the hall when I go talk to this guy Leslie, whom I'd just assumed was going to be a woman because of the name and also because here was someone whose job was to talk to predominantly female *rape victims*.

Amber But it wasn't.   **Tom** But I wasn't.

Tom And Leslie says if the panel determines that a preponderance of the evidence suggests I did it, he will be brought in to help determine my penalty. And I'm like, "What?" and he says: "If they find that the claim is more likely true than not true," which is still sounding kinda opaque to me, and he's like, "Fifty percent plus a feather, that's what it's like," and I picture this two-sided scale, and each side has the same amount on it, the very same shit, but wait, what's that up there? Oh, it's a feather, and it comes drifting down from the sky . . . and lands on one side of the scale and suddenly that side is weighted down beyond belief. Suddenly there's no contest.

Amber I tell Leslie that *Bob*, my stepdad, says I have to be really careful about accusing a Black man of . . . And the way Leslie looks at me, even though he doesn't say anything, makes me worry that Tom isn't gonna get a fair trial, like he's gonna be one of those Black men just tossed recklessly into the tornado of a broken system, but then I realize that shouldn't really matter to me. I can't fix the system, can I?

Tom So the panel of three neutral appointees is made up of a white dude who's like the assistant *assistant* dean of students, this hippy-ish art professor who looks white to me but her last name is Diaz, and a Black woman in the *women's studies* department. Which is like, really?

Amber And then Leslie is like: "But are you sure you clearly expressed your 'lack of affirmative consent'? This is, after all, a very serious accusation, young lady" and he's staring at me hard, like it would suit him just fine if I walked right on out of his office and his life, and for the first time I flash back to the night in question and to the way I felt the next morning, how I wanted to get out of Tom's room as quickly as humanly possible, and dig a hole and just live there forever, and I'm like, "I'm sure, Leslie, but thank you for reiterating the gravity of my actions."

Tom   He puts his hand on my shoulder and is like, "Call me if you need anything" and I have the sensation I always have when someone tries to be paternal, which is pretty much uncontrollable rage mixed with deep-seated resentment and I brush his hand off my shoulder as though it was a bug and he flinches like I hit him or something.

Amber   Linda is also there with me, at the trial. She's my lawyer. That creeper Leslie told me I could bring one person with me to any discussion related to the investigation—a friend, a relative, an advisor or a lawyer. So duh I go with a lawyer.

Tom   I am all alone. I don't even tell my mother about this. It reminds me of this time in 9th grade when my mom came to see me in the school play and she got all dressed up and was so proud but the thing is—I never stepped foot on that stage. I was in the third-floor computer room making out with this girl Julia, who was also in the chorus and when we realized we missed the beginning we didn't know what to do so we just stayed there and later my mom was like, "You were just so good in that play." And I never told her it wasn't true.

Amber   Bob found Linda for me. He's a lawyer too and needs to feel important so he's always like, "Lemme help you with that." Bob is this tiny man and so maybe he has to compensate. I don't know what my mom was thinking. It might seem weird to say so, but my dad was a very attractive man. Even when he was frail. Like I once overheard my mom on the phone snorting and saying, "Well, at least he's still virile." Which is not really the way you want to think about your dad. Or maybe it is?

Tom   I think I went to a debate in the first week of school in this room. It was on whether or not Guantanamo Bay was constitutional, and this one dude was so crazy passionate about it being unconstitutional that I started to agree with the other side, just because they weren't so annoying, and the whole time then and the whole time now I'm like how do you defend yourself? Is it what you say or how you say it?

Amber   So when we're all there—

Tom   The chair of the panel stands up and says, "Welcome, all." As though we're at a church service or something.

Amber and Tom   "Welcome."

Tom   "We're here today to decide whether or not Thomas Anthony committed a violation of the sexual misconduct policy on October 23rd in connection with his interactions with his fellow student—"

Amber and Tom   "Amber Cohen."

Amber   And when they say my name it's like, whoa. This is really happening.

Tom   Then I guess we're each supposed to make a statement. I am made aware of this because the panel chair is like, "Tom. Amber. Now you will each make a statement."

Amber   Here's a statement for you: the beginning of college was *insane*. I can barely remember it; that's how insane it was.

I drank a lot. Like, a lot a lot. And it tastes so foul but you just keep drinking it.

It's not peer pressure so much as fear. Like, if I don't do this, I might have to think about who I am and where I am and all of that is just too . . .

It was nice to be on the squash team, because you have this kind of . . . this built-in group of friends. Or at least people who could be your friends if you liked them. I mean, you see them all the time. The thing about doing a sport in college is that you do it all the time.

And, like, Heather was on the team too and she lived on my hall, so it actually would have been like weird and conspicuous if we *weren't* friends.

And Heather came from a lot of money. You could just tell. And that's not a knock on her at all, it was just . . . you could tell.

And she had a boyfriend from home, Dave, who was at Georgetown now, and she was always getting What'sApp messages from him and laughing hysterically. I guess Dave was really funny or something.

I don't know. Heather and I spend a lot of time together, and she shows me how I've been plucking my eyebrows all wrong and she shows me how to drink demurely from a flask. Also she buys me a flask.

We go out every night because everyone goes out every night. And then you go to classes and then you read—and there is so much to read; every day you have like hundreds of pages assigned but you only have between let's say 4 and 7 to do all that reading because after 7 you have to go out and drink til you're sick but those afternoon hours are exactly when, if you're on a team, you're at practice. So there's no time to do any of that reading and it starts to build up and even by the end of the first week there's this voluminous amount of reading you haven't done and this equally voluminous terror and *that's* what keeps you drinking.

Tom   Amber makes a really brief statement about how regrettable this whole thing is and how she wishes it hadn't come to this. And I'm like, you know, if you wished that you had it in your power to make it happen.

Amber   And then Tom makes his statement. He's like a) we were drunk and b) I would never rape someone. He can't even say "rape"—he takes this enormous pause before he says it like there's something in his mouth that's causing him great pain but which would be even more painful if it managed to escape.

Tom   I don't want to be here. It's all that goes through my head. I don't want to be here.

Amber   I don't like that Tom is all alone. He's like all alone at this long table.

Tom   I start thinking about when I first got to school, and how . . . yeah, how nervous I was. I mean, nobody brought me to college. My mom didn't, like, come with me and unpack my clothes and make my bed for me. Nobody took me to the store to buy that sticky stuff you use to put up posters, that doesn't leave a mark on the walls. Nope, I took the bus and then dragged myself and two crappy suitcases across campus.

And then halfway across the quad, one of those shitty suitcases just cracks wide open so there I am gathering as much of my stuff as I can in my arms and trying to look like it doesn't matter one bit. Finally this guy who's like the Indian Channing Tatum or something comes over and is like, "Need a hand?" and that was Sunil. He went and got me some garbage bags and we shoved everything into them so I show up to my room hauling what looks like this gigantic load of trash, but, you know, it's how I met the best friend I ever had, so I guess, in a way, I'm grateful.

Not that Sunil and me were tight from the start. I didn't see him again for a week, and it was possibly the weirdest week in my life, when you're sort of trying to fit in but you're not sure yet you even want to. I mean, seriously—part of you just wants to put all your stuff in your one remaining suitcase and go back the way you came. It's overwhelming—people are *all over you* to join their newspaper or their Motown-only a capella group, or the Black Student Union and you feel sort of sorry for them and also guilty for not wanting any of it. I mean, *you're* just like trying to figure out where the damn bathrooms are. And how to get from your room to where you can *eat* things. And yeah, maybe you kinda miss home. Or not like, home, but the idea of it.
Like, maybe you start to realize you've moved on from something. And you're never going back.

Amber   Linda, my lawyer, told me not to mention enjoying myself for some of the night. So I didn't say anything about my emotional state. About how just looking at Tom makes me tingly all over, so much so that sometimes I need to go home and change my underwear, which is gross but also a totally natural phenomenon as any high school health teacher would have you know. I didn't say that every night I imagined Tom slipping into my dorm room, unannounced, crawling into my bed and just having me.

Tom   Oh, and thank you, Princeton. I almost forgot. They gave me a Black roommate. Wasn't that thoughtful? Only Jayson was from San Francisco and into, like, fashion and didn't know a thing about music. He was always telling me how I could "dress for success," which apparently meant never wearing any of the clothes I actually owned, and of course I assumed he was gay so on one of the first nights I'm like, "So what's it like being gay?" and he gives me this weird look. Whatever. I'm sure he figured it out sooner or later.

So at the end of that first week the only thing I wanted was to find a piano and be alone. I'm hung-over from all the Jell-o shots; I can't get the taste of keg beer outta my mouth; I can't find my jacket which I musta left somewhere. So I'm cold and I have this headache and so far the food—it's like there is just never enough food to fill me up, or I feel like I have to leave the dining hall because I have a sense that I need to do something but almost immediately after I've left I realize I'm starving.

I'm just feeling depleted, you know? And my mom sounds a little tired on the phone, like not as interested in what's going on with me as I would expect. But whatever. If I find a piano, I'll be okay.

So I'm wandering like a jackass up and down Nassau Street looking for Woolworth, the music department, which isn't even on that street but me and maps, we do not get along—when I hear my name. And it's Sunil. And he's leaning against a wall under this stone arch and he's like, "You have to hear this" and he shoves his iPhone at me and I kid you not the guy is listening to Mozart's Piano Concerto No. 9, which is one of my all-time all-time favorites. And he's like "Isn't that *astonishing*?" And it was.

Amber   And then they start asking questions. And the questions are almost as embarrassing as the answers.

Tom   The white dude is like: you're saying it was consensual? And I'm like, yeah . . . what I can remember was consensual. That's right.

Amber   And then the art professor asks how much I had to drink and when I drank and how much time elapsed between drinks.

And I wanna be like—that's the point of drinking! So you don't remember how many drinks you've had and how much time has elapsed between drinks. But I know I can't say that.

Tom   Some of the questions we wrote ahead of time to ask each other.

Amber   I think this must be one of Tom's questions: Amber, did you feel you had something to prove that night? And I'm like, "No." And Linda puts her hand on my knee, which is her way of saying, "No need to elaborate." But when I think about it, I guess I think that when I got to school I should've said I had a boyfriend at home because *Heather* got to be this outside observer, staring down at us all. And by night ten or twelve the pressure is huge and Heather was always next to me going, "What about him?" and invariably pointing to some loser and I'd be like, "*That's* what you think of me?" but end up hooking up with him anyway just to get her off my back.

Tom   They ask whether anything else was going on with me that might have contributed to my behavior that night. And because Amber isn't really answering the questions, I'm just like, "Nope." Nothing else going on with me.

Amber   I look at him, and I'm like, "Really, Tom?" Because it really really seemed like something was going on with him. That night.

Tom   Sunil is like my spirit guide, my maestro, my first base coach, my brother. I follow him around like a fuckin' cat in heat. I just have this *reverence* for the guy.

He's from Florida, some town where he was the only person under, like, ninety-five for miles around, and his family owns a few restaurants now but for so many years they were just poor, just like dirt poor. His dad couldn't get work and at one point his mom and one of his sisters moved back to India. They went back to *India* because shit was gonna be better *there*. So Sunil was left with his dad. They literally started with a cart. One of those food carts and the two of them cooked everything and it took years but then it caught on.

He said the violin saved him. He played it all his life. And to hear him play is a fucking miracle. That's how good he is.

You know how some people love a book and they read it again and sorta get new things out of it? That never really happened to me. But with music. With music, it happens all the time. And Sunil. He wasn't anything like me but he got that and so he was completely like me.

And it occurred to me how lucky it was that I didn't realize, growing up, you know, like, how alone I'd been.

I tried to explain it, on the phone, to my mom, and she was just like, "Tommy, you had friends. You've always had friends" so yeah, she didn't get it. And you know, she was just sounding so tired.

But then I thought it was just that I was so fatigued myself because I wasn't sleeping because, you know, every night it was one of these parties, or three of them. And every night I was having sex.

Amber   I notice him for the first time in Intro Psych. He's sitting off to my left, a couple rows ahead of me, and his head is jerking forward every few minutes in that way that happens when you can't stay awake. He's making a really valiant effort though and at one point I see him literally hold his eyes open with his fingers and he is also constantly shifting in his chair. So all of that catches my attention, and also, and this probably sounds, like . . . but yeah, that he's Black. I notice that too.

Tom   At some point Sunil is like, "Man, you should slow it down." And I'm like, "Why?" And he points out—because *he's* a nice guy—that a couple times, these girls have sent these crazy transparent messages like, "Hey, did I maybe leave a lip gloss in your room?" or, "I wasn't gonna get in touch but I had this weird dream last night and you were in it!" but I'm like screw that. I'm a freshman. It's the first month of school.

And instead I start to get on him about why he's *not* hooking up. Because these girls are just there for the picking and every night he hangs back. I'm like, "Dude, what're you doing?" and one night he says he's not feeling well and another night he has a leg cramp and another night he doesn't see anyone "remotely interesting." And I'm like, "Interesting? These girls don't gotta be interesting." And I can tell there's some part of him that thinks I'm a dick and also some part of him that likes that about me. But he doesn't give in. He's just like, "Tommy-boy, you do your thing. I'm heading home." And after five nights of that, I pounce. I'm drunk off my ass and I get in his face, like, "Yo, what the fuck are you doing? This isn't gonna happen every day for the rest of your life, you know" and by this point we've walked out onto the quad and I'm so wasted that I'm seeing stars or maybe there really are that many stars over New Jersey, and I am so pissed at him and love him like a brother—maybe even more than my actual brothers—that I am shaking him a little, like shaking his shoulders and feeling really righteous and like I'm helping a brother out and teaching him what's right while at the same time justifying all the choices that *I've* ever made, that when he kisses me I am more shocked and repulsed and freaked out than I've ever been in my entire life.

Amber   But, like, I'm a big fan of Black people. I don't want to be so naïve as to say Jews and African-Americans have all this stuff in common, but they have some stuff in common, like not really wanting to go camping, or to Nantucket, and also the deep and unwavering fear that at any moment they will be rounded up and killed.

And like, I just, I notice him. That's all.

Tom The weird thing is that after Sunil like *assaults* me with his tongue, we're actually okay.

We don't even talk about it.

I mean, it was clear that I didn't want anything to do with any of that, but he didn't seem hurt or anything. Which is actually kind of amazing, right? And I start to have a little insight. Like maybe this is why guys do that. Something doesn't work out, you just move on. Not like every single female I have ever known who is physically incapable of moving on even if you make out once for five minutes on a fucking dance floor.

Amber After I notice him in Intro Psych, I start seeing him everywhere. I turn around and he's a few people behind me in line in the dining hall with like five waffles on his tray; he's walking across the quad with this ripped Indian guy, who looks kinda like Channing Tatum if he was Indian, like he's really bulked up, which you don't expect with Indian guys, no offense.

Tom And then one day at the end of Intro Psych, Sunil's like, "Dude, you *are* aware of the fact that this girl can't stop staring at you" and I'm like, "Who?" and he points to someone a couple rows behind me and she's really hot, like kind of a Chrissy Teigen/Kate Upton type, skinny but with enormous tits, and I'm like, "Wow" and he's like, "No, the one next to her" and the one next to her is not as good, but you know, I'm equal opportunity.

Amber I see him sleeping in Firestone, the library, and I see him in the doorway of PJ's Pancake House, and I see him at the gym where he's maybe technically lifting weights but mostly just talking to that Indian guy. One night I see him making out with this tiny Korean girl at T.I. and he's so into it it's like he's *eating* her face, and normally I would think that was gross but for some reason this time I *don't*.

Tom So I go and talk to her. Why not, right?

Amber He comes up to me after Psych and is just like, "Hey."

Tom And she's like, "Hey."

Amber And it occurs to me that maybe he's been seeing me everywhere too!

(A new disappointing discovery.) And maybe he thinks I've been stalking him?

And then I get self-conscious. And *then* I think that maybe actually he's talking to Heather, and I just hugely embarrassed myself, but no . . . it really does seem like he's talking to me.

Tom For some reason, I lose my smooth. Like, I don't know what to say next. And we kinda stare at each other until finally I'm like:

So how's Psych treating you?

Amber Oh! It's okay.

Tom Yeah?

Amber Yeah.

Tom Cool.

Amber Yeah.

Beat.

Tom So, so far we're having a really interesting conversation.

Sunil's right behind me and kinda jumps in. He makes a bad joke, at least I think it's a joke, about how we're probably missing out on some critical exploration of the human condition by always falling asleep in this lecture so maybe she could help fill us in, and I'm thinking, holy shit, Sunil is not good at talking to the ladies. And then this girl, this—sorry—kinda mousy girl who looks like she could be any of the girls at Carpenter whose Bat Mitzvahs I went to every weekend of 8th grade—this girl turns to me and is like, "I'm afraid you might have gotten the impression that I've been following you or something"—which by the way I hadn't, *at all*—"but I really have just been struck by how we seem to move along the same paths or in the same circles or something, like I saw you in the gym and at PJ's and weren't you at the Bent Spoon too—the ice cream place? And isn't it crazy" and all that and I'm just, like, who is this girl?

Then her friend, the hot one, is like, "Amber, I think he just wants your notes" and poor Amber turns beet fucking red and you can see her mind just unraveling. She's like:

Amber and Tom Oh, right, duh.

Tom And then these kinda splotchy spots start to appear all over her neck and before I can even help it I'm like, "Nah, I wasn't after yer notes. I saw you that time, at the Bent Spoon, right?" even though I haven't once gotten ice cream since I got here and would never pay five dollars for a tiny scoop of gourmet anything, but I don't know what's up with me; I keep going: "And I was thinking we could go back there together, like on purpose this time."

Amber The funny thing or maybe it was just weird was that I'd never actually seen him at the ice cream place. As soon as I said it I knew it was wrong; I was just running at the mouth the way I do sometimes, and sometimes as a result not everything I say is 100 percent wholly and completely true. I mean, maybe it's just that ice cream is never far from my mind. Or maybe I just wanted it to be true but either way we do end up getting ice cream the next day and he offers to buy mine, which even though I demur because I'm the product of feminists who worked really hard to have the right to buy their own ice cream, the offer means we're on a real date, right? Me and "Thomas Anthony," who, I mean, even his name is hot, and who knows, maybe he's gonna be my first real boyfriend, not counting my camp boyfriend, which in all honesty was a relationship based almost entirely on correspondence. Anyway I can't really believe it, and I'm trying not to think about all the other things I should be doing, like seriously the call of those books stacked on my desk is deafening, and also I didn't work out as hard as I usually do this afternoon, I don't know why, and now this ice cream that I can't help but eat all of is gonna make me fat, I can feel myself getting fatter as I eat it, not that I have eating issues, I mean, I don't, aside from the way all girls have eating issues, which is that we think about what we eat 100 percent of the time and always wanna kill ourselves.

Tom   Okay, so she's, like, weird.

I mean, she talks fast, like Usain Bolt-fast, and she doesn't really look at me.

But she's not shy, exactly. I've been with shy girls before. This isn't really shy. This is more like . . . yeah, weird, I guess.

Amber   But it doesn't matter. I'm on a date with this guy who for some reason I noticed and it turned out he noticed me too, and *this* is why I'm here, right? For experience, not just to read books I'll forget a month after reading them, and life is short, I know it is; I've had that feeling in my gut since I was a little kid, and it's not just because my dad was older and was always maybe about to die, it's something that was in me, was just *in* me, this sense that you can't hold onto anything and every moment is over before it's even begun.

Tom   Not like there's something wrong with her. She's just *awkward* and I'd like to say I find it cute or something, but really I just feel awkward too, until she's like, "God, I'm so awkward, aren't I" and without meaning to I'm like, "Yeah, I guess" and she apologizes and laughs in this way that *is* kinda cute and says she's gonna stop eating her ice cream because she's *so* full, and she puts it down, but a minute or two later she picks it up and finishes it anyway.

And then she's like:

Amber   So what's up with your friend?

Tom   What?

Amber   That hot Indian guy.

Tom   You mean Sunil?

Amber   How many hot Indian guys do you hang around with?

Tom   And for a second I'm sorta taken aback, like despite myself, because does she think Sunil is hotter than me?

But then she adds:

Amber and Tom   Not that he's hotter than you, Thomas Anthony.

Tom   I mean, she is already calling me *Thomas Anthony*! Which is something only my mom has called me, and only when she's mad or like being really lovey with me, but this weird girl starts it up right away, which is what I mean when I said she wasn't really shy; I mean, she's actually kinda straight up confident except that she can't look me in the eye and she can't stop talking.

Amber   A little thing about Judaism? When something good happens to you, you just assume something bad is on the way. That's the way Jews exist in the world, and also we have a very hard time walking around knowing about all the bad things happening at every moment in every part of the world, like if you watch that Naomi Watts movie about the tidal wave in 2004, then afterwards you're gonna Google the *shit* out of it and find this account of a guy who stayed up in a *tree* while everyone he knew got swept away, at which point you can't stop thinking about the last moments those people had alive and their fear, and also the pain they left in their wake. When this kid I didn't know well, but had known since preschool, so I *knew* him, you know? . . . when he killed himself in 11th grade, it occurred to me just how deafening and enormous the grief must be that emanates off the surface of this earth. Like, our atmosphere must just be filled with all this airless sorrow.

Tom   "Is he a nerd in a not nerd's body?" She's *still* talking about Sunil, and I really don't wanna be thinking about his body right now, I mean cool it, girl, who just took you for ice cream?, so I'm like, "Nah, he's chill" and she's like, "Okay but, like, didn't I notice he had a violin case" and so then I have to get into the whole music thing and she's all, "Wow. WOW, you two sound like professional musicians. So is that why you came to Princeton? To pursue music?" And she's looking at me in this way that I can't explain and before I know it I'm saying "I can't think about music like it's work because I need *something* in my life that's an escape from everything else." I mean, I tell this girl that I need to *escape*. And she nods like she understands, and then says:

"So why did you come here?" Which to me is, like, obvious: because I aced my SATs, and I got in; you don't *not* go to Princeton, and she's like, "I was attracted to the university's very strong English and creative writing department. See, my only minor talent is in writing so I have to pursue that path because really I think we pursue what we feel we're decent at because why set ourselves up for total abject failure." That's what Amber Cohen is like.

Amber and Tom   I'm telling you.

Amber   Like after that kid died, and his name was Jonathan, I feel like I should say his name, I was Skyping with Rachel about how horrible it was, how we just felt empty and like we had no business being alive, when one of my camp friends messaged me too, wondering if I could send her a photo of me from 9th grade because she was about to get that same haircut and wanted to show her stylist, so I'm having these two simultaneous conversations, one about the utter existential pain of living and the other about whether that was my haircut in 9th grade or maybe she means the one during the 10th grade chorus trip to Budapest—and really that just about sums up life, doesn't it?

A new idea, definitive.

Only it doesn't. Because it leaves out so much. Like when my dad died, I was just numb for so long. For so long I walked through my life without really living it, just years of school, squash, homework, in this endless cycle, and feeling like if I had something great to say there wouldn't be anyone there to hear it because my dad was many things—a product of his time and of growing up Jewish in the South, which probably made him irascible and insecure but he would always listen to me and seemed to care what I had to say and when he was gone . . . that was gone too. And somewhere deep inside, I think I felt like I was due for something good to happen, and when I got into Princeton it seemed like maybe that was my dad's doing, like a balancing of the scales.

Tom Never in the past, not once, yo, have I gotten such a hard time for *not* making a move on a date. I mean, I went with her for fucking ice cream, for godsake.

Amber But Thomas Anthony felt like too much. I mean not only was he by far the hottest person who had ever noticed me, but behind that layer of swagger and charm, he was also frankly the nicest. All of which is to say: he didn't kiss me that night. And I couldn't tell what that meant. I mean, maybe it was because all we'd done was get ice cream like fifth graders so afterwards it made sense to go our separate ways.

Or . . . maybe it was . . . me.

Something to do with me.

Tom An *hour* later, I get this message on Facebook:

"Dear Tom."

Amber (*bashful*) I couldn't help myself.

Tom "Just to be clear, I really enjoyed hanging out with you. I wasn't sure, based on the way our date (was it even a date?) ended—the way you said, 'Okay, so see ya around' that you would wanna see me again but I wanted to let you know that I'd be more than game to give it another go because I feel like I still have so much to teach you about the world, Thomas Anthony, like the proper way to eat an ice cream cone (which is not all in one bite) and how to pronounce your linguistics teacher's name. (I spent a summer in Wales.) And if that doesn't tempt you completely, I don't know what will. ☺"

Amber I was really torn about the use of an emoticon, which any self-respecting person should be, but then again I was torn about sending the message at all, so I figured what the hell.

Also the hour I spent writing that message was more time than I'd spent focused on any single thing up to that point in my college career.

Tom I don't know if I'd been planning to go out with her again. Probably not, if I'm being honest. Some guys get off on a girl being aggressive but for me it's the other way around. If I'm being honest. Like, you know, let *me* make the moves.

But in the case of Amber, I remembered this thing she'd said when we were ordering our ice cream, like, "Isn't it funny how incapacitating having choices is" or something like that, and also she isn't quite as, like, mousy as I first thought, like actually her eyes are sorta weird and sad and pretty when she actually looks at you, and the one time she actually looked at me, when I was saying goodbye, I was so taken aback that I just took off.

So I wrote her back. I mean, I waited a week, but I wrote her back.

Amber He waited *a week*. And, like, I saw him around and had to pretend I hadn't written that stupid thing.

Tom Sunil was like, "Dude, you're blowing her off" and he seemed really amused by the whole thing, and strangely, like, interested in Amber. Like in what I knew about her, and I was like, "I don't know, dude, she's just sort of a weirdo" and he's like, "But you like her" and I'm like, "I don't know." And he seems really suspicious about why I haven't had a real relationship before and I'm like dude I'm eighteen; I don't need to settle down. And he's like, "But I bet your mom would like if you did" and I don't know how he knows that, but my mom *is* always like, "Thomas, you could make some young lady so happy, why do you insist on torturing these women?" But I can't admit that so I'm just like, "Get off my back" and then he says, really simply, "What are you looking for, man? What do you think you're gonna find?" And I almost tell him the truth, which is that I have this sort of 3 a.m. fear, this desperate like night of the soul fear, that I will never really find my way around this world and that whatever I do I won't amount to anything . . .

And this might be why I write Amber back. Because she looked at me as though I really might pursue something.

Amber   He Snapchats me: "Amber, wanna meet at Cap tonight? Kegger."

And I can't help it. I write back

Amber and Tom   right away

Tom   I get a message back. Like, within two minutes.

This girl has no fucking game, right?

But that's okay, I guess. I mean, so she has no game. So what.

Amber   I don't know what to wear so I just go with a sort of tried and true look—the tank under a blazer with tight jeans and tall boots look. And I used the more expensive of my two shampoos and I even read two pages of my psych textbook before going out and they happened to be about the pratfall effect which explains why people actually are *attracted* to people who aren't perfect, who are clumsy or flawed in some way, and I found that really encouraging and the timing, like, really fateful.

And that afternoon I'd spoken to my mom, which is hit or miss because sometimes she only talks about herself, which is my fault for asking her so many questions but I always want to see if she'll realize she hasn't asked me anything and turn it towards me of her own accord. But this time I think there was some undeniable quality in me—happiness, I guess—and she could just tell and she was like, "Amber?" and I said, "You know, I think I'm gonna like it here" which is obviously a quote from *Annie*, a movie I watched about a zillion times when I was a kid, so much so that I think the movie and my childhood are sort of synonymous. Which made her cry a little. To think of me happy. Because that's just not always true. Of me.

Tom   Right before I'm supposed to meet up with Amber, I'm pre-gaming with Sunil. We're three shots of Jagermeister and a couple Sam Adams in when my phone rings and it's my mom—and she's just like, "Tommy, I've got it." The big fucking C. Cancer. She says she doesn't want me to give it a single thought and she's fine; it's not such a bad kind of cancer and I should enjoy college and I'm like you know I can't do that and she starts to cry and she says, "Tommy, what'll kill me quicker than cancer is if you don't take every advantage of your time at school" and what can I say to that? My brothers didn't go to college, my dad—nope—and the closest my mom came was three months of nursing school. So she's wailing and I'm all, "Okay, okay, of course I'll enjoy college" so I'm trying and Sunil and I go back to pre-gaming and talking and I'm already kinda drunk and it comes out, what she just told me, and Sunil—he just flat out bursts into tears. I mean, *I'm* not even crying but he cries for me and for my mom, who he's never even met and that moves me—that fuckin' moves me—and our man Mozart is playing in the background, Piano Concerto number 9, and Sunil puts his arms around me and I start to let it out; I let it out because I can't lose my mom; I can't lose my mom; she's been the glue binding me to this earth, I know it even if I've never said it out loud . . . and it's good to be held, it's nice to be held by my friend, to be in his arms; I even have this passing thought about how nice it must be to be Sunil's violin, this is how gentle he is, and even when he, like, rubs my back, that's okay; he's just there for me; he's just feeling it, but yeah . . .

When he tries to kiss me again . . . I mean, that's too much, that's a line crossed, that's me being taken advantage of right there and so I say so; I jump back and I say so, and he's like, "Tommy. Come on, Tommy. You know you're in love with me. It's okay. We're in love."

Amber Heather walked me to Cap even though I told her not to, and when we get there I'm waiting for her to leave. I just don't want to be with her when Tom arrives. Like I don't need a) the comparison and b) the suggestion that I didn't want to meet him on my own. I didn't want to seem nervous. Precisely because I was so nervous.

But Heather isn't getting the picture. So finally I have to just be like, "So maybe you should go now?" at which point she gets really huffy and is like, "Suit yourself" and as she walks off adds, "Nothing's gonna happen tonight anyway" which, like, infuriates me, because how does she know that? And so I call after her, "Who died and made you Humbert Humbert?" and then to clarify, "an omniscient narrator" and she looks back at me like, "What?" and walks away.

Tom And then there's this long pause and finally I'm like nope. Nope you've got that wrong. I say you don't know the first thing about me and you never will. I say you're an asshole and a fag and my mom has cancer and what the fuck were you thinking? And I can't help it but I pick up his violin and I smash it; I smash it into the ground and pieces of it fly everywhere and Sunil screams as though I've hit him, or worse, and my mother is sick and my friend, my only friend, is not my friend anymore and I wanna puke it all up and get it out of my body, just out, just gone, all of it, and then cleaned up and away, I want someone else to please clean it up—please.

Amber I was standing in the quad, waiting, taking little ladylike sips from my flask and watching this kid—like he was definitely too young to be a freshman—walk along the fence but he kept falling off it so it wasn't really so impressive but still strangely compelling—to watch someone keep failing at something—and I was like nota bene, Amber. The pratfall effect at work again. How human it is to fail.

Tom I don't know why but I kept thinking about Richard Wright's *Black Boy.* We read it in 10th grade English. Like you know, even the title. Even the title alone. I felt like everyone was looking at me because, you know, they were. I mean, there were other kids from "under-served communities" who got into Carpenter through this program prep but my year I was the only guy. And so most of my friends were white. And no. I never told them that I felt at all . . . like, weird, going to their houses after school and playing Xbox while their Black babysitters cooked and cleaned and made us dinner.

And in English class we'd read aloud. And I remember having to read this part of *Black Boy* that was like: "I live in this country where black people's aspirations are limited. So I had to go somewhere else to do something to redeem my being alive." *To redeem my being alive.* I remember that part. And I felt so much shame. And I felt so much shame that I felt so much shame.

Amber   When Tom got there I could immediately tell he was in a bad way. And in my head I was like, "Please don't end this. Don't say you have to go home. Please." I tried to just keep him drinking so he wouldn't leave. And, amazingly, that worked and eventually we went inside and danced. He had his hand on my waist and he was kind of holding on. Digging in. And I liked it. Feeling needed like that. But I think I also knew that something wasn't right? And it made me so sad, that Tom might be sad. I mean what in the world should make Tom sad?

Tom   And suddenly she just takes her shirt off.

Amber   I mean, yeah I was drunk, but I'd been drunk before and never done that. I just had to do something to get rid of that look in his eyes.

Tom   I was like *what is going on*. Did we just walk into some alternate fucking universe where Amber Cohen takes her top off? . . . But she looked happy. And free . . . To this day, I'm not sure I've ever felt free like that.

Amber   We were in this crush of people. We were inside of it and moving with it and I loved it because I don't usually feel . . . part of things in that way. And being there with Tom. That was like.

Tom   She looked . . . yeah, she looked sexy, and I was like, let's get out of here.

Amber   And I took his hand and led him away. I felt like a character in someone else's story: Daisy and Gatsby, or that woman who worked at the department store in season one of Mad Men and Don Draper. I was just a girl pulling an attractive man out of a party with her.

Tom   Where do you wanna go?

Amber   Where do *you* wanna go?

Tom   I think I must've said we could go back to my place.

Amber   But first we just walked around. And made out. All over campus. It was . . . amazing. I remember my hand in his, and the total thrill of wondering when we'd kiss next combined with the equal thrill of knowing it was going to happen. The *gift* of that.

Tom   When we got to my room, Jayson was there, sleeping; I must've thought he was sleeping. Or maybe I just wasn't thinking about Jayson.

Amber   He was sleeping. And we sort of tiptoe in, trying not to laugh. But there's this enormous poster on the wall, this Calvin Klein ad with Justin Bieber like naked, and I'm like what? And Tom is like, "That is NOT mine I swear" and that cracks me up, and his roommate was like, "Shut the fuck up I'm trying to sleep" and then Tom was kissing me again.

Tom I remember these little flashes of what came next . . . Her back, this streak of white. And the light going on in the room, but I don't know who turned it on. I remember how good it felt to turn off my mind. The way you feel when you get lost inside a piece of music and the texture of it just envelops you and you're not in the world anymore; you're just part of the music.

Amber I remember the weight of him on top of me and thinking he was different from Zach—not necessarily heavier, just different, like he was giving me more of himself, letting his weight just completely cover me up. I remember kissing him. I remember at some point really kissing him and thinking this guy was an excellent excellent kisser and worrying a little about that tuna sandwich I'd had at lunch while feeling simultaneously proud of myself for experiencing this unexpected thing, and very lucky.

Yeah. I think mostly I just felt really lucky.

Tom The Latino one only uses the word coitus, not sex. Did Amber say anything, she asks, trying to sound neutral, when you were mid-coitus? Not that I remember, I tell them, always trying to smile as though I'm Mister fuckin' Rogers over here. How about "actually" the women's studies woman suggests. Did she say "actually" at any point?

Amber There was this moment when suddenly it all just felt a little bit . . . wrong.

Tom No, I don't remember what she said or if she said anything but yeah, she probably didn't say yes. But, like, who says yes? Who in these situations is like, "Yes do that, please." We were drunk. She was into it . . .

And if she wasn't into it at some point . . . well, then my body, my brain, convinced me she was. I wasn't knowingly . . . I didn't do anything knowingly . . . I know that.

Amber Why would I have asked him to stop? You were into it at first. On this everyone agrees. And I really think about this. This zone of wanting something and not wanting it at the same time. Like I didn't ask Zach Lieberman to stop, and it's not like he was so gentlemanly. And now I am always silent during sex. I didn't ask Robby O'Neill in the 8th grade not to put his fingers inside of me on a dare in a closet, even though his thumbnail dug into me and it killed. I didn't say stop in 5th grade when Rachel and these two other girls were pulling my hair to see how long I could take it. I didn't say stop when my high school advisor suggested I take French and Latin and Ancient Greek *and* Japanese my junior year, even though when it comes down to it I much prefer English to any foreign language because how can you express yourself fully in a language that isn't your own? It's hard enough to express yourself in your own language. I didn't say stop when my mother told me not to eat carbohydrates if I ever wanted to get married. I didn't say stop when my dad died because I knew that was one thing I couldn't stop even if I tried, but still . . . I didn't even

Amber and Tom Try

Tom to remember what happened next they keep asking. And I am trying. But I can't get this moment out of my brain, this moment in the really early morning, when I woke up, and my face was tangled in her hair, like it was in my mouth and stuff. She was sleeping. Peacefully. And I saw the condom wrapper on the floor and was breathing a sigh of relief because I thought shit, Tom, you were so gone, something bad coulda happened. And then she opens her eyes and when she sees me she kinda startles a little, like she'd forgotten where she was. Then it's like she's about to say something but instead she just throws up all over the floor, just everywhere.

Amber and Tom "I'm so sorry"

Tom She keeps saying:

Amber and Tom "I'm so sorry"

Tom And I'm holding her hair back and I see just a little of the back of her neck and I swear I wanna, like, touch it, just a tiny bit with my thumb, which is weird because there she is puking but I feel something, like a longing for . . . Like maybe I do actually like this girl. After that she runs outta there pretty quick but I'm thinking she's embarrassed. And I clean it all up. It's fucking disgusting but I don't mind too much.

At some point, Jayson walks in like he's been up for hours already and run ten miles and designed a new messenger bag or some shit, and he's like, "Good night?" in this snide little Jayson way and I don't say anything, and he's like, "Next time try not to fuck someone when I'm literally in the top bunk," and I'm like, "I'm sorry, man," which I really was, and then, just to be sure, I say, "But she was into it, right?" And he gives me this look like, "You're really gonna ask me that?" but still he said, "Well, she wasn't *not* into it, if that's what you're asking." And I *guess* that was what I was asking. And I was relieved.

Amber At one point during the trial they start reading our text messages.

Tom Like, *out loud*. And let me tell you it is really fucking weird to hear your own idiotic texts read out loud as, like . . . evidence.

Amber "Hey Amber. I guess that was kind of weird. Ha. But I hope you're feeling better and you never vomit like that again in your life because that looked like deeply deeply unpleasant.

I'm sorry I was in a sort of weird frame of mind yesterday. I hope I didn't freak you out or anything. I'm not really such an asshole. I promise. See you soon.—T."

And the even crazier thing is? I wrote back.

Tom "Hey Tom. No worries. I mean yes it was a little weird but it's okay. I don't think you're an asshole.—A."

So, like.

Amber and Tom I don't know.

Tom But I think: that's gotta score me some points. Her text back to me.

Amber And then this awful professor—I've repressed her face she was that awful—I think she was in women's studies so she thinks she and I are . . . she thinks we are on, like, intimate terms. And she just asks the most graphic questions in the most matter-of-fact way, like "Amber, at what point did you feel Thomas Anthony's penis inside of you?"

Tom (*incredulous*) Thomas Anthony is what my mom calls me.

Amber I mean, let's just be clear. We had sex. And I didn't say, like, "Yes, fuck me. Do it in any way you want." So when they ask: "Did this boy do this to you without your consent?" even though I might not have chosen that exact phrasing it seemed like the honest answer was yes, especially because I was probably too drunk to give any meaningful consent anyway—

Tom You think *I* wasn't drunk?

Amber And because Olivia, my RA, sat me down after Heather told her and I guess Olivia had been raped once too and she said, "Amber you have to take this very seriously. If women don't take this very seriously it hurts all women. It affects all women."

Tom Jayson comes into the hearing wearing this bow-tie like he's about to go have tea with the queen but what comes out of his mouth is low-down and dirty; he says Amber couldn't have been conscious when we were . . . He says he didn't hear a thing from her. But I'm like . . . who would have a better sense of that? Me, or the guy on the top bunk? I think there are things the body just *knows*, you know?

Amber And then the assistant dean of students is like, "Amber, I want you to pay very close attention to what I'm about to say" and he looks around the room really intensely like a poor man's Gregory Peck giving his closing statement in *To Kill a Mockingbird* and he says: "So everyone agrees that earlier that night you took your shirt off. That you drank to excess. That you very willingly went back to Tom's room and got into his bed. Which makes me wonder: why do you think these actions that you admit you freely took don't amount to some kind of tacit consent?" And the panel is staring at me, one of the women looking kind of annoyed with the tenor of the question, and the other one doing her best to appear really neutral—which is when it occurs to me that maybe it doesn't even matter what I say. Maybe these people will hear what they want to hear no matter what. Maybe they decided in the first five minutes what they thought happened, or even last week. And I'm processing that and am just like "What?" and he says "You heard me" kind of harshly, like a dare. And for the first time I really wanna leave the room, but I can't, here I am, so I look down at my hands, and . . . I tell the truth. Which is that I do remember it. This moment when all of a sudden he was inside me, and it's not like I expected him to ask my permission but I didn't expect him not to either. And it hurt and it kept hurting, and eventually I just jumped out of bed.

Tom Wait a second. No you didn't.

Amber What?

Tom You didn't jump out of bed.

184   Actually

Amber (*slowly*)   I thought you didn't remember.

Tom   I would remember that.

Amber   But you don't. You obviously don't because it happened. I jumped out of bed and you grabbed me, hard, and I was like, "Actually, um" but you pulled me back into bed and you just . . .

Tom   I didn't!

That's a lie—she didn't get out of bed; I know she didn't, and she certainly didn't *jump* out of . . . Amber, tell them.

Amber   No I did. I had this strong physical impulse to get away from you, I did—

Tom   What are you talking about?

Amber   I'm just saying what happened—

Tom (*not able to help himself*)   You are such a privileged bitch, do you know that?

Amber   *I'm* privileged? I am? I know you want people to think you've had this awful life, but you haven't.

Tom   I want people to think that?

Amber   I bet you've always had friends. You've always had girls in love with you. You've always felt good about how you look. You get to be comfortable in your own body. And that's a privilege. *That's* a privilege.

Tom   It's a privilege to have everyone always looking at you? Is that right, Amber?

Amber (*really sincere*)   No one ever looks at me. So yeah. I think it is.

Tom   You're crazy if you think I'm comfortable in my own body.

Amber (*trying to figure it out*)   Well, if you're not that might explain why you did this to me.

Tom   Why are *you* doing this to me? Because you think I've had it easy or something?

Amber   I don't think you've had it easy. I think you raped me.

Long beat.

Tom   And I hate her. In that moment I really fucking hate her. And I say so.

Amber (*suddenly quiet*)   You don't mean that . . . do you?

Tom   You're like this . . . flood of feelings that you just dump at people's feet. You don't get what it's like to have to be careful; you don't get that it matters how people see you.

Amber   I never stop thinking about how other people see me.

Tom   I know I have to calm down but I can't. And I can't hide. Holy fuck, there is just nowhere to hide! I can't have any body but this one; I can't be anybody but who

I am—this man in the world who everyone assumes will make a mistake, if they just wait long enough!

And then Diaz is like, "Both of you sit down! And, Amber, speak only to us and explain what happened next. When you were back in the bed." And Amber, out of breath from fucking me over, is looking at her hands like they're the most fascinating things she's ever seen.

Amber   I don't know how to say out loud what happened next. Which is that I let him do what he wanted. I mean, I lay there as he *pounded* into me, this vacant look in his eyes, just thinking, "You idiot, Amber" because I'd let myself believe that he actually liked me. And also, "Fuck you, Tom" because stupidly I thought he could see that I'd spent my entire existence feeling . . . invisible, and that he would therefore know how amazing it would be just to look at me right now.

And I felt so profoundly, like desperately . . . sad, like am I the only one aware of the fact that I'm on this earth, in which case am I really on it? And if I don't exist then who *is* this, what is the point of this brain constantly torturing me with all this self-doubt if there is no self; what is this body I'm inside of, this body I *hate*, that never does what I want it to and doesn't look good in the clothes I put it in, that I don't like to look at too long in the mirror, that seems so wholly inadequate to the task of housing a person in this awful, fucked-up world.

And Tom didn't see any of that . . . He didn't see or forgive anything of my body or my soul. And I wanted to die.

Tom (*with reluctance*)   Yeah, so.

There are things the body just knows.

Amber (*then, quietly, realizing*)   So of course I didn't say anything else that night. I wasn't even there.

Tom (*quietly, a fear/a discovery*)   So maybe I knew. Maybe I knew. That she wasn't . . . And that's the . . . That's the thing that I . . . I mean, I thought . . . Deep down, I thought I was a nice guy.

Amber   But I'm here, now. And I can't just be silent anymore. I can't do that to myself.

Tom   She's crying, all of a sudden, these sort of animal cries that make everyone deeply uncomfortable.

Amber   But the cost of not doing that to myself anymore is . . . Tom. Which is just . . .

Tom   I don't like seeing her cry like that. It's all just . . . It's too much.

Amber   And then *he* starts to cry, and we just . . .

Amber and Tom   So now we're both

Tom   sitting there just . . .

Amber   and Tom is all alone and I wanna . . .

Tom I mean there's Amber, and she's gazing at me with this unmistakable . . . love. Which is like . . .

Amber I remember this Kierkegaard quote we learned in Intro Phil. "It belongs to the imperfection of everything human that man can only attain his desire by passing through its opposite."

But I don't know what it means.

Beat.

Tom Isn't it crazy, the idea that every single thing leads to everything else?

I played the piano for the first time when I was eleven. This was back at 261, when I was in a class with thirty other kids, and none of us paid any attention, just no one did anything anyone told us to, but still this one teacher, Mrs. Landrieu, still she, like found me.

Mrs. Landrieu was sweet and in over her head, like all those kinda offensive movies you see of well-meaning white ladies in inner-city schools trying to control this, like, pack of beasts.

But yeah, we probably were a little like beasts. And she *was* sweet. And she was trying. And one day towards the end of a particularly, I mean, a particularly fucked-up class—Elijah, who was the worst of the worst and also my best friend—might've implied that he was gonna go to her house and mess her up when he was like, "Mrs. Landrieu, I'm gonna go to your house and mess you up."

And then Mrs. Landrieu, she says in this tiny voice: Elijah, go to the office. Go straight to the principal's office, but here's the thing—he won't go. He just stays there. And the whole class laughs. And this is when she starts to cry.

And the next day, Elijah sits right up front, like an asshole, just to show her who's boss. And yeah, it was funny, but the look on her face like she wanted to die right there on the spot made it not the least bit funny. And so when she calls on me—and I'm telling you her voice has gotten even tinier since yesterday—I'm just like, "I think that's a really interesting question, Mrs. Landrieu," which doesn't win me any popularity points but, you know, I see a chance to do something nice for someone and I take it.

That's the kind of guy I thought I was, after all.

Of course she wants to talk to me after class. And I think she's gonna thank me but instead she's like: "Tommy, I wondered if you might like piano lessons."

I'm like, "What?" Turns out she teaches piano on the side. So when I show up at her apartment the next day and sit next to her on the piano bench—by the way, I had no interest in the *piano*, zero, but I would also never turn down something that's free—that's like my modus fucking operandi—when I sit next to her and she says really gently and really kindly, "I know your father left a few months ago" I just . . . I break down.

I mean, I didn't even like the guy. I didn't even like the guy.

And . . . after that, like . . . what else can you do. So you just play.

Suddenly they are in a scene—the college party that took place the night of the incident. **Tom** *is agitated and irritable. They have to shout a bit to be heard over the music in the quad.*

Amber (*waving awkwardly at him*)   Tom!

Tom   Sorry—I got a little held up.

Amber   That's totally fine. I've only been here . . .

Looks at her watch—she's been here forever already.

Like, yeah, not very long.

She holds herself, shivering.

Tom (*annoyed*)   You're cold?

Amber   I'm always cold.

He rolls his eyes.

Tom   You want a drink?

Amber   Like from, the, um, keg?

Tom   Yeah.

Amber   Well, it's so delicious, I don't know how anyone could turn it down.

Tom (*peeved*)   Is that a joke or something?

Amber   Are you okay?

Tom (*angrily*)   Yeah I'm just trying to figure out if you want a beer. Is that okay by you?

Amber   You don't seem like you're in the best frame of mind tonight.

Tom   Who talks that way: "the best frame of mind"?

Amber   I do.

Tom   I know. It's weird.

Amber   Is it?

Tom   We could also just get outta here.

Amber   Sure.

I mean, we could go inside and like, dance. Or find another party. Or get someone to go to Varsity and pick stuff up for us.

Tom   Why would we do that when there are free drinks right here.

Amber   Good point. We wouldn't. I'm just happy to do what you want to do.

Tom   I'm gonna get a beer for the road.

Amber   I also have a, um.

She pulls out her flask.

Heather got it for me.

Tom   Heather's the hot one, right?

Amber   I mean, yes, she is very attractive. Like, objectively attractive. She has a lot of qualities men would find attractive, I guess. Like she has a very nice body—

Tom   Can I just . . . Lemme just see that flask.

He drinks from it; she drinks from it; this relaxes him.

That's good. What is that?

Amber   I'm not sure because Heather just gave it to me so . . .

Tom   It's tequila.

Amber   If you knew, why'd you ask?

Tom (*smiling*)   Maybe I was testing you.

Amber   Why would you be doing that?

Tom   See if you're up to my super-high standards.

Amber   From what I hear you have no standards at all.

Tom   Now who told you that.

Amber   I think there's a whole website at Princeton devoted to it.

Tom (*dry*)   That's hilarious.

Amber   I thought so.

Tom   What can I say? I like women. That's not a crime.

Amber   No it's not.

Tom   And I like you.

Amber (*out of awkwardness at being complimented*)   So, how much do you know about the pratfall effect?

Tom   What?

Amber   I was reading about it tonight in our psych book and it's actually really interesting: it's about how a person's attractiveness increases or decreases after he or she makes a mistake. So a highly competent person, like, say, a celebrity, would be *more* likable after committing a blunder, while the opposite would be true if—

Tom   God, do you ever stop talking?

Amber   What?

Tom (*with a small smile*)   Just stop talking.

Amber Okay.

Tom I'm gonna kiss you now.

Amber Oh.

Okay.

He does; it's actually kinda tender. When it's over, **Amber** *doesn't know what to say.*

Amber Let's play a game. Let's play Two Truths and a Lie.

Tom Um. No.

Amber Come on.

Tom Okay. I have two truths for you . . . I hate games and I hate that game.

Amber But you'll play it.

Tom And why would I do that?

Amber (*slower and more pointed than the first time around*) If you wanna sleep with me tonight, for one thing.

Tom (*slower and less of a joke than the first time around*) Who goes first?

A light gray feather falls from above, right in between **Amber** *and* **Tom**. *Before it hits the ground—blackout.*

End of play.

Where Storms Are Born

Harrison David Rivers

Introduction

Where Storms Are Born premiered at the Williamstown Theatre Festival in the summer of 2017 under the watchful eye of artistic director Mandy Greenfield, the compassionate direction of Saheem Ali, and featuring a galvanic central performance by Myra Lucretia Taylor.

The play began with a photograph published in *The New York Times* in 2014 of a woman embracing two of her sons on the steps of a courthouse where both men had just been exonerated of murder. They had spent a combined total of sixty years in prison. The woman's third son had died inside.

Something about the image—the emotion of it, the simultaneous joy and profound sadness of it, the bittersweetness of it—stayed with me. Haunted me, really. Wouldn't let me go. Much like Bethea, the mother in *Where Storms Are Born*, refuses to let go of her sons: Myles, her firstborn, who died mysteriously in prison, and Gideon, her baby, who is still very much alive.

I have (and have had) a number of Betheas in my life. Women who have loved me fiercely.

This play is for them.

Characters

Bethea Solomon, *fifties. African-American. A fearsome momma bear. Engaged and protective. You'd be a fool to cross her.*

Gideon Solomon, *twenty-seven. African-American. A sensitive, dutiful son. He has a beautiful smile—he should smile more.*

Myles Solomon, *thirty-one. African-American. Charming and charismatic. Could have been anything.*

Worthy Bell, *late twenties. African-American. Calls it like she sees it. Ride or die.*

Benton Massey, *early thirties. African-American. Knows how to use what he has to get what he wants. Sexy as fuck.*

Luke Jacobs, *late twenties–early thirties. Non-white. A Corrections Officer. A Boy Scout with an edge.*

Setting

New York City, 2015.

Notes on Production

Where Storms Are Born had its world premiere at Williamstown Theatre Festival (Mandy Greenfield, artistic director; Michael Sag, general manager) opening on July 15, 2017. The director was Saheem Ali, the stage manager Ellen Goldberg, the set designer Arnulfo Maldonado, the costume designer Jessica Pabst, the lighting designer David Weiner, the sound designer was Miles Polaski. The cast was as follows:

Bethea	Myra Lucretia Taylor
Gideon	Christopher Livingston
Myles	LeRoy McClain
Worthy	Joniece Abbott-Pratt
Benton	Joshua Boone
Luke	Luis Vega

Where Storms Are Born was developed with support from LAByrinth Theatre Company.

Scene One

A prison cell.
It is small. And gray.
And fluorescently lit.

Bethea And this is where . . .?

Corrections Officer Yes, ma'am. Just there. Over in that corner.

Bethea *crosses to the spot.*

Bethea Here?

Corrections Officer Yes, ma'am.

Bethea Can I ask um . . .? How was he . . .?

Corrections Officer How was he . . .? I'm sorry / I don't—

Bethea I mean, can you tell me . . . Can you tell me where his head was?

Corrections Officer Ma'am?

Bethea His head. When he was found. How was his head positioned?

Corrections Officer Oh. Right. Um . . . Well, it was near the wall.

Bethea *moves closer to the wall.*

Bethea I'm sorry. I'm having a hard time visualizing. Would you mind showing me how you found him?

Corrections Officer Ma'am?

Bethea I mean, you *were* the one who / found him, yes?

Corrections Officer Yes, ma'am, I was. But I—

Bethea It's just that I have so many pictures in my head. Pictures of him in this place. In this place . . . And, well, see I'm afraid that none of them are quite the right picture. And I'd like to have the right picture because he was my son. You understand? He was my son and to not know exactly what or how . . . I know it's odd. That it's an odd request. But please, Officer Jacobs. Please.

After some time, **Jacobs** *lowers his body to the ground.*

Jacobs He was like this, ma'am. When I found him. He was . . . legs this way. Head here. Arms . . . He was like this.

Bethea Thank you.

Jacobs Yr welcome.

Jacobs *returns to his post near the door.*
Bethea *moves to the indicated spot, then begins to lower her body to the ground—*

Jacobs   Ma'am? Ma'am, you can't! Miss Solomon, please!

Bethea *lies resolute on the floor of her son's cell as the scene shifts to:*

Scene Two

Later that day.
A brownstone in Harlem.
Bethea *and* **Gideon** *at the dining room table.*
Their hands are held and their heads are bowed.

Bethea   For this and all that we are about to receive, make us truly grateful, Lord. Through Christ we pray—

Bethea/Gideon   Amen.

They begin to eat.

Bethea   How's it taste?

Gideon   Good, ma. It tastes good.

Bethea   Well, good. You know, it didn't occur to me until we were in the car on the way home that we haven't sat down to a proper meal together in weeks. Things have been so hectic, what with the funeral and everything—

A siren. They both look toward the sound.
I thought—

It's still going.

What in God's name is going on out there?
Baby, go see.

Gideon *crosses to the window.*
Well?

Gideon   Nothing. Cops just dicking around.

Bethea   Harlem.

Gideon   Mm-hm . . .

Gideon *sits back down.*
Bethea *watches her son eat.*

Bethea   You know we useta have some good times at this table. Yr father, God rest his soul, he useta make all this noise. You probably don't remember, but he would take a bite of something, whatever I'd prepared, and it would taste sorta good to him, you know, so he'd kinda—

She demonstrates.

And he'd be just a grunting and a moaning and shaking his head. "Mm Thea girl, is this a new recipe? Cause *damn*! You really put yr foot in this meatloaf. Both feet!" Ooo and in public, too! Lord, I couldn't take that man anywhere. Useta drive me crazy all his carrying on. I'd say, "Carter, hush. Yr embarrassing me." But he'd just keep right on doing his thing.

She chuckles to herself.

Back when we started dating yr father took me to a different favorite restaurant for dinner every Thursday night for a year. A year! Can you imagine? That man had *fifty-two* favorite restaurants and a favorite dish at every one of those favorite restaurants!

Beat.

I remember practically starving myself in anticipation of our dates. I was determined to finish everything on my plate. I wanted him to choose me.

Gideon And he did.

Bethea Well, of course he did. Yr father wasn't a fool!

They laugh together. It's a nice moment.

It's good to hear you laugh. I haven't heard you laugh in . . . You know I love yr laugh.

Gideon Okay, ma.

Bethea What? I do. *I do!*

Gideon Yeah, all right. I heard you. Everybody on the whole damn block heard you.

A shared smile.

Bethea You know, you got it from me. Yr laugh. Yr brother, he got yr father's laugh, but you? You got mine.

Beat.

It's funny how different parts of yrself find their way to yr children. I look at you sometimes and I can see yr father plain as day. I see myself. I see yr brother.

Beat.

There's a face you get sometimes when you think no one's looking. It's sort of a . . . faraway look. Like yr . . . oh I don't know . . . like yr seeing something that no one else can see. Something no one else even knows is there. Myles useta get that same look.

Bethea *gestures to* **Myles**' *place at the table.*

He'd be sitting here at the table . . . at *this* table . . . and he'd look off sometimes and I'd think, Lord, if my boys aren't a pair—

Gideon's *fork hits his plate. It is definitive. Intentional.*

Bethea Gideon—?

Gideon Sorry, I—

*He reaches for **Bethea**'s plate.*

Are you finished with / yr plate—?

Bethea No, I am not. What the hell was that?

Gideon Nothing. I just . . . It was / nothing—

He moves to exit.

Bethea Boy, I know what nothing looks like and that was definitely *not* it.

And then—

Gideon, you better turn around and look at me when I'm talking to you—!

Gideon Why does every conversation have to lead back to him, huh? Every single . . .

*He gestures to **Myles**' place at the table.*

It's like he's still here. Only he hasn't been here for thirteen years. He hasn't sat at this table. He hasn't eaten yr food. He hasn't walked through that door / in thirteen years—

Bethea Gideon, he's yr brother!

Gideon I'm not talking about Myles, ma. I'm saying his name. I know I'm saying his name, but I'm *not* talking about *him*. *I'm talking about you.*

He exits.

Scene Three

Later.
***Gideon**'s bedroom.*
***Bethea** tries the door knob.*

Bethea So we're locking doors now?

Gideon *opens the door, then returns to his bed. He does not look at his mother.*
***Bethea** enters the room.*
Look, I'm not gonna apologize for the way I feel. Just like I won't ask you to apologize for the way you feel. We're just gonna have to cut each other some slack.

Beat.

Do you know what I pray for, Gideon? What I've prayed for every night / for thirteen years—?

Gideon Justice. You pray for / justice—

Bethea That's right. Justice. And I'm gonna keep right on praying until God sees fit to answer.

Gideon Do you ever think that maybe he already has? That maybe he just said no?

The question hangs in the air for a while and then—

Bethea You got plans tonight?

Gideon Seriously, ma?

Bethea Yes, seriously. You ain't been out of this house for any length of time these last three weeks except to run to the Rite Aid or to Fairway for groceries. You need to *get out*, baby. Yr young and its Friday night. You should call up one of yr little friends and meet them out somewhere. Go dancing.

Gideon You know I don't dance—

Bethea Yeah, well, you *should*. It'd be good for you. Good for you to get out and unbutton a few of those buttons. Move those hips I know you have. Those hips you try to hide—

Gideon Okay, mama.

Bethea And that cute little butt!

Gideon Ma!

Bethea Well, it *is* cute! I should know. I've been looking at it for twenty-seven years!

Gideon *can't help but smile.*

Gideon You talk too much you know that? Too damn much.

Bethea There ain't no such thing as too much truth, baby. No matter what folks say. There is no such thing. You remember that.

A moment and then—
I can't do this without you, Gideon. I can't. Yr all I have left.

Bethea *exits.*

Scene Four

Later.
The pier.
Gideon *lights a cigarette.*

Worthy Can you believe these motherfuckers? Locking the fucking bathrooms like folks ain't gotta pee in October same as they do in July. I had to piss standing up in the bushes over there. Pretty much flashed the whole of the West Side highway.

Toward the street:

YEAH YR WELCOME!

She takes the cigarette from **Gideon**'s *mouth.*

She takes a drag and then—

I couldn't be homeless. Sleeping outside. Pissing outside. Uh huh. It's too fucking cold for that shit. You got something to warm me up?

Gideon   You know I do.

He produces a bottle from his coat pocket.

Worthy   Gideon Solomon, looking out!

She drinks.
You know it's been a minute since we've been down here. You remember the last time?

They both start to laugh.
What was that boy's name / again—?

Gideon   I don't think he ever said.

Worthy   Yeah, I don't think he *said* much of anything.

More laughter.
You were a mess that night. / A fucking mess—

Gideon   ME? What about you?

Worthy   All Ima say is thank God the shit that happens at the pier STAYS at the motherfucking pier.

More laughter and then—

We've had us some good times, haven't we?

Gideon   Yeah. We have.

Worthy   And we've always been there for each other.

Gideon   Yeah . . .

Beat.

Worthy   You wanna talk about Sing Sing?

Gideon   You mean about how I was dragged there by you know who?

Worthy   She's yr mother, Gideon. She lost a son.

Gideon   Yeah and I lost a brother.

Beat.

Sorry. That was a little—

Worthy   Yeah, it was. But given the circumstances, I'll let it slide.

Beat.

I think it's good you went. Good you took her. No matter how pissed you think you are at her.

Gideon   Think?

Worthy   You heard me. Plenty of sons *don't* do that for their mamas. Plenty of *non*-pissed-off sons. None of my brothers do. You've got all these women crowding onto buses heading upstate cause the men in their lives, the one's not already locked up, can't be bothered to take them where they need to go. Yr a good son, Gideon.

Gideon   Okay—

Worthy   Oh shut up and let me compliment you. You stuck by her when they closed Myles' case. You moved in with her to make sure she was all right. Yr a good man. And good men are to find.

Gideon   I'll drink to that.

They toast—cigarette to liquor bottle.
And then—

Worthy   So . . . I did something bad.

Gideon   Do I wanna know?

Worthy   I let Maurice come by the other night. And by come by I mean . . .

She demonstrates.

Gideon   Ew . . . why?

Worthy   What do you mean *why*? 'Cause he's my ex-boyfriend. 'Cause he says he still loves me.

Gideon   Yeah and what do *you* say?

Worthy   Nothing . . . Yet.

Gideon   Yeah, well, when you do, you better say fuck off.

Worthy   Hey! Be nice. We're celebrating—

Gideon   Seriously, Worthy? / Be nice—?

Worthy   Yes, seriously! He's not all bad.

Gideon *gives* **Worthy** *a look.*
Worthy   What? He's not!

Gideon   Yeah, OKAY.

Worthy   You know there's a laundry-list of shit I could call you out on, too. / Got so much to say about my fucking life—

Gideon   Excuse me? Like what?

Worthy   Like what? Like when was the last time *you* got some? See there. I can't do like you be doing. Going *without* for months on end. Shit closes up.

Gideon   Shit doesn't close / up—

Worthy Shit closes up. Believe me. I've heard stories.

Beat.

I fucking hate it when you get like this.

Gideon Get like *what*?

Worthy Like this! Moody, aloof, ill-tempered. Pick an adjective. It ain't cute.

Beat.

Gideon Six months.

Worthy *looks at* **Gideon**.

Worthy What you talking about?

Gideon Six months. That's how long I've . . . You know . . .

Worthy Jesus, Gideon.

Gideon I know.

Worthy But like seriously / Jesus—

Gideon Yeah, seriously, I know!

A moment and then—
Worthy *slides closer to her friend.*

Worthy Damn, girl, we gotta get you laid.

Scene Five

A gay club.
Loud music.
Gideon *and* **Worthy** *dance.*

Scene Six

A bathroom.
Gideon *at a urinal.*
Luke *appears.*

Luke Hey.

Gideon Um . . . hey.

Luke It's crazy out there. So many guys.

Beat.

I noticed you on the dance floor. You looked good.

Gideon   ... Thanks.

Luke   Do you come here a lot?

Gideon   Do you mind? I'm actually trying to pee.

Luke   Oh, sure, of course. Sorry.

Luke *moves a distance away, but doesn't exit.*
Gideon *flushes and moves to the sink.*
Luke   You don't remember me, do you?

Gideon   Um ... should I?

Luke   I'm told I look different out of uniform. I was the one that took yr mom back to see yr brother's cell.

Gideon   You ...? Is this a joke?

Luke   Look, I don't mean to disrupt yr night ... It's just that I saw you and I *knew* that it was you. I mean, you look so much like him, like Myles, and he talked about you all the / time—

Gideon   Yeah, I have to go.

He moves to exit.

Luke   Gideon. Please.

Gideon *stops.*
Luke   I know this is weird. I'm sorry that it's weird, but um ... you must have questions or, you know ... things you wished you knew about ...

Luke *produces a cocktail napkin from his pocket.*
This is my number. If you ever want to talk. About Myles or whatever. I'm around.

There's nowhere to set the napkin so **Luke** *places it in* **Gideon**'s *hand, then exits.*
Gideon *stares at the piece of paper as the scene shifts to:*

Scene Seven

A grief support group.

Bethea   Um ... hello.
My name is Bethea
And this is my first time here.

Beat.

I have two sons.
Gideon, my youngest, is still—
Well, he's still with me.
My eldest, Myles, died three weeks ago.

Beat.

People ask me all the time now, "How . . . *are* you?"
With that certain inflection?
That gap between *how* and *are* that's code for
How fragile are you?
How likely are you to break if I give you a hug?
How messy is this interaction going to be on a scale from one to ten?
People care, sure.
They try their very best to care.
But they don't like mess.
People don't like mess.
And I'm perceived as a ticking time bomb of a mess.

Beat.

My son died in prison.
But he was a good boy
My Myles
He was good
And he was sweet
And he was smart
He was so . . .
And he didn't do what they said he did
I know
Because I'm his mother
And mothers know.
But what I don't know
What I've asked myself again and again and again is
How?
How does a good boy . . .?
How can you have two children
Two sons
Who are loved the same
Taught the same
Prayed for the same
How can you want every good thing for them the same
And one ends up in a cell
And the other one doesn't.
Did I do something wrong?
Where did I go . . .?

Beat.

I love both of my sons.
I love them like breathing.
I love them like I breathe.
But the love I have for Myles doesn't transfer.
I wish it did.
I wish I could just shift it over, you know?

Give it to my baby.
Cause I know—I can see—that he needs it.
But I can't.
I can't.
Cause it won't.
So I'm left just . . . holding it.
This extra love.
Holding it.
Wondering what do I do?
What do I do with this love?
Where am I supposed to put it now that Myles is—?
Because it's heavy.
My love for my son.
It's heavy.
It's a burden.
It's a curse.
And it's what saves me every single day.

Scene Eight

Later.
The fire escape.
Gideon *smokes.*
Myles *appears.*
He points to the sky.

Myles Ok so . . . see there? To the right? Those three little ones? That's the handle. And then those four rhombus-y looking stars . . . You *do* know what a rhombus is, right?

Gideon Well, duh.

Myles All right, all right. Just checking. Well, those four rhombus-y looking stars make up the ladle. That's like the spoon part of the spoon—

Gideon I know what a ladle is, Myles. Don't be a dick.

Myles Who me?

A shared smile.
Anyway, when you put 'em all together. All seven of those stars. *That's* the Big Dipper. It's cool, right?

Gideon Yeah, it's cool.

Myles Mom and Dad lucked out with this place. Who needs a balcony when you've got a fire escape with a view. This spot up here? This shit? Is sacred. You hear me, Gid? Sacred. Like church.

Gideon Like church?

Myles   Yeah, like church. Only not everyone's invited. This church, number two? This church is only for a select few.

Gideon   You mean like Benton?

Myles   Yeah. Like Benton. And like you.

Gideon *smiles.*

Myles   Hey. You doing okay? With school / and everything—?

Gideon   Yeah, school's good.

Myles   No one's giving you any trouble?

Gideon   Why would anyone give me / trouble—?

Myles   No reason, little brother, I'm just . . . you know . . . checking in. Asking the questions big brothers are supposed to ask.

Beat.

You know if you ever need anything. Like if you ever need me to have a little chat with someone. Rough 'em up / a bit—

Gideon   Myles—

Myles   I'm just saying . . .

Benton *pulls himself up from below.*

Myles   *If* you need me . . . for any reason . . . I'm here. I'm looking out for you, Gid. I'm always looking out. You know that, right?

Myles *disappears.*

Benton   Big ass moon out tonight.

Gideon   Bright as fuck.

Benton   Bright. As. Fuck.

Gideon *offers* **Benton** *the cigarette.*
Benton *takes it.*
They smoke.
A long while and then—

Gideon   My parents got Myles a book about the stars for his birthday one year. You remember that? He'd come up here every night after dinner with a flashlight and a magnifying glass and he'd learn the sky. The constellations. And star configurations. More celestial shapes than I can remember the names of.

Beat.

He wanted to be an astronaut. You remember that, Benton? How he wanted to be an astronaut?

Benton   I didn't come up here to talk about yr brother.

Benton *takes one last drag of the cigarette, then enters* **Gideon***'s room through the window.* **Gideon** *takes a breath, then follows. They undress in tableau.*

Scene Nine

The next morning.
Gideon's *room.*
Benton *begins to pull on clothes.*
Gideon *stirs.*

Gideon   Hey. Yr still here.

Benton   Yeah . . .

Gideon *watches* **Benton** *dress.*

Gideon   You could stay if you want.

Benton   I've got work.

Gideon   Last I checked dealing wasn't a twenty-four-seven gig.

Benton   Yeah, well, that's 'cause you don't know.

Gideon *slips out of bed and begins to dress.*

Gideon   Maybe we could do breakfast sometime?

Benton   Say what?

Gideon   I mean, we both eat, right? We both gotta / eat—

Benton   Can you imagine me at yr table with yr mama? Eating scrambled eggs? Drinking French pressed coffee?

Gideon   Why not?

Benton   Why not? Shoot. Yr crazy, you know that, Gid? Crazy.

Bethea *appears at* **Gideon**'s *door. She knocks.*

Bethea   Gideon?

Gideon (*shit*)

The men scramble to pull on clothes.

Bethea   You awake?

Gideon   Yeah, but hold on—

Benton
(Yo where's my fucking shirt?)

Gideon
(I don't fucking know!)

Benton
(Fuck!)

Bethea   Will you open the door?

Gideon   Ma, I'm not dressed.

Bethea   Baby, you ain't got nothing I ain't seen / before—

Gideon   TMI, ma. / TMI—

Benton
(Fuck the shirt. I'm out—)

Gideon
(No, wait—)

Bethea   Gideon!

Benton *exits out the window. A moment and then* **Gideon** *opens the door.*

Gideon   Ma, I don't have a lot of time so what do you want?

Bethea   I wanted to thank you for yesterday. For driving me to Ossining. I know you decided a long time ago not to go up there and see yr brother like that. In that place. And I've always respected that. Yr decision. I always have. But I'm grateful that yesterday you made an exception.

Beat.

Gideon   Yr welcome.

Beat.

Bethea   You know, I stood in the spot where yr brother . . . Where Myles . . . I stood there in that cell. In that *box*. That . . . And I thought, somebody *put* my baby here. And somebody made him feel like he had no other choice but to . . . All those boys he useta hang around with. Cedric and Rasun—

Gideon   Yeah, ma, I know—

Bethea   Little Benton Massey with that sweet face of his. I told yr brother time and time again, ain't nothing good gonna come from that. Ain't nothing good gonna come from hanging around with that boy. And I know it's in the past. And the past is the past. And we can't change it. Ain't nobody but God's got the power to change it. But it's like yr father useta say, "God ain't the kind to begrudge a little help."

Bethea *helps* **Gideon** *into his work vest.*

Bethea   You've always been so sweet. You stayed just as sweet as you were the day you were born—

Gideon   All right / ma—

Bethea   Don't you "All right, ma" me. It's a compliment, Gideon. Learn to take a fucking compliment.

She locates **Benton**'s *shirt in* **Gideon**'s *bed.*

Bethea   Is this new?

Gideon *turns to look.*

Gideon Uh . . . yeah—

Bethea I don't think I've seen it before. Kinda big, isn't it?

Gideon Nah. That's the style.

Bethea The style, huh? Why young people refuse to wear clothes that fit I'll never understand.

She holds the shirt to her face and inhales.
You trying out a new cologne / too—?

Gideon OKAY, ma.

He attempts to take the shirt from **Bethea***, but she holds onto it.*

Gideon Visit's over. Thanks for coming. / Bye now—!

Bethea All right, all right! I'm going! Contrary to popular belief I *can* take a hint. Ima put this in with the next load of laundry—

Gideon Nah, you don't have to / do that—

Bethea Oh hush, baby. It's done. It's already done.

She exits.

Scene Ten

A hotel.
Gideon *and* **Worthy** *behind a counter.*
The phone rings.
Neither of them wants to answer it.
They play rock, paper, scissors.
Worthy *loses and answers the phone.*

Worthy Mercer Hotel front desk.

The person on the phone yammers on. **Worthy** *is over it.*

One moment please.

She transfers the call then hangs up the phone.

So, are we gonna talk about it?

Gideon Talk about what?

Worthy *punches* **Gideon** *in the arm.*
Ow—what was that for?

Worthy Why do you do that?

Gideon Do what?

Worthy Answer my perfectly legitimate questions with other questions?

Gideon I don't / do that—

Worthy Yeah, you do. You just fucking did!

Beat.

Well?

Gideon Well, what / Worthy—?

Worthy Boy, I'm gonna slay / you—!

Gideon What? I don't know what yr talking about!

Worthy The guy, Gideon! The guy / from last night—!

Gideon What guy?

Worthy The one who was looking at you like he wanted to eat you for breakfast, lunch, dinner, and dessert—

Gideon Okay, why do you always gotta make everything so nasty?

Worthy Because life is nasty, Gideon. Life is fucking nasty.

Beat.

So?

Gideon So what?

Worthy Unbelievable!

Gideon What? There's no story there.

Worthy Bullshit, Gideon. I call / BULLSHIT ON YR ASS—

Gideon Okay, OKAY! He knew Myles, all right? He's a guard at Ossining and he knew Myles. That's it.

Worthy That's not nothing / Gideon—

Gideon I didn't say it was nothing. I said that's it.

Beat.

Worthy What did he want?

Gideon I don't know.
To talk.

The phone rings.

To buy me a drink.
Does it really matter?

He answers.

Mercer Hotel front desk. One moment please.

He transfers the call then hangs up the phone.

Scene Ten

Worthy Um ... yeah, it fucking matters.

Gideon I don't wanna talk about this / anymore—

Worthy It fucking matters when a fine ass man of color wants to fucking dialogue with you.

Gideon He approached me in a gay bar bathroom.

Worthy So? / What is that got to do with anything—?

Gideon So ... Ew!

Worthy Boy, I KNOW firsthand you've had worse in worse / places—

Gideon Look who's fucking talking! Port Authority? The Chase Bank lobby with the ATMs on 118th? That hand job you gave Maurice on the A train / while I was sitting right fucking next to you—!

Worthy Okay, OKAY! YEAH, ALL RIGHT ALREADY! Damn. You made yr point.

Gideon *moves to say more—*

Gideon AND YEAH, I'm figuring out my Maurice shit okay so pipe the fuck down.

I wasn't gonna say anything about / Maurice—

Worthy Yeah you fucking were. Don't play, Gideon.

A moment and then—
Worthy *dials a number on the hotel phone.*
Gideon*'s cell phone begins to ring.*
He pulls it from his pocket and sees that it's **Worthy**.

Gideon Yr stupid, you know that?

Worthy Answer the phone.

Gideon Worthy—

Worthy JUST DO IT!

He does.

Gideon I repeat, yr stupid—

Worthy So ...

She pulls her cell phone from her pocket.

What was his name?

Gideon Who?

Worthy *punches him.*

Gideon Ow—what the fuck?

Worthy Don't try me, Gideon Solomon. I beat the shit outta you in third grade and I will do it again.
(*Into the hotel phone.*) The gay guard from the club. What's his name?

I SAID / WHAT'S HIS FUCKING NAME—?

Gideon (*into his cell phone*)   LUKE, OKAY! LUKE!

Worthy Luke what?

Gideon Jacobs, I think? Luke Jacobs. (**Worthy** *types on her phone.*) Damn, yr pushy today.

Worthy Shut up.

Gideon What are you even doing?

Worthy Don't worry about it.

Gideon Don't worry / about it—?

Worthy And . . . done.

Gideon Done? What did you do—?

Worthy I sent him a Facebook message / You know you really should change yr password—

Gideon A Facebook message? I can't believe you just did that!

Worthy He knew yr brother. He wants to talk. And you *need* to talk.

Gideon That's not yr call.

Worthy Not my call? I'm yr *best* friend—

Gideon Yeah, but—

Worthy You know what this is like? This is like that moment where the mama bird pushes the baby bird out the nest. Fly, motherfucker!

Scene Eleven

A street.
Bethea *carries a bag of groceries.*
She is on her phone.

Bethea Now see that's yr problem right there. What you need to do is stop watching those *Law & Order* re-runs on TNT. The "Criminal Intents" and the "Trial by Juries" and especially the "SVU's" cause that shit'll mess you up. And I don't mean nightmares. I mean, warp yr perspective. Girl, we are living in the absolute safest moment in the history of history. No, not according to me, according to statistics! Listen to me. Safer than ever. And folks are still walking around with guns like they got something to be scared of. Like there's some criminal lying in wait around every street corner when it just ain't true—

Her bag breaks and the contents spill onto the sidewalk.

Oh shit. Nah girl, I'm fine. My grocery bag just ripped. I'm gonna have to call you back.

She bends to gather the fallen items. **Benton** *appears.*

Benton   Here let me help you with that—

Bethea   Well, thank you. That's very kind of—

She sees who it is and stiffens.

Oh.

Benton   Hey, Miss Solomon.

Bethea   Benton.

Benton   Been awhile.

Bethea   It sure has.

Benton   How you been?

Bethea   Fine. I've been fine.

Benton   Doing some shopping?

Bethea   Well . . . trying to anyway.

Benton   Yeah, I guess they don't make grocery bags like they used to.

Bethea   No, they most certainly do not.

Benton *has gathered up the fallen groceries.*

Benton   You know you should try cloth.

Bethea   Excuse me?

Benton   They're less likely to break on you and they're better for the environment. My mama swears by 'em.

Bethea   Yes, well I'll keep that in mind. Thank you for yr help. You have a nice day.

She reaches for the grocery bags. **Benton** *withholds.*

Benton   You want me to run back to the store for you? Grab you some more eggs?

Bethea   No, it's okay.

Benton   'Cause I've got time.

Bethea   I'll make do.

Benton   You sure? / It's really no trouble—

Bethea   I am, Benton. Very sure. But thank you.

She reaches for the bag again. A moment and then **Benton** *relents.*

Benton Well, all right then. You take care.

Bethea I will.

Benton Oh and Miss Solomon? Remember: Cloth. That's where it's at!

He exits. **Bethea** *takes a breath.*

Scene Twelve

The pier.
Luke *on a bench looking out at the water.*
He's holding an envelope in his hand.
After a while, **Gideon** *appears.*
He watches **Luke** *for moment and then—*

Gideon Luke?

Luke *quickly tucks the envelope away and stands.*

Luke Gideon, hey.

Gideon *goes in for a handshake.*
Luke *goes in for a hug.*
They try again.
It's awkward.
Eventually, they shake hands.
And then—

Luke I hope this is okay. I wasn't sure if you had a favorite bench / or—

Gideon Nah, this is fine.

They sit. They look out at the water.

Luke It's funny you picked this place. Or well, maybe not funny exactly, but . . . like a strange coincidence? The pier's always been one of my favorite places in the city. I come here when I need to clear my head. I mean, it's crazy in the spring. People everywhere. And in the summer, forget it. But now, you know, late fall? It's quiet. You can hear yrself think. You can . . . hear yrself figure things out.

Beat.

Can I be honest with you? I didn't think I'd hear back. I mean, I hoped I would. I hoped you'd reach out, but—

Gideon I didn't . . . actually.

Luke You . . . / what—?

Gideon That Facebook message?

Luke Yeah—

Gideon It wasn't from me.

Luke   It . . . Sorry, it wasn't from / you—?

Gideon   See my friend—the woman who was with me at the club last night? She thought it would be good for me to meet with you or whatever so she sent you a message / from my account—

Luke   *She* sent the message.

Gideon   Yes.

Luke   Well . . . Yr here, right? That's what matters.

Beat.

God, I feel like I know so much about you.

Gideon   I'm sorry I can't say the same.

Luke   Well, what do you want to know? I'm an open book.

Gideon   No one's an open book.

Luke   Try me.

And then—
I like music.
All kinds.
And movies.
Comedies, mostly.
Old school.
Charlie Chaplin.
The Marx Brothers.
Carole Lombard.
Uh . . . I'm a pisces
So I love the water.
Spots like this.
The beach.

Beat.

Kittens.

Gideon *smiles.* **Luke** *smiles.*

Luke   I definitely talk too much so . . . there's that.

He gestures.
See?

Open book.

Beat.

Let's see . . .
What else can I tell you?

Gideon Did you always want to be a prison guard?

Luke Wow, okay, you just dive right in, don't you?

Gideon Hey, you asked.

Luke No, yr right, yr right, I did. Um . . . Did I always want to be a guard? Nah. My parents wanted me to be a lawyer. And I didn't have any real objection to the idea so I got my JD and I signed with a big firm, but . . . it didn't feel right. It wasn't a good fit. So I quit. When I told my them I was taking the job at Ossining my dad said, "But you have so much potential." Like it takes no skill, right? No aptitude whatsoever to do what I do. To work with these men.

Beat.

I don't know. Maybe one day I'll go back to it. Maybe one day I'll wake up and I'll be like, you know what, I think it's time for a change. But until then . . . I'm happy where I am. Doing what I do.

Gideon I hate my job. Answering phones. I hate customer service. This vest. This tie. I *hate* this tie.

Luke It looks good on you.

Gideon *gives* **Luke** *a look.*
Luke I'm serious. You wear it well.

A moment and then **Luke** *pulls a bag of Skittles from his jacket pocket.*
Luke Skittle?

Gideon *considers, then holds out his hand.* **Luke** *pours several into his palm.*

Gideon Thanks.

Luke Yr welcome.

They eat. After a while—

Gideon Myles useta come here. That was his bench over there. His spot. You know, where he would . . .

Luke The way he talked about you, you must've been close.

Gideon When we were kids, yeah. We were. He was the cool one, of course. The superhero. I was the sidekick. The Robin to his Batman. Jimmy Olsen to his Superman.

Luke I always wanted a brother. I useta ask Santa for one every year, but my parents weren't having it.

Gideon What'd you get instead?

Luke Socks, mostly. A shit ton of socks.

They laugh and then—

Myles was always telling some story. I remember he told this one about yr father. I guess you and Myles were home on a break from school. And yr dad thought it would be funny for the three of you to play a trick on yr mom—

Gideon *(freely)* Oh my God . . .

Luke So you hid all the furniture in the house so it would look like you'd been robbed, right—?

Gideon *(freely)*   Oh my God . . . / I can't believe he told you that . . .

Luke And the idea was that yr mom would come home, freak out. And then you'd all jump out and say "gotcha" and have a good laugh. Only yr mom got off work early that day and you, Myles and yr dad / had—

Gideon We'd gone out for ice cream—

Luke Right, in anticipation of yr successful prank. And when you got back to the house there were—

Luke/Gideon Squad cars lining the street—

Gideon Mom had called the cops for real for real.

Luke Priceless.

The men laugh.
And then—
Luke *offers* **Gideon** *another Skittle.*
Gideon *extends his hand.*

Scene Thirteen

The dining room.

Bethea Heavenly father, thank you for keeping me safe in yr hands and close to yr heart—

A knock.
Bethea *lifts her head.*
Another knock.
She moves to the door.

Who is it?

Benton Benton Massey.

Bethea *takes a breath.*
Come on, Miss Solomon, open up. I'm not leaving 'til you do.

Beat.
Miss Solomon?

Beat.

Miss Solomon—

Bethea *cracks the door.*

Bethea   What do you want?

Benton   Is that anyway to greet a friend?

Bethea *gives* **Benton** *a look.*
Benton   Yeah, all right, all right. We'll skip the pleasantries.

He produces a cloth bag.
I've got something for you.

Bethea   What is it?

Benton   Go on and see for yrself.
Well go on . . .

Bethea *takes the bag and looks inside.*

Bethea   Benton, I told you I didn't need eggs—

She tries to hand back the bag.

Benton   And I'm telling you, don't nobody with any kind of kitchen know-how *not* need eggs.

He pushes the bag back toward her.
Consider it a peace offering.

Beat.

Bethea   Thank you.

Benton   Yr welcome. See, that wasn't so hard, was it?

Beat.

Bethea   Well, if that's / all—

Benton   I meant to say earlier . . . I was sorry to hear about Myles. For a while there we were . . . we were real close.

Bethea   Yeah, I remember.

Benton   I meant to make the funeral. I did. I got dressed and everything, but well . . . you know how it is.

Bethea   I certainly do. Life so often gets in the way. Good night, Benton.

Benton   Look, Miss Solomon, I'm not the enemy here. Folks be running their mouths, spewing all kinds of hateful things about me, but saying 'em . . .

A siren.
Saying 'em don't make 'em true.

Bethea   They looking for you?

Benton   Funny, Miss Solomon. Very funny.

Bethea   Believe me any humor was unintentional.

Benton   Look, I'm trying to be nice here.

Bethea   It would be nice if you let go of my door. My dinner's getting cold.

Beat.

Benton   Yeah, all right. All right.

He removes his hand from the door.
You have a nice night, Miss Solomon. Enjoy yr eggs. Oh, and say hey to Gideon for me.

He exits.

Bethea   To Gideon?

A buzzer.
The visiting room at Sing Sing Correctional Facility.
Myles *appears in a green jumpsuit.*

Myles   Mama.

Bethea   Hey, baby.

They embrace.
Yr looking good.

Myles   You always say that / ma—

Bethea   And I will continue to say it as long as it's true. Truth, baby. You can't never have too much truth. Now sit on down here and tell me what's going on. How you doing? How was the week—?

Myles   Fine, mama. Everything's / fine—

Bethea   Nah, baby. Don't you "fine mama" me. Fine don't tell me nothing.

Myles   Ain't nothing else to tell.

Bethea   Myles.

Myles   Come on, ma. We've been doing this a long time. You know the answers to the questions cause they're the same answers I gave last month and the month before that and the month before that. It's the same. Everything's the same. The same guys on the Unit. Same food. Same lights out. Nothing ever changes in here. It's fucking purgatory / up in here—

Bethea   Don't talk like that.

Myles   Or what? You gonna stop coming?

Beat.

Shit, ma.

He takes her hand.
I'm sorry. I just . . . I'm just not feeling it today.

Bethea   Course, baby. A person can't be up every day.

Beat.

Anybody come to visit you this week?

Myles   You know they didn't.

Bethea   What? Somebody could've come by. One of yr little friends. Cedric. Or Rasun.

Myles   Rasun's in Lincoln.

Bethea   The one on a hundred and tenth?

Myles   That's what I heard anyway.

Bethea   I had no idea. His poor mother.

Myles   His poor mother?

Bethea   Yes, his poor mother. Just because I don't like yr friends—

Myles   He's *not* my friend!

Bethea   Yeah, well, he *was*. And just because I never liked him doesn't mean I can't feel sympathy for his mother.

Beat.

You heard from Benton?

Myles   Oh, sure. He sent me a letter just the other day.

Bethea   He did?

Myles   God, mama, no! Ain't no one's come to visit. Ain't no one's written. Ain't no one's sent a package, but YOU.

Beat.

How's Gid?

Bethea   He's all right. He sends his love.

Myles *gives his master a look.*

Bethea   Just because he doesn't say it does not mean he doesn't send it.

Beat.

I heard from the lawyer yesterday. She said she found something that might be helpful with yr case. She sounded real excited on the phone.

Myles   Ma—

Bethea   I have a really good feeling about this one. You wait and see.

A buzzer signals the end of visitation. **Myles** *stands.*

Bethea   Is it just me or do these visits get shorter and shorter?

Myles   It's just you, ma.

He embraces his mother.

Bethea   I love you, son.

Myles   I love you, too.

Bethea   You be good. And stay safe—

Myles   I will.

And then—
Hey, ma?

Bethea   Yes, baby?

Myles   Tell Gideon I say hey.

Bethea   I will.

Another buzzer.
Bethea *breathes.*
She looks back toward the door.
And then—
She breaks her dinner plate against the table.

Scene Fourteen

Later.
The dining room.
Gideon *appears with a laundry basket.*
He notices the broken plate.

Gideon   What happened here?

Bethea   Oh you know me. Just a clumsy mess. I completely missed the table. I'll clean it up later.

Gideon   Nah, I'll get it.

He begins to clean up the mess.

Bethea   You hungry? I could make you up a plate—

Gideon   It's okay. I ate while I was out.

Bethea   Oh. Well, good. Were you with anyone I know?

Gideon   Nah. Just some people from work.

(*Re* **Benton**'s *eggs*.) You want me to take these to the kitchen?

Bethea Thank you, baby.

Gideon *exits.*
Bethea *pulls* **Benton**'s *shirt from the laundry basket.*
She holds it in her hands.
It's still too big.
She holds it up to her face.
It still doesn't smell like her son even after washing.
Gideon *returns.*

Gideon I think I'm gonna turn in.

Bethea So early?

Gideon It's been a long day.

Bethea Well, all right then. Here. Take yr laundry.

She hands him **Benton**'s *shirt.*

Gideon . . . Thanks.

Bethea Course, baby.

Gideon *moves to exit.*
Bethea You been hanging around with Benton Massey?

Gideon What?

Bethea Have you?

Gideon *turns back.*

Gideon Have I—? No! Are you / serious—?

Bethea You sure?

Gideon You don't think I would know if I was hanging out with Benton Massey? He's a thug.

Bethea Damn right, he's a thug. But he's a charming thug. And it's the charming ones you've gotta watch out for.

Gideon I don't know Benton like that.

Bethea Gideon—

Gideon What? I don't!

Bethea Yeah, well, I think it's best to keep it that way, you hear?

Beat.

BOY, YOU BETTER ANSWER ME WHEN I'M / TALKING TO YOU—

Gideon YES, MA'AM! YES, MA'AM—!

Bethea Okay then.

Beat.

Gideon Why would you even ask me that? I mean, what would make you think / that I—?

Beteha Because he came by.

Gideon He came *here*?

Bethea And he asked about *you*.

Gideon Well, I don't know why / he would do that—

Bethea Gideon, that boy ain't been on my porch in thirteen years. And I tell you it brought back some memories. Some good. But most of them . . . Mothers know. When something isn't right we . . . You stay away from him, you hear me? Ima tell you like I told yr brother. Ain't nothing good gonna come of that. Ain't nothing good come of *that* at all.

She exits with the laundry basket.

Scene Fifteen

Later.
The fire escape.
Gideon *smokes a cigarette.*
Myles *appears.*
He points to the sky.

Myles It's got lots of names. The pole star. The steadfast star. The guiding star. Since it lies in an almost direct line with the Earth's rotation above the North Pole it looks like it doesn't move. And all the Northern stars appear to rotate around it, which makes it an excellent fixed point for celestial navigation. If you ever get lost, little brother, and you need to find yr way . . . the North Star, baby. That's where it's at.

He watches **Gideon** *smoke.*

Myles Yr getting good at that.

Gideon I've been practicing.

Myles Not where Mom can see you, I hope.

Gideon You think I'm stupid?

Myles Nah, boy. I *know* yr not.

And then—
Give it here.

Gideon *hands* **Myles** *the cigarette.*
Myles *takes a drag, holds, then releases the smoke into the air.*
They watch it dissipate.
Myles One of these days, Ima be up there.

He gestures to the sky.
Just like Robert H. Lawrence.
Discover some shit.

Beat.

What *you* gonna do, number two?

Gideon Ima come with you.

Myles *smiles.*

Myles Yeah, I like the sound of that. The Solomon Brothers in space!

He stands and yells to the sky.
Hey, universe! Y'all better get ready! Cause the Solomon brothers are coming for ya!

Gideon Son!

Myles and **Gideon** *laugh together as* **Benton** *pulls himself up from below.*

Benton Hey.

Gideon *doesn't reply.*
Benton I said, hey.

Beat.

You sick or something?

Gideon No.

Benton Well, something's up. You usually bombard me with salutations and shit when I come over here.

Beat.

Gid, what's up?

Gideon My mom found yr shirt in my bed. The one we couldn't find?

He tosses the shirt at **Benton**.

Gideon She asked about it. I told her it was mine. Good. Done. But then you came by the house. You came to *my* house and now she's asking more questions. Other kinds of questions.

Benton Like what kind / of questions—

Gideon Like "Are you spending time with that thug?"

Benton Called me a thug, did she? Well, I guess she's entitled to her opinion. Lemme have some of that.

He takes the cigarette. He takes a drag, then exhales.

Gideon What else did you do with my brother?

Benton What you mean, *what else*?

Gideon You sold drugs together.

Benton   Allegedly.

Gideon   Yeah, whatever. What else?

Beat.

Benton   Yeah. That was pretty much it.

Beat.

Gideon   Did you fuck him?

*The cigarette pauses part way to **Benton**'s lips.*

Benton   Did I / what—?

Gideon   Fuck him? Like you fuck me?

A moment and then—
Benton *advances on* **Gideon**.
Gideon *flinches.*

Benton   Yeah . . . Yeah, we're done here.

He moves to descend.

Gideon   Yeah, don't worry. I won't tell anyone yr little secret. I wouldn't want to make things difficult for you—

Benton   Me climbing up here
Sitting with you
Laying alongside you
Ain't shit.
You hear me, it ain't shit.
You want to know about yr brother?
I'll tell you about yr brother.
He was loyal.
Like a motherfucker.
You made a pact with him
That was it.
That was it.

Beat.

Grieve however you need to grieve, but this shit ain't osmosis.
Ain't nothing to be learned about yr brother by fucking with me.

Gideon   Get off my fire escape.

Benton *takes a drag of the cigarette, then blows the smoke in* **Gideon**'s *face.*
Gideon   GET THE FUCK OFF!

A moment and then **Benton** *descends as the scene shifts to:*

Scene Sixteen

The pier.

Worthy And I'm standing on the corner, right?
The fucking corner
And I hear
Huh
I hear that he's fucking another bitch
And not just any other bitch
He's fucking Candace
You know
From down the block?
Oh but he's not *just* fucking her
Uh uh
That motherfucker
That motherfucker got her
Fucking
Pregnant.
Pregnant, Gideon!
Can you fucking believe that shit?
I'm with him three years
Three years
Off and on, yeah okay
Off and on, but still
For three years I paid his rent
His phone bill
I put gas in his motherfucking car
Got lied to
Cheated on
Went through the motherfucking ringer with that motherfucker
AND HE PROPOSES TO HER!

Gideon Wait. He proposed?!

Worthy Proposed, yeah.
Motherfucker put a ring on it.
He put a fucking ring on it.

Beat.

I hate the fucking corner.

A long moment and then—
Worthy *sits next to* **Gideon**.
Worthy I didn't tell you this before
'Cause I know how you feel about Maurice but
The other night?
When he came over?

He was real sweet
Telling me he loves me
That he still wants to be with me
Telling me he wants to try again
He got me to a place where I was like
Okay, okay, maybe Ima reconsider this fool
Give him another chance
'Cause it finally felt like he was stepping up, you know?
And then this shit.

A moment and then—
Worthy *produces a bat from her bag.*

Gideon   Um . . . Why do you have a bat?

Worthy   I was thinking . . .
I know where that bitch lives.

Gideon   You . . .?

Worthy *gives* **Gideon** *a look.*
Gideon   Are you fucking crazy?

Worthy   WHAT? We ain't gonna hurt her. Just scare her a / little bit—

Gideon   Uh-uh. No way.

Worthy   What you mean, no way? Why the fuck not? Bitch stole my man!

Gideon   Technically she didn't / steal anything—

Worthy   Technically? TECHNICALLY! I'd do it for you. HELL, I'VE *DONE* IT FOR YOU.

Beat.

Yr my best friend, Gideon. *Be* my best / friend—

Gideon   That's what I'm doing.

Worthy   NAH, THAT'S NOT WHAT / THIS IS—

Gideon   Do you hear yrself? Do you? That fool's been a fool from jump. He treats you like shit. He's always treated you like shit. That's why you broke up with him over and over and over again. He consistently fucks up yr life. What the fuck do you care if he's fucking up someone else's?

And then—
Worthy *punches* **Gideon**.
Again.
And again.
And again.
Until.
Gideon (*Explodes.*)   YO, Worthy, STOP!

Worthy *is stunned.*
A long moment and then—
Gideon I'm sorry.
Worthy, I'm . . .
I'm real / sorry—

Worthy You know what . . .? Save it. I've gotta go.

Gideon Worthy . . . Worthy, come on.

Worthy You need to figure yr shit out, Gideon.
I have my shit
Yeah
CLEARLY I have my shit
But you—
You . . .

Beat.

You call me when you get good, okay?
Call me when yr good.

She exits.

Scene Seventeen

The next morning.
Bethea *at the dining room table.*
After a while, **Gideon** *appears.*

Bethea There you are. I thought I was gonna have to send up a search party.

Gideon *sits, then holds out his hand.* **Bethea** *takes it. They bow their heads.*

Bethea For this and all we are about to receive, make us truly grateful, Lord. Through Christ we pray. Amen.

Gideon Amen.

He begins to eat. **Bethea** *watches her son and then—*

Bethea You know I always knew when something was bothering yr father 'cause he would sort of pick at his eyebrow. Only ever did it when something wasn't right. Oh, he'd deny it, of course. He hated the fact that I could tell he was bothered. He'd say, "Thea, ain't nothing wrong with me. You go on and mind yr own business." But, of course, there *was* something wrong. And it *was* my business because he was my husband. And *you* are my son.

Beat.

Is this about last night? About Benton?

Gideon I don't want to talk about last night.

Beat.

Bethea Baby, look at me.
I said, LOOK.

A moment and then—
Gideon *looks at his mother.*
Bethea Why does it feel like everything I say to you is wrong?

Gideon *does not reply.*
Bethea Please don't shut me out.
Please.

And then—

Gideon I'm sorry, but . . .
I'm gonna be late.

Gideon *pulls away from* **Bethea**. *He exits.*
A buzzer.
The visiting room at Sing Sing Correctional Facility.
Myles *appears in a green jumpsuit.*
His eye is bruised.

Myles Mama.

Bethea Hey, baby. Oh my God, Myles yr eye!

Myles It's not as bad as it looks.

Bethea Not as bad as it looks? Yr black and blue. What happened?

Myles I fell.

Bethea Into what? And how many times? Has someone looked at this?

Myles I'm fine, ma. It's just a . . . It'll heal.

Bethea That's not what I'm concerned about. What I'm concerned about is how yr face got this way. What I'm concerned about / is who did this to you—?

Myles Ma! Ma / you've gotta—

Bethea What, Myles? What?

Myles Let it go.

Bethea Let it go? You want me to let / this go—?

Myles Yes.

Bethea How am I supposed to / do that? Yr face looking all—

Myles Ma, listen to me. Nothing good will come of questions or . . . I'm handling it, okay? It's handled. *Sit.*

Beat.

Bethea Does it hurt?

Myles Ma, stop. Please.

Bethea *sits.*

Bethea Yr better than this. You hear me? Better than this place. Better than the people yr protecting—

Myles Ma—

Bethea Listen to me. When you were ten months old you would wake up in the morning and recite yr words. Dog, bus, apple, slippery. Ten months! You were destined for big things, baby. Big things. Don't give up.

She takes his hand.
Don't you dare give—

A buzzer signals the end of visitation.
Myles *pulls away from his mother.*
Myles Ma, I . . . I have to go—

He moves to exit.

Bethea "Now may the God of hope fill you with all joy and peace in believing, that you may abound in hope by the power of the Holy Spirit."

Beat.
You take care of yrself. Promise me you'll—

Myles I will, ma. I promise.

He moves to exit, then turns back.
Mama?

Bethea Yes, baby?

Myles Tell Gideon I say hey.

Another buzzer.
Myles *has disappeared, leaving* **Bethea** *alone.*

Scene Eighteen

The pier.

Gideon I visited once. Right after he got put in. I was fourteen. And I remember on the bus on the way up mom said, "He's still yr brother, baby. The only thing that's changed is the setting." And I remember I nodded. Cause when my mama says something you nod. And we got to Ossining. And we showed our IDs. And we went through the metal detectors. And the scanners. And we sat in the visiting room. And he came out and . . . And he looked like . . . And he hugged me real tight. And he hugged my mom. And then the two of them just went in, you know? They just starting talking like . . . like we were sitting at the breakfast table and not in a maximum-security prison, which . . . well, I didn't know what to do with that. The . . . normalcy of that. In that place. In that place. And then eventually he turned to me. Myles turned to me and he said, "Well, aren't you gonna say anything, Gid? Aren't you at least gonna tell me how you are?" And the only thing I could think to say was, "Why didn't you tell them you didn't do it?" And he didn't answer my question. So, I never went back.

Luke How did yr mom feel about that?

Gideon She'd've preferred I'd been there, I'm sure. Wished I'd been there. But she never said anything.

Beat.

She always believed he was innocent. She never lost faith. Not for a second. What does it say about me that I did?

Luke That yr human.

Gideon Huh. What a thing to be.

Beat.

I've been doing a lot of apologizing recently. Like every other word out of my mouth is a sorry. I've been a real dick.

Luke Not to me.

Gideon Yeah well . . . yr the exception.

Beat.

Sometimes I feel like if I could just smash the shit out of something . . . punch a hole in a wall or break a chair . . . that then I'd feel better.

Luke When I was a kid, there'd be days when I'd come home from school in a mood, you know? Just like . . . attitude attitude attitude . . . And my mom would be like, "*Ay no, papito! No me vengas con esas chavienda! Te me largas y te me regresas de nuevo!*" And I'd go back out on the porch and I'd yell. At the passing cars. At the sky. I'd just—

He yells.
Eventually, **Gideon** *joins.*
They yell together.
An unexpected moment of connection.
And then—

Luke Look, Gideon.
I don't know what it's like to lose the way you've lost.
I still have both my parents.
Both sets of grandparents.
And I'm an only child so losing a brother is . . .
Well, it's unimaginable.
But I did lose an inmate that day . . .
And that . . .
That's not nothing.

Beat.

I liked him.
Yr brother.
He was a good guy.

A long moment and then—

Gideon   Thank you.

Another long moment and then—

Luke   I know this is probably the absolute wrong thing to say right now, but . . . well, it's like this. You know how you can have like five hundred conversations with a person and they can still feel like a total stranger and then you can have one conversation with a different person and you feel like you've known them yr whole life? I feel like that with you.

A moment and then **Gideon** *kisses* **Luke***.*

Scene Nineteen

The next morning.
Luke *and* **Bethea** *set the dining room table together.*

Bethea   Back when I first started dating Gideon's father, God rest his soul, he took me to a different favorite restaurant for dinner every Thursday night for a year. A year! Can you imagine?

Eventually, **Gideon** *appears. He watches the scene.*
That man had *fifty-two* favorite restaurants and a favorite dish at every one of those favorite restaurants—!

Gideon   Good morning?

Luke   Hey. Good morning.   **Bethea**   Well, look who's finally up.

Bethea   We were just about to start without you. I hope yr hungry.

Gideon   I could eat.

Luke   Yr mom made a feast.

Bethea   Nah, Luke. Come back at Thanksgiving. *Then* you'll see a feast.

She checks her table-setting work.
I'm forgetting something. Syrup! I swear my mind is going. Talk amongst yrselves.

She exits.

Luke   I'm so sorry I disappeared. I was on my way back from the bathroom and yr mom cornered me in the hallway and asked me to help her set the table.

Gideon   And when Bethea Solomon asks you to do something you just say yes, believe me, I know.

Luke *kisses* **Gideon** *on the cheek.*

Luke   Good morning.

Bethea *returns bearing syrup.*

Gideon   Good morning.

Bethea   All right you two, take yr seats.

They do.
Do you come from a praying family, Luke?

Luke   Um . . . not really, no.

Bethea   Well, Gideon does. If the Solomons do *anything*, we pray.

Gideon   And pray and pray / and—

Bethea   Boy, hush. And give me yr hand. Luke.

Hands are held and heads are bowed.
Dear heavenly father,
We are asked to accept so much on faith
By faith
We are asked to accept the ugliness of this world
Right alongside the beauty of it
The hatred
Alongside the love
The senseless acts of cruelty
Of carelessness
Alongside acts of compassion
We are asked to accept death
The deaths of loved ones
The deaths of our children.
The too-soon deaths—

Gideon   Ma—

Bethea   Gideon, I'm praying!

Gideon *mouths an "I'm sorry" to* **Luke** *across the table.*
They both re-bow their heads.
Bethea   We are asked to accept
To believe that there is a greater purpose
A larger plan
A context wherein these things
These . . . happenings
These sometimes very ugly happenings
Make some kind of sense
A kind of sense that is clearly beyond human understanding
Beyond mine anyway.
We are told that you are going to use them
That all this ugly will one day be used for yr glory.

Luke *lifts his head, struck by* **Bethea***'s words.*
Bethea   I hope, by the grace of God, that I live to see that day.
But until then, Lord.
Until then.
Please help us to be patient.
Please help us to be patient and to see each day for what it is.
A gift.
Amen.
Gideon/Luke   Amen.

Bethea   Well, all right. Everybody dig in. Don't be shy, Luke. I made plenty.

They begin to eat.
After a while, **Gideon** *notices that* **Luke** *is not eating.*

Gideon   You good?

Luke   Oh. Yeah. It's delicious, Miss Solomon.

Bethea   Thank you, Luke. That's very kind of you to say.

A moment and then—
Luke *sits back in his chair.*
Bethea   Is there something you need, baby?

Luke   No, ma'am, I'm . . .
Um . . .

Gideon   Luke, what's going on?

Bethea   Luke . . . ?

Luke   Look, I don't know exactly how to . . .

He produces an envelope.
I've been holding on to this for uh . . .
He sets the envelope on the table.
This is for you.
For both of you.
It's from Myles.

Bethea   . . . Myles?

Bethea *reaches for the envelope. She opens it.*

Luke (*to* **Bethea**)   He asked me to give it to you before he . . .
(*To* **Gideon**.) I'm sorry.

Bethea   "Dear number two—"

She looks at **Gideon***, then continues.*
Bethea   "I was the corner man that night."

Myles *appears in a green jumpsuit.*
His eye is slightly bruised.

Bethea/Myles   "I was corner—"

Myles   Benton was point
And Rasun was the muscle.
It was a Monday so things were quiet.
A couple cop cars on Adam Clayton Powell
But no blue on the street.
It should've been easy
Easy as shit
Pass the product
Grab the cash
And go.
But the guy was mouthy
And short five hundred
And Benton was feeling itchy
So, they got into it
And then Rasun and the other guys' man got into it
And I heard the shouting
Bitch ass nigga this
And faggot ass that
And then
Pop
And I stepped out into the street to make sure it wasn't one of my guys
You know?
That it wasn't Benton.
And Rasun is flying toward me
Running like a motherfucker
And he's like
Let's go let's go let's go
And then we're running down one thirty third
And then we're running down Lenox
And then we're ducking into our man Doug's spot on like one twenty-seven
And we're panting
Gasping for breath
And we're dripping sweat everywhere
And Benton shows up like ten minutes later
And Rasun's like, what the fuck?
And Benton's like, whatever.
Like what the fuck ever.
And that very same night.
Walking home.
Not a block from the house.
I'm picked up by the cops.

Beat.

I've had a lot of time to think

To think about loyalty
To question my idea of it
My eighteen-year-old self's idea of it versus my thirty-one-year-old self's idea of it
People I thought were friends
People I thought I owed—

Beat.

This place'll change you, Gid
It'll make you hard in places that were soft
It'll make you afraid
To move
To speak
To feel—
It's not a safe place
Or a kind place
There is no forgiveness here
Even love—
Even love looks different here
It feels different.
Smells different.
Like sweat.
And shit.
And blood.
It's hard.
Rough.
Rougher.
It's muscle
And bone
And stubble
And hot breath
And concrete
And stainless steel.
And shit.
It's about domination.
And dominating.
And being dominated.
And pussy.
Love is pussy.
Love here is about the holes you have
And how those holes are filled.

Beat.

You know the worst thing about being in here?
It's the shit you miss.
Dinners around the table

And nights on the 'scape.
The fact that you can't see the sky.

Beat.

I fucked up.
I fucked up and—

Beat.

You know, Dad was tenderhearted
We're like him in that way
We see the good in people
We see the good
And miss the bad
The inconsistent
The dangerous
It's not really a weakness.
It doesn't have to be a weakness.
Don't let it be a weakness.

Beat.

Love,
Number one.

A long moment and then—
Gideon *stands.*
Luke *stands, in response.*
And then—
Gideon *exits.*
Luke *watches him go.*
After a while, **Luke** *begins to clear the table.*
Gideon *appears at the pier.*
He lights a cigarette, inhales, then blows smoke into the air.
Luke *finishes clearing the table.*
Before his exit, **Luke** *looks back at* **Bethea**.
In that moment, **Gideon**, **Bethea**, *and* **Luke** *in tableau.*
Bethea *produces a Bible and begins to read.*

Scene Twenty

A knock.

Bethea *closes her book and crosses to the door.*

Benton I heard you were looking for me.

Bethea That's right. Come on in.

He does.

Benton   This place. All these years and it still feels the same.

Bethea   Can I get you something? Water? Tea?

Benton   Nah, I'm good.

Beat.

You know I've gotta say, I was surprised to hear you wanted to talk. My boy said, Bethea Solomon wants to see you. And I was like, uh-uh, that woman ain't nothing to say to me. Not after the other night with the eggs and the door.

Bethea   And yet yr here.

Benton   I don't like tension, Miss Solomon. I never have. And I felt tension between us. And not like a surface of the skin kinda tension. Nah, something deeper. Like on account of me not making it to Myles' funeral or whatever. And like I said before. I wanted to be there. I did. I tried to be there—

Bethea   Life just got in the way.

Benton   Exactly. See, you get it! I just want to move past all of that, you know? *That's* what I'm interested in. Moving forward. Cause I mean, I loved Myles. I loved him like— Well, like family. He was my family. I mean, that's why I'm here.

Bethea *offers* **Benton** *a chair. They both sit.*

Bethea   I've been thinking about this one moment.
I can't stop thinking about it actually.
You and Myles couldn't have been more than twelve
Maybe thirteen
I was on my way home from the library
And as I was passing the bodega on the corner
I happened to glance inside.
It wasn't more than a glance.
But I saw you and Myles inside
Standing at the counter.
And I remember I smiled because
For the longest Myles wasn't allowed to go to Mister Ahmed's by himself
And I got a bit nostalgic
And that's when I saw him grab a handful of candy bars and stuff them into his pocket.
Just—

She gestures.
And at first I couldn't believe it.
My son?
A thief?
Nah, there must be some explanation.
Because Myles had never done anything like that before.
Because he was a good kid
And because I had taught him better than that.

Because his father taught him better than that.
Because *we* taught our son the difference between right and wrong.
I confronted Myles about it later.
I said, "I saw you at Mister Ahmed's."
I said, "I saw you take that candy."
I said, "What the hell did you think you were doing?"
And do you know what he said to me?
What my son said to me?
"They were just candy bars, ma."
Just candy bars.

She stands.
Mothers know, Benton.
We do.
We know when our children change.
When their sweetness . . .
We know.
You say you loved him.
You say you loved my son like family.

Benton That's right.

Bethea Then why did you let him steal?

Benton Sorry, why'd I / what—?

Bethea Why did you let him sell? / He went to prison for you. Died for you—

Benton Yeah, nah, Miss Solomon. Look. LOOK!

He stands.

If I'd known that this was why you called me over here, I could've saved you the trouble. I maintain the same story I told the cops thirteen years ago. I don't know what Myles was into.

Bethea *produces* **Myles'** *letter and begins to read.*

Myles And I certainly wasn't there / when whatever went down went down so I can't help you—

Bethea "I was the corner man that night. I was corner. Benton was point. And Rasun was the muscle . . ."

Benton What is that?

Bethea "It was a Monday so things were quiet . . ."

Benton Miss Solomon, I asked you a question! What are you playing at?

Bethea "A couple cop cars on Adam Clayton   **Benton** WHAT THE FUCK
                                                        ARE YOU PLAYING AT?
Powell but no blue on the street—"

Bethea *evades* **Benton**, *continuing to read.*

Bethea "It should've been easy / Easy as shit—"   **Benton** Hey! HEY!

Gideon *enters the house.*

Bethea You're a liar! YOU FUCKING LIE!   **Gideon** Ma, I'm home.

Gideon *rushes at* **Benton**.

Gideon GET THE FUCK OFF HER!   **Benton** Gideon, GET THE FUCK OFF—!

Gideon *pulls* **Benton** *from his mother.*
Benton *and* **Gideon** *engage.*
Gideon *is pushed onto the table.*

Benton YOU SOLOMONS ARE FUCKING CRAZY!
All of y'all.
Fucking crazy.
We're done here.

Bethea *produces a gun.*

Benton Holy shit—!   **Gideon** Jesus, ma—!

Bethea Nah, Benton. We're not done until *I* say / we're done.

Benton All right now, Miss Solomon. Go on and put the gun down—

Bethea I visited Myles in that place every month for thirteen years. Thirteen! Every month. I never missed a visit.

Benton Miss Solomon—

Bethea LET ME FINISH!
Whatever arrangement the two of you had
He honored it.
He never said a thing.
Had me fighting for him and . . .
The law has washed its hands of it.
Of me.
They say they got the right man.
They say justice was done.
But I know different.
I know because I know justice when I see it
And that—
You and I both know that justice wasn't what that was.
I want the truth, Benton.
That's what I want from you.
That's all I want.
And I want to hear it from yr mouth.

A moment and then she advances toward **Benton**.
Bethea BOY, YOU BETTER START / TALKING—!

Scene Twenty

Benton   ALL RIGHT, ALL RIGHT!   **Gideon**   MA, NO—!

All right.

Beat.

It was me.
Okay?
I shot the guy.
It's just like you read there.
Myles wasn't even . . .
He wasn't even there.
He was on the corner.
He didn't even see it go down.

Bethea   But you told the cops that he was the one—

Benton   Myles knew what he was into. / He knew the risk—

Bethea   And that makes it okay? That makes what you did / okay—?

Benton   I SURVIVED!
That's what I did.
I survived.
I wish Myles had, too.
I wish . . .
I wish lots of things.
I wish survival was easier.
I wish it was a guarantee for folks around here.
Good, bad or whatever.
But it's not.
What you want?

He walks into the gun.
For another Black man to go to prison?
Another Black mother taking the bus upstate?
What's that solve, huh?

Beat.

Look, I'm sorry for yr loss.

Bethea *lowers the gun.*
Benton   Truly, I—
But it's done.
It's been done.
He's gone.
And the truth won't bring him back.

Bethea *re-points the gun.*
A moment and then—
Benton *moves toward the door.*
Bethea *keeps the gun trained on* **Benton** *as he exits.*

Gideon *intercepts his mother's arm, lowering it to the table and removing the gun from her hand.*
They breathe and then—
Gideon *breaks.*
Bethea *holds her son.*
She holds his face—a reassuring gesture.
We're going to be okay.
After a while—

Gideon   I'm sorry, mama.

Bethea   Oh, baby, I know.
I'm sorry, too.

And then—
Everything falls away except the fire escape.
Gideon *and* **Bethea** *look up at the sky.*
Gideon *points.*

Gideon   See there? To the right? Those three little ones?

Bethea   Mm-hm . . .

Gideon   Well, that's the handle. And then those four rhombus-y looking stars . . . You do know what a rhombus is, right ma?

Bethea *gives* **Gideon** *a look.*
Gideon   Just checking / just checking—

Bethea   Uh huh. You better check yr attitude is what you better check. Smart ass. Now finish showing me the damn stars.

Gideon   Well, when you put 'em all together. All seven of those stars. The handle. And—

Gideon/Bethea   The rhombus—

Bethea   Yeah, I got you.

Gideon   *That's* the Big Dipper.
It's cool, right?

Bethea   Yeah. It's cool.

Beat.

Gideon   Myles useta complain that he couldn't see the stars he really wanted to see cause of the lights.
He useta say there were too many lights in the city.
"You gotta get out, Gid," he useta say.
"You gotta get out of New York City, outta Harlem—"

Myles *appears on the fire escape.*

Myles See, what you do is you rent a car
(Once you have yr license, of course, and not before)
Or you Metro North-it up to Westchester or somewhere
Some white neighborhood right
Where everyone's asleep by like ten o'clock
So it's real dark outside
Like inky black
And you park by the Hudson River
One of those overlooks, you know?
You park by the Hudson
And you lay out on the hood of the car
And you look up.

He looks up.
Gideon *and* **Bethea** *look at each other.*
The night sky is suddenly illuminated by countless stars.
It is breathtaking.

End of play.

Selling Kabul

Sylvia Khoury

Introduction

This play was informed by encounters with Afghan Special Immigrant Visa (SIV) applicants in 2015. Each of these men was navigating the difficult process of applying for this visa—one that had been guaranteed to individuals who had collaborated with American forces at tremendous personal risk. All were hiding from possible retribution at the hands of the Taliban as they waited for this promised paperwork—for visas that were seldom granted.

I wrote *Selling Kabul* out of two conflicting responses that these encounters generated in me. The first was empathy—their longing for safety, for improved circumstances was a deeply American one, one that has fueled immigration to this country since its inception. My own family would not be in this country were it not for the promised security and opportunity of the American dream. The second response to these encounters was guilt—my understanding that it was the long arm of American imperialism that had reached into their homes in Afghanistan and thrust their lives into chaos.

I hoped that audiences would ask themselves, as I had asked myself—are we so readily separated from the actions of our government? Once the American dream is attained, and generations have lived here in relative security, are we fated to become myopic? It is fitting that the first production of *Selling Kabul* occurred at the Williamstown Theatre Festival in 2019 under the tremendous leadership of Mandy Greenfield, who has never shirked from asking audiences difficult questions.

After an almost two-year delay due to the pandemic, the Playwrights Horizons co-production with WTF took place in late 2021. It was a mere three months after America's precipitous exit from Afghanistan, and the devastation left in our wake. As I write this at the beginning of 2022, Afghanistan is in the throes of a humanitarian crisis. Thousands of Afghans who collaborated with American forces remain in hiding, fearful for their lives. I ask again—are we, as Americans, so readily separated from the actions of our government?

Characters

Taroon, *early thirties, an Afghan man who worked as an interpreter for the American military.*
Afiya, *early thirties, his sister, a seamstress.*
Leyla, *early thirties, Afiya's neighbor and childhood friend.*
Jawid, *late thirties, Afiya's husband, a tailor.*

Setting

Kabul, April 2013.

The United States has begun a major withdrawal of troops from Afghanistan.

Notes on Production

Selling Kabul had its world premiere at Williamstown Theatre Festival (Mandy Greenfield, artistic director) in association with Playwrights Horizons (Tim Sanford, artistic director) opening on July 13, 2019. The director was Tyne Rafaeli, the stage manager was Brett Anders, the set designer was Arnulfo Maldonado, the costume designer was Dina El-Aziz, the lighting designer was Jen Schriever, the sound designer was Beth Lake. The cast was as follows:

Afiya	Marjan Neshat
Taroon	Babak Tafti
Jawid	Omid Abtahi
Leyla	May Calamawy

The play was subsequently produced in New York City by Playwrights Horizons, opening on December 6, 2021. The cast was as follows:

Afiya	Marjan Neshat
Taroon	Dario Ladani Sanchez
Jawid	Mattico David
Leyla	Francis Benhamou

Selling Kabul was a recipient of the L. Arnold Weissberger New Play Award.

Evening.

A small but well-decorated living room in Kabul.

A large oriental carpet covers most of the floor. A floor couch wraps along the perimeter of the room, with corresponding cushions propped up against the walls to lean against. Noticeable on the carpet is a nice television set—slightly too large for its modest surroundings—as well as three large piles of folded Afghan army uniforms, each pile stacked so high in a basket that it threatens to topple over. Elsewhere, a router and a tangle of wires. There are also two large fans, one close to the entryway and one in the living area. Upstage from the living room is a kitchen with a sink visible to the audience. The room also has a closet, a door to the bedroom, and a door that gives out onto the hallway shared with other apartments.

As the play begins, **Taroon** *is trying to fix the router. He has a laptop open beside him and clicks furiously, trying to connect to the internet. It doesn't work. He unplugs the router, then plugs it back in. As he waits for the router to reboot, he stares vacantly at the television. Light from the television flickers on his face, but no sound comes from it. A baby cries from a neighboring apartment.* **Taroon** *turns back to his laptop and tries to connect once again. It doesn't work.*

Frustrated, he slams the laptop shut. Wincing at the sound, he casts a worried glance towards the door. The baby next door cries louder. **Taroon** *springs up, anxious, and paces. He feels his face and notices he missed a spot when shaving. He goes into the bedroom, and comes out shaving a small patch on his face without shaving cream. He opens his laptop back up and checks his internet connection again. Nothing. He unplugs the router once more. As he moves to replug it:*

The sound of movement outside the door. **Taroon** *abandons the router and quickly turns off the television, shoving the razor in his pocket. From offstage, we hear his sister,* **Afiya**, *conversing with a neighbor,* **Leyla**.

Afiya
(*offstage*)
He won't sleep?

Leyla
(*offstage*)
He won't even close his eyes.

Hearing **Leyla**, **Taroon** *springs into silent, practiced action.*

He rushes to the closet, opens the door, goes inside it, and closes the door from inside—

All without making a sound.

Afiya
(*offstage*)
Poor thing.

Leyla
(*offstage*)
You mean me!
I am the poor thing.
I'm telling you, he's trying to kill me.

Afiya
(*offstage*)
He's not sick?

Leyla
(*offstage*)
No, no,
Just vindictive.
(*To the child.*)
Aren't you, Nabil?
Aren't you vindictive?

Afiya *unlocks the door and opens it a crack—we hear them a bit better.*

Afiya
(*offstage*)
I hope you get some rest, / Leyla.

Leyla
(*offstage*)
I started some tea,
Set your things down!
Come join me.

Afiya
(*offstage*)
I can't.

Leyla
(*offstage*)
Come on,
Amir's mother just left!
There is so much to tell you.

Afiya
(*offstage*)
I've got this headache, Leyla,
I'd better go close my eyes.
(*To the child.*)
Like you should, Nabil!
Sleep for your mother.
She needs her rest.

Afiya *enters the apartment alone, chadaree and purse in hand, and closes the door behind her.*
She takes the nearest fan, places it in front of the door, and turns it on.
Satisfied that she won't be overheard, she moves over to the closet.

Afiya
I'm alone.

Taroon *emerges from the closet, eager.*

Taroon
So?

Afiya
A boy!

Taroon
Healthy?

Afiya
Yes.

Taroon
And Bibi?

Afiya
Healthy.

Taroon
Ten fingers?
Ten toes?

Afiya
Yes.

Taroon
Our cousin—
He was missing a pinky.

Afiya
I counted them.

Taroon
A boy.

Afiya
A boy.

Taroon
You held him?

Afiya
No, but I touched him.
He's too small to hold.

Taroon
Too small?

Afiya
(*warm*)
He's normal, Taroon.
I asked.
Everything is normal.

Taroon
And when you left?

Afiya
She was holding him.

Taroon
Wow.

Afiya
Bibi, she looks like she was meant to look.
Like a picture.

Taroon
And she's well?

Afiya
Tired, but she can't stop smiling.

Taroon
Was it difficult, for her?

Afiya
Yes.

Taroon
Did she ask where I was?

Afiya
(*regretful*)
She knows better.

Taroon
Was she looking around, hoping I might come?

Afiya
No, Taroon.
She was accomplishing the considerable task
Of pushing a child into the world.

A moment.

Taroon
This isn't right.
. . .

I should have been there.
The birth of my son, Afiya!

Afiya
Your son will be glad to see you alive one day.

Taroon
He'll think me a coward
Too scared to show my face in the light of day.

Afiya
Please, Taroon, for me.
Raise your son without the word "coward."
Or "hero," now that I think of it.

Seeing him distraught:

He has a full head of hair, your son.

She ruffles his hair.

Taroon
Really?

Afiya
You'll have to get a spray bottle, like Mama had.

Taroon
Never!
I will never do that to my son.

Afiya
God, you would cry!

Taroon
Well, I was wet all day!
You try being wet / all day!

Afiya
(*gentle mocking*)
"Mama, no, please, no!"

He laughs.
Afiya *straightens her chadaree and goes towards the closet to put it away.*

Taroon
(*touching his hair*)
It never even worked!
It only made it expand.

Afiya *feels the television as she passes it.*
She stops short.

Afiya
Taroon, why is the television hot?

Taroon
I don't know.

Afiya
Taroon.

Taroon
I don't know!
It was warm in the apartment?

Afiya
Were you watching the television?

Taroon
This is some congratulations for the new / father.

Afiya
Were you watching it?

Taroon
No.

Afiya
Taroon, how many times do I have to tell you?
If someone sees it flickering from the street—

Taroon
It wasn't on.

Afiya
If someone sees it,
With Jawid and I both out for the day—

Taroon
It wasn't on.

Afiya
They would know someone was here!

Taroon
I'm telling you!
It wasn't on.

She scrutinizes him.

Afiya
You swear on your son's head?

Taroon
(*offended*)
Two hours old, you want me to swear on his head?
If I said I didn't watch it, I didn't watch it.

She considers him.

Afiya
Okay.
Okay.

She puts her chadaree away before moving into the kitchen and rummaging around.

Taroon
So who's with her?
At the hospital?

Afiya
Jawid, her family.

Taroon
Come on, show me a picture.

Afiya
Bibi's aunt was taking them.
She said she'd send them to me.

Taroon
You didn't even take a / picture?

Afiya
My phone ran out of battery.
Two weeks early, your wife surprised us, Taroon.

Taroon
Two weeks early, but he's not too small?

She brings a box of dates and a plate of cookies to the floor couch.

Afiya
No, he's not too small.
I asked the doctor five times.
He's perfectly healthy.
A beautiful, hairy baby boy.

She sets them down and sits.

Afiya
Congratulations.

She motions for him to sit with her.
He remains standing but looks with interest at the sweets.

Taroon
Where did these come from?

Afiya
I've had them since your wife entered her eighth month.

Taroon
Here?
That's impossible.

Afiya
Why, because you've pilfered every drawer?

She motions for him to sit again.
Instead, he takes a cookie and eats it, standing.

Taroon
Mm.
Have.

As he takes another one:

Afiya
I'm not hungry.

Taroon
(*mouth full*)
Have!
I can't celebrate alone.

She takes one and motions for him to sit again, but he ducks into the bedroom.
*She deflates momentarily before **Taroon** emerges, putting gel in his hair.*

Taroon
Four months.
Four months, I haven't seen her.
I'm starting to think I dreamed her up.
Is she really as good looking as I think she is?

Afiya *gives a weak smile that **Taroon** doesn't clock.*
Finished with the gel, he motions to his appearance.

Taroon
What do you think?
This is how Bibi likes it.

Afiya
It's good, Taroon.

He smiles, satisfied, then sits next to her.
As he reaches for another cookie, she blurts:

Afiya
Taroon, you can't go see them tonight,
It's too dangerous.
I'm sorry.

Taroon *freezes, cookie halfway to his mouth, then looks at **Afiya**.*

Afiya
I'm sorry.
It's not what I wanted—
You know that—
But it's too dangerous.

Taroon
(*trying hard to be steady*)
We have the plan, Afiya.
Wait until dark,
Wear a chadaree,
Go to the hospital once everyone has left.

Afiya
You can't.

Taroon
And that's what we're doing.
Waiting until dark,
I'll wear a chadaree—

Afiya
Your son came two weeks early.
We aren't ready.

Taroon
(*half to himself*)
I really thought you might not do this.

Afiya
Taroon, going at night, dressed as a woman,
It's not so simple.

Taroon
It is.
It is simple.

Afiya
It isn't!
I don't know the best way to get there,
Without getting stopped.
The best person to accompany you,
Who we might trust as a lookout,
What entrance to use, of the hospital,
It takes time.

Taroon
You're inventing problems, Afiya.

Afiya
Four months, you haven't set foot outside this apartment.

Taroon
And when I do,
All anyone will see
Is a woman walking into a hospital.

Afiya
And if you're stopped?

Taroon
I won't be.

Afiya
How can you say that?

Taroon
I won't be.

Afiya
Taroon your name was on a list!
Everyone who collaborated with the Americans,
Do I have to go find it?

Taroon
I don't think you understand
My son was just born.

Afiya
Exactly.
Your son was just born.
We can't take any chances.

Taroon
I'm sorry, Afiya, I have to be there.

Afiya
No.
You are not setting foot outside this apartment.

Taroon
Jawid said he would drive me.

Afiya
I spoke to him at the hospital,
He will not drive you.
Not tonight.

A moment.

Taroon
(*barely concealed rage*)
You spoke to Jawid?

Afiya
For you to go tonight, Taroon,
It would be madness.
We aren't ready.

Taroon
Without speaking to me, asking me,
Just like that, your husband won't drive me?

Afiya
I'm telling you, it's too dangerous!

Taroon
This is my son, Afiya!

Afiya
So you had a son, and you can't see him yet.
It has happened before, it will happen again.

Taroon *goes into the bedroom and slams the door shut.*
Afiya *turns on a second fan, then opens the bedroom door a crack, and angrily whispers:*

Afiya
Are you crazy?
You can't go around slamming doors!
. . .
Taroon, I didn't mean to upset you
. . .
I promise,
I'll make sure you see him soon
It's your son, of course you should see him.
. . .
Taroon?

Taroon *emerges from the bedroom.*

Taroon
Thank you, Afiya,

Afiya
For . . . ?

Taroon
For everything you've done.

Afiya
Taroon.

Taroon
You've fed me, you've put up with me.

Afiya
What, now you're playing houseguest?

Taroon
I know that everything you've done,
It's been to keep me safe.

Afiya
That's all I want, Taroon.
To keep you safe.

Taroon
But I am going to the hospital tonight.

Afiya
How?

Taroon
I'll walk.

Afiya
It's all the way across the city!
Are you crazy?

Taroon
I spent two years in Helmand, Afiya,
Carrying a gun,
Coming under fire.
I think I can navigate the streets of Kabul
For thirty minutes,
At night,
Under a chadaree.

Afiya
Taroon,
This isn't about your ability,
This isn't even about you!
You have a child now!

Taroon
Afiya, you and your husband?
You don't decide if I see my son and my wife.

Afiya
That's right,
You do, Taroon.
You decide.
That door isn't locked from the outside.
But remember,
Now you have a son,
And that son has a father to lose.

This hits him.
After a moment:

Taroon
Well, what am I supposed to do?
Sit here, while my child passes from hand to hand?
While my wife imagines how this all should have gone?
That I should have been there?

Afiya
Yes.

She softens.

Afiya
In a few short days, Taroon,
You will see them.
You'll meet your son, hold your wife.
You'll be a family, Taroon.
Your family.
I promise.

He sits, somber.
After a long while:

Taroon
This is not how it's supposed to go.
This is not how any of this is supposed to go.

Afiya
Let me make you tea.

Taroon
No.

Afiya
I'll make you tea.

Taroon
I want to scream.

Afiya
Don't.

Taroon
I know I can't.
But knowing I can't,
It makes me want to scream more than I've ever wanted to.

Afiya
I'll bring you tea.

She goes to the kitchen and begins to make tea.

*The phone rings in **Leyla**'s apartment.
Hearing it:*

Taroon
Mama called.

Afiya
I was going to ask.

Taroon
Calling five times in five minutes.
What is wrong with her?

Afiya
She left a message?

Taroon
After the fifth time, yeah.
A baby, she said, what a blessing.
She sounded like she was smiling.

Afiya
I'm sure she was.

Taroon
I almost picked up.

Afiya
Taroon.

Taroon
Almost.
I said almost!

Afiya
You cannot answer the phone.

Taroon
Afiya, I know!

Afiya
Don't scare me like that.

Taroon
Scare you?
What, I can't talk anymore?
I was just talking!

*A moment of tea making, **Taroon** slumped on the couch.
He checks the time.*

Taroon
That was an hour ago.
You think she'd try again.
A grandson, and she hasn't called in an hour.

Afiya
She knew I was at the hospital.

Taroon
Still.
A grandson, and she hasn't called in an hour.

After a while, she returns with a steaming cup of tea for her brother.
She places it in front of him, then sits beside him.
He stares at it.

Afiya
Well?

He looks at her.

Afiya
Drink.

Taroon
It's hot.

She eyes him suspiciously.

Taroon
What do you want, it's too hot!

Afiya
Fine.

Taroon
You want me to burn my tongue, so I can't speak?

She makes a dismissive gesture and goes to the phone.
She dials her mother.
No one picks up.

Afiya
She must have gone out.

Taroon
Gone out, and she has a grandson.

Afiya
She'll call back.

She sits back down.

Taroon
And now for news, what?
We wait for Jawid?

Afiya
Yes.

Taroon
That's most of my life,
Waiting for your husband.

She picks up sewing work from one of the baskets and begins to work.
***Taroon** fidgets, restless, then looks at his sister, motioning to the router.*

Taroon
It still doesn't work.
I tried to fix it

Afiya
Jawid will look at it when he gets home.

Taroon
It's been three days, Afiya.
They may have sent / a message.

Afiya
I understand.

Taroon
Could you imagine if they've sent / a message?

Afiya
I'll call someone tomorrow.

Taroon
If you don't want to call someone,
I'm sure Tariq would come by.

Afiya
Enough, Taroon.

Taroon
You don't want me to hear from them.
Just say it.

Afiya
Taroon.

Taroon
I heard Jawid last night.
I heard him telling you that you should get it repaired.

Afiya
I know the walls are thin, Taroon.
But my affairs are still my own.

Taroon
Who knows, they may have already sent a message!
They may be inviting me and Bibi and our son—
They may be inviting us to America!

Afiya
I'll call tomorrow.

A moment.

Taroon
You don't want me to go, is that it?
You want me to stay?

Afiya
Of course I want you to go.
Don't be stupid.
You think I want you here?

Taroon
I can handle whatever they send, Afiya.
Good, or bad, or nothing.

Afiya
Nothing!
Exactly.
I hate it, seeing your hope when you check for messages.
Watching it crack when there's nothing.
There's always nothing.

Taroon
Until one day, there's something.

Afiya
We repair that box and you won't have an invitation to America,
Just a message from Jeff.

Taroon
Jeff is my friend.

Afiya
Jeff is not your friend.
Jeff got to go home to America.
Jeff abandoned you.

Taroon
Jeff didn't abandon me.
Listen, Afiya.
America, their word is good, okay?
So it takes some time, it takes some time.

Afiya
He fills your head with dreams.
I don't like it.

Taroon
You know what Jeff and I went through together.

Afiya
Yes, yes.

Taroon
You've seen in my folder.

He pulls out a binder from a cabinet.
As he opens it:

Afiya
Taroon.

Taroon
All the letters he had them write me.
Taroon translated for us here—
Taroon came under fire there—
Taroon is a strong man—
Brave man—

Afiya
Repetitive man,
I've heard this before, Taroon.
Please, you're making my head hurt.

He puts the binder away.

Taroon
They will get me this visa, I know it.
They will.
For me, for Bibi, for our son.
Jeff promised.

Afiya
(*absently, tired*)
Yes, of course.
Jeff promised.

A moment.

Taroon
Four months and suddenly this place seems so small.

Afiya
It is small.

Taroon
No, today it's like the walls are pressing in on me.

Afiya
You'll get used to it.
Drink your tea.

She motions to the tea.

Afiya
Go on, it's going to get cold.

Taroon
I don't want it.

Afiya
You let me make tea,
and you don't want it.

Taroon
I never want it,
I don't like tea.

Afiya
Stupid.

Taroon
You drink it, then.

Afiya
I don't want it.

Taroon
You don't like it!
You just like to make it!

This surprises **Afiya**.
She smiles.

Afiya
That's true.
I do like to make it and not to drink it.
That's true.

An easiness between them.
Afiya *pulls a dress she is working on out of a basket.*
Taroon *grins.*

Taroon
Well, that's an interesting color combination.

Afiya
It's our mother's new dress.
She picked them out.

Taroon
She's colorblind, then.

Afiya
She is not colorblind.

Taroon
She is getting older.

Afiya
You don't become colorblind with age.

Taroon
Explain these colors to me, then.

Afiya
She has bad taste.
She's always had bad taste.
Remember the dresses she would have me wear?

Taroon
You looked nice.

Afiya
I looked ridiculous.

Taroon
Yeah, it was bad.

He smiles.
They sit for a while.

Taroon
I wish she could come with me and Bibi, to America.
She would make sure my son speaks English.

Afiya *laughs.*

Afiya
If you make it to America, Taroon,
Americans will teach your son English.

Taroon
That's true.

Afiya *holds up the completed dress.*
It is ugly.

Taroon
Well, I should thank her.
When my son becomes an American, it will be because of her.

Afiya
Thank her *if* you get your visa, okay?

Taroon
I will get my visa, Afiya.
And then, who knows
Maybe you'll follow!
You could go back to school.

Afiya
Yes, yes.
And we'll all break out in song about dreams coming true.

She stands and goes to the closet to hang the dress up.
While at the closet, she pulls out **Taroon***'s pack.*
She finds a nutritional bar wrapper in the closet behind the pack.

Afiya
Taroon, what is this?

Taroon
I got hungry.

Afiya
These aren't for eating!

Taroon
Now, Afiya?
This is what we're doing now?

Afiya
This is from your pack!
What have we said?
We said, don't touch your pack!

Taroon
Oh, what does it matter?
I was hungry.

Afiya
And what if you have to run away?
Now you have one less meal!
(*Finding another wrapper:*)
Two!
Two less meals!

Taroon
Today I am a father.
We can celebrate.
We can eat everything in the pack.

Afiya
Don't be stupid.
Now you have a baby, we need a bigger pack!

Taroon
I got nervous.
I got nervous, so I ate.

Afiya
That's fine.

Taroon
It's a baby, I got nervous!

Afiya
I said, it's fine.

After throwing away the wrappers, she sits back down to resume her work. As she is threading a needle, **Taroon** *looks at her suspiciously.*

Taroon
You haven't checked my pack in a while.

Afiya
What?

Taroon
My pack.
You haven't checked it in a while.

Afiya
I checked it yesterday.

Taroon
You did?

Afiya
Yeah.

Taroon
Huh.

He watches her pick her work back up, unsteady. She glances at her phone.

Taroon
Do you have the picture yet?

Afiya
Of what?

Taroon
Of what?
My son!

Afiya
Not yet.

Taroon
Of course not, it's just my child.
Why should I care what he looks like?

Afiya
They're busy, Taroon.

Taroon
Too busy to send a picture?

Afiya
Yes, they're taking care of your wife.

Taroon *sits back down, restless.*
He looks at the uniform **Afiya** *is working on.*

Taroon
I don't know why you have to do that in front of me.

Afiya
Because this is my house and I have nowhere else to do it.

He shakes his head.

Taroon
I can't see my son
Because these men want my head,
And my sister is outfitting them.

Afiya *doesn't respond.*

Taroon
Making army uniforms.
Army uniforms for the Taliban.

Afiya
Please, Taroon.

Taroon
Afiya, the uniform you're holding?
It lets Taliban access official places.

Afiya
I don't want to talk about this.

Taroon
People think they are the army!
People trust them!
They see the uniform and just like that—
They trust!

Afiya
Taroon.

Taroon
Tell me, why should I be here,
Caged like an animal?
Away from my son and my wife,
While they run free, destroying our country?

. . .

Army uniforms for Taliban,
For what?

Afiya
For you.
To keep you safe.

Taroon
To keep me safe?
Afiya,
There were stacks of uniforms in this house
Months before I was in any sort of danger.

Afiya
Times are hard,
They're hard for everyone.
Jawid has to keep food on the table.

Taroon
He's doing more than keeping food on the table.
Watching your husband wipe down that screen once a week, so careful—

Afiya
Taroon.

Taroon
People have died to pay for that television set.
It runs on blood.

Afiya
Well, I don't see you looking away when a soccer match is on.

Taroon
What am I supposed to do?
Make excuses to leave the room, like you do?

Afiya
Please.
Try to relax.

Taroon
I know you won't watch it.
I know you don't approve of what he does.
Why should you?
That was our father's shop, Afiya.
He's making uniforms for the Taliban in our father's / shop!

Afiya
Enough!

She continues her work.
He flings himself back, frustrated.

Taroon
Your hands are shaking.

Afiya
They're not.

Taroon
They are.

Afiya
Because you're making me angry, Taroon.
That's what happens.
You make me angry,
My hands shake.

He continues to watch her.

Taroon
You're going to stab yourself with the needle,
Your hands shaking like that.

Afiya
If I stab anyone, make no mistake,
It will be you.

Taroon *looks in the basket.*
He pulls out a tiny sweater.
He holds it up, moved.

Taroon
Is this—?

Afiya
It's for your wife.

Taroon
Afiya.

Afiya
I'm not in the mood to give you a present.
So it's for Bibi.
For her child.

Taroon
It's very small.

Afiya
He's very small.

Taroon
(*concerned*)
Small but—

Afiya
Normal, Taroon.
Don't worry.

He looks at it, then at her.

Taroon
I heard you talking to Leyla.
About women's . . . things.

Afiya
Oh, God.

Taroon
That you might be . . . ?

Afiya *closes her eyes.*

Taroon
I didn't mean to overhear.
My ear wasn't at the door.

A moment.

Afiya
I'm not pregnant.
I thought I might be.

Taroon
I'm sorry.

Afiya
No, no.
Don't be sorry.
Not today.
Today, I have a nephew.
A healthy, normal-sized nephew.
With cheeks too big for his face.

Taroon *smiles.*
He helps himself to a cookie.
While chewing:

Taroon
You will have a child, Afiya,
I can feel it.
My son will have a cousin.

Afiya
God willing.

Taroon
Yes, God willing.

Afiya
Don't say God willing with your mouth full, Taroon.
You're trying to curse me?

Taroon
What did I do?

She starts swiping at the crumbs on his shirt.

Afiya
Crumbs everywhere,
Speaking God's name—

Taroon
Stop, stop!

Afiya
Never pray for me, please,
If this is how you do it.
The shame.

She shoves a shirt into **Taroon**'s *hands.*

Taroon
I am not helping—

Afiya
It's Jawid's.
I haven't had the time to mend it.

Taroon
You want me to mend your husband's shirt?

Afiya
I want you to occupy your hands,
And occupy your mind,
With something other than tormenting me.

Taroon *takes the shirt from her.*
He begins to sew.
They work side by side for a while.
Afiya *glances over at* **Taroon**'s *progress.*

Taroon
Are you checking my work?

She makes a noncommittal movement.

Taroon
I'm better at mending than you are.

Afiya
You work too fast.

Taroon
Too fast?
Tell me, Afiya.
Are my stitches straight?

She inspects them; they are.

Afiya
Depends what you mean by straight.

Taroon
It means my stitches are in a straight line.

Afiya
They look like a machine did them.
Mine are . . . expressive.

Taroon
You mean yours are terrible—
That's what you mean?

They keep working.
Afiya *glances at her cell phone.*

Taroon
I forgot how good at this I am.

The house phone rings.
In the split-second that **Taroon** *looks up:*

Afiya
(*violently*)
Don't!

Taroon
Afiya?

Afiya
I just meant—
Don't pick up the—

Taroon
I never pick up / the phone.

Afiya
I'm sorry / I just got

Taroon
Afiya.

She turns to the phone.
It stops ringing.
They look at each other.

Afiya *breaks it.*

Afiya
Are you hungry?
I haven't even thought about dinner

She goes into the kitchen, avoiding eye contact.

Taroon
Afiya.

Afiya
And I didn't go to the market today—

Taroon
What's going on?

Afiya
Nothing.
Nothing is going on.

Taroon
Did something happen?

Afiya
No, no

Taroon
Something at the hospital?

Afiya
No.

Taroon
Afiya, look at me.

She finally does.

Taroon
What happened at the hospital?

Afiya
Taroon—

Taroon
What was it?
Was someone there?
Who was there?

Afiya
Just her sister.
The doctor.
The nurses.

Taroon
Afiya.

Afiya
No one bothered us.

Taroon
Was anyone else there?

Afiya
I told you everything was fine, will you rest?

Taroon
Who was there?

A moment.

Afiya
There was a man.

Taroon
You recognized him?

Afiya
No.

Taroon
You'd never seen him before?

Afiya
No.

Taroon
A cousin of Bibi's, maybe?
Family?

Afiya
Taroon.

Taroon
Taliban?

Afiya *nods.*

Taroon
What did he do?

Afiya
Nothing.
He circled the floor a few times.

Taroon
Did he speak to you?

Afiya
To me?

Taroon
To anyone?

Afiya
No.

Taroon
Was he with anyone?

Afiya
No.

Seeing her look away:

Taroon
But?

Afiya
The doctors looked wary of him.

Taroon
How do you mean?

Afiya
They jumped out of his way.

Taroon
The doctors?

Afiya
Yes.

Taroon
Was he armed?

She looks down.

Taroon
He was armed?

Afiya
Jawid is there now.
He brought people with him.

Taroon
Near my son?

Afiya
And the doctors said she can leave soon
They said it was uncomplicated.
Your son is healthy.

Taroon
He's circling the floor?

Afiya
This is why I didn't want to tell you.

Taroon
I want him away from my son and my wife.

Afiya
They are well, Taroon.
Jawid will move them soon.

Taroon
I have to go.

Afiya
Jawid said you can't
But we can put bodies between them.

Taroon
Oh, is that what Jawid said?

Afiya
Taroon—

Taroon
How dare you not tell me?

Afiya
I'm sorry.

Taroon
How dare you decide not / to tell me?
This is *my* son and *my* wife—

Afiya
Lower your voice!

Taroon
I'm leaving.

Afiya
No.
Nearly everyone we know is there.
Everyone protects them.

Taroon
What room is she in?

Afiya
I won't tell you

Taroon
I'll try each one, then.

She grabs his arm.

Afiya
Be reasonable, Taroon!

Taroon
Get off me.

Afiya
You walk into that hospital,
And that gun will be fired.
Is that what you want?
Shots fired near your son and your wife?
But this way—
Quickly in, quickly out,
The bustle of friends
The joy of a child
It's the safest they can be.
You know it is.

He glares at her.

Taroon
Where is Jawid taking her?

Afiya
To her uncle's, I told you.
He has a house, outside the city.

Taroon
And this house is safe?

Afiya
Yes.

Taroon
You're sure?

Afiya
Yes.

Taroon
How do you know?

Afiya
Because it's safe, Taroon,
It's safe.

He stands.

Taroon
I'm leaving.

Afiya
No.

Taroon
You don't know anything.
I'm leaving.

Afiya
Sit down.

Taroon
I won't!
I won't sit here and let them terrify my family!
Circling the hospital?
I'll break his neck.

He moves halfway towards the door.

Afiya
You think you're going to break his neck?
You think he's the one who will suffer?

She blocks his way.

Afiya
My stupid brother.
If you step outside that door,
You murder your child.
You murder your wife.
You murder my husband.
You murder me.
With one step you kill
Every person who has helped you.
Because they will know.
You know they will.

Taroon *glares at her, then continues towards the door.*
Just as he's about to reach it—
A knock.
The tension of the moment dissipates as **Afiya** *frantically ushers a protesting* **Taroon** *into the closet.*
She turns off the fans, makes sure the apartment is in order, and opens the door.
It's their neighbor, **Leyla,** *holding a pill bottle.*

Afiya
Leyla!

Leyla
I brought you something, for your headache.

She extends the pill bottle.

Afiya
(*taking it*)
Thank you!
(*Loud, hoping* **Taroon** *hears*)
Come in!

Leyla
Nabil finally slept,
And I never see you like that, head down!

Afiya
Oh, I'm feeling much better.
As quickly as it came, it went.
(*Throwing her voice for* **Taroon**'s *benefit*)
Please, sit!

Leyla
Jawid's not home?

Afiya
No, no,
I'm alone.

Leyla *sits, removing her headscarf.*

Afiya
Tell me, how was her visit?

Leyla *groans.*

Afiya
That good?

Leyla
She wants me to die.
She looks at me, and I can tell,
She still wishes Amir married that girl from Herat.

Afiya
What a terrible woman.

Leyla
She only stands me now because of Nabil.
Amir would go to work and she wouldn't look at me
Except for when I was feeding him.
I am just the feeding station for her grandson.

Afiya
I've said it before
And I'll say it again
She can't be Amir's mother.

Leyla
I told you, Afiya.
The nose!
They have the same nose.
Sometimes I look at my husband and I shiver because I see her nose on his face.
Nabil doesn't have it, thank God.
Listen to me, I sound awful.
I used to be nice.

Afiya *shoots her a look.*

Leyla
Fine, nicer!
Nicer, at least.

Afiya *begins to prepare* **Leyla**'s *tea.*

Afiya
I should have come help, Leyla.
I said I would, and I didn't.
I've been so busy.

Leyla
Oh please, why torture yourself?
You didn't marry her son.

Afiya
Still.
It sounds like it was worse than when she came for the wedding.

Leyla
So much worse,
And in new and interesting ways.
Do you know what she kept repeating?
You're going to love this, Afiya.
Every day,
"You hug him too much."
"You sing to him too sweetly."
"You shouldn't coddle him, he needs to grow up strong."
My son is five months old.
What,
She wants him to do pushups?
To learn to fight?
Honestly, sometimes I wish I'd had a girl,
So she would leave me alone.
. . .
When Bibi has the child,
She'll see.
It's not easy.

Afiya *tenses at the mention of Bibi.*

Leyla
What?

Afiya
You're going to kill me, Leyla.

Leyla
What?

Afiya
Just remember, I hadn't even told my mother—

Leyla
What is it?

Afiya
Bibi just gave birth.

Leyla
What?!
When?

Afiya
Today!

Leyla
And you didn't tell me?

Afiya
(*apologetic*)
I had to call my / mother!

Leyla
And you let me ramble on and on?
Have you hit your head?

Afiya
I'm sorry
But the birth went well!

Leyla
Thank God.
. . .
I can't believe you didn't tell me.

Afiya
Everyone is healthy.
Bibi, the child—

Leyla
And?

Afiya
Leyla.

Leyla
(*expectant*)
Come on, just say it!

Afiya
(*smiling, despite herself*)
A boy.

Leyla
A boy?!
And you didn't tell me?

Afiya
I had to tell my mother!

Leyla
Well done, Bibi!
A boy.
Your family must be so happy with her.

Afiya
Weren't you just wishing you'd had a girl, Leyla?

Leyla *waves this off.*

Leyla
So who does he look like?

Afiya *smiles.*

Leyla
Come on, who?

Afiya
He has something of each of them, I think.

Leyla
No, someone always wins.

Afiya
He looks like Taroon.

Leyla
He does?

Afiya
He really does.

A moment.

Leyla
Oh, I feel for Bibi, Afiya.

I really do.
I can't imagine,
Having to bring a child home without your husband.
. . .
I hope you know, Amir and I,
We're here to help,
We're always here to help.

Afiya
I do know that.
Thank you.

Leyla
I can make extra when I cook for a while.
And when I go to the store, if she needs anything—
Oh, we have extra diapers,
Clothes that Nabil's outgrown!
You know what?
I can bring those over tomorrow.

Afiya
Thank you.

Leyla
A baby,
It's a lot.

Afiya
I know.

A moment.

Leyla
(*quieter*)
And listen, Afiya.
If you ever needed more help,
Maybe bringing the baby to Taroon, or—

Afiya
(*shocked*)
Leyla!

Leyla
I just wanted to extend the / offer

Afiya
I don't know where my brother is.
You know that.

Leyla
Right.

Of course.
I know.

A moment.

Leyla
It's just the most natural feeling, Afiya.
To want to be with your child.

Afiya *stands to get tea.*

Leyla
You'll see soon enough!
Oh, come over for lunch tomorrow, before your appointment.
I'm making that rice you like, with the lamb.
I had Amir pick up the cherries yesterday.

A moment.

Afiya
Oh.
I had to cancel it,
The appointment.

Leyla
Afiya.

Afiya
It's fine.
I'm fine.

Leyla
How are you / feeling?

Afiya
I'm fine.
I bled, that's all.
It wasn't painful.

Leyla
I'm sorry.

Afiya
Three weeks late,
When I think about it,
It's nothing.
I shouldn't even have made the appointment.
…
Stop looking at me with those eyes, Leyla!

Leyla
Sorry, I'm sorry.

Afiya
If that's how you look at me,
I'm definitely not coming for lunch tomorrow.

Leyla
Not even for sweet rice?

Afiya
That depends.
How ripe are the cherries?

Leyla
They're perfect.

Afiya
It's early in the season.

Leyla
They're perfect.

Afiya
I'll consider it.

An easy moment.

Leyla
Can I just say—

Afiya
Please—

Leyla
It *will* happen for you.
I'm certain of it.

Afiya
I think I want to be
Realistic, now.

Leyla
Stop.
You've had a hard year, that's all.

Afiya
Have we had easy years, Leyla?

Leyla
No, but I'm telling you.
This year?
Between Taroon,
The visa,
Bibi pregnant—
I could smack your brother,

Bibi pregnant, right as they started giving him problems.
Typical Taroon,
Putting all this stress on you.

Afiya
It's not so bad.

Leyla
Oh, please.
The doctor said it himself, didn't he?
He said the stress makes it difficult to conceive.
Didn't he say that?

Afiya
He did.

Leyla *scrutinizes her.*

Leyla
Oh my God.
You don't think it's the stress.
You think it's you.

Afiya
Leyla.

Leyla
What, you know better than the doctor now?

Afiya
Maybe I waited too long.

Leyla
No, I'm sorry,
I can't even entertain this.
The way you've looked this year, so tired.
And Jawid!
Afiya, I've never seen him so exhausted.

Afiya
We're fine.

Leyla
You aren't.
You're too good, the both of you.
I don't know if I could do it.
A brother, his wife, their child,
The worry of it all.

Afiya
You would do the same.

Leyla
All I can say is don't give up yet.
Let these worries pass, Afiya,
And then you'll see.
You'll try again,
And you'll see.

Afiya
Maybe you're right.

Leyla
Afiya, you forget,
I'm always right.

Afiya *smiles.*
A moment.

Leyla
But to be serious, Afiya,
With the baby born,
Maybe it's time Taroon start sending something.

Afiya
Leyla!
What are you saying?

Leyla
I just thought he might be in touch—

Afiya
He isn't!
Wherever he is, he knows not to contact us.
Leyla, you know this!

Leyla
(*apologetic*)
Amir and I, we assumed he was sending word—

Afiya
(*harshly*)
Well, he isn't.
He isn't.
Get it through your head!

An awful moment.

Afiya
I'm sorry.

Leyla
No, I am.

Afiya
I don't mean to be—

Leyla
Sometimes it's just hard.
To know what I can and can't / say

Afiya
I know.

Leyla
I mean, his son was just born.

Afiya
I know.
I'm sorry.

A tense moment.

Leyla
Have I upset you, Afiya?

Afiya
No, I told you, I overreacted.

Leyla
These past few months,
Between us,
Things have been—

Afiya
Leyla—

Leyla
Difficult.
When Amir's mother was here,
And you didn't come visit—

Afiya
I'm so sorry.

Leyla
No, I'm sorry.
I started thinking,
How could I have been so insensitive?
Complaining about Nabil every waking moment
Asking you to help.

Afiya
I love to help, and you're entitled to complain!

Leyla
But Afiya, every day there's a headache, a phone call,
Some reason to dodge me in the hallway.

Afiya
There *was* a phone call today,
And a headache.

Leyla
Afiya.
You were the first to know I was pregnant.
I knew before your mother, when you were getting married!
I was here when Bibi found out she was pregnant.
And now if I hadn't come over,
God knows when I would have learned about your nephew—

Afiya
Tonight! I would have told you tonight!

Leyla
There's this wall between us,
And it turns me into the court jester,
Hoping I can at least keep making you laugh.

Afiya
Oh, Leyla.

Leyla
Please, tell me what I've done.
Why you never want me here anymore.
If I've been insensitive, bringing around my child—

Afiya
No. You haven't done anything.

Leyla
You can tell me.

Afiya
It's me.
I've been overwhelmed.
Taking care of Bibi, making sure she has everything she needs.
Making sure her child will have everything it needs.
And you're right, I haven't checked in enough on you.

Leyla
I don't need that
I want to help.
I want to know what's happening in your life.

Afiya
Well I can assure you, Leyla, there is nothing else that you don't know.
And not even Jawid knows that I cancelled my appointment.
(*Sudden.*)
So don't tell him.

Leyla
I would never.

Afiya *looks at her, skeptical.*

Leyla
I would never, Afiya!
When something's *really* serious, I keep my mouth shut.

Afiya *smiles.*

Afiya
I've missed you, Leyla.

Leyla
I've missed you, too.

She reaches for the sewing, picks up a uniform to help mend.

Leyla
Here, let me make myself useful.

Afiya
No, you've had the child all day.

Leyla
I want to.

They work together in silence.

Leyla
Feels like a long time, since we've done this.

Afiya
Yes.

Leyla
How many years were we stuck here sewing?

Afiya
I don't even want to count.

Leyla
Come on, we kept ourselves entertained.

Afiya
You kept us entertained, Leyla.

An easy moment.

Leyla
I can stay until Jawid gets home.
I don't have to rush back, Nabil is / sleeping

Afiya
Good!
Stay as long as you'd like.

Taroon *scratches from the closet.*
Leyla *looks.*

Afiya
Mice.

Leyla
Mice?
You're not serious.

Afiya
I know, it's disgusting.
Have you had any?

Leyla
No, thank God.

Afiya
Well, we've only seen the one,
I don't think you have to worry.

She turns on the nearest fan.

Leyla
This building, I swear.

Afiya
(*re: fan*)
Do you mind?

Leyla *shakes her head.*

Leyla
Remember when we had those ants?
What was it, two years ago?

Afiya
Please, don't remind me.

Leyla
It *was* two years ago.
That was the summer I'd help you clean,
Before everyone came over.

Afiya
That's right.

Leyla
Your brother and Bibi, me and Amir, Jawid,
You were always cleaning,
But I don't think I ever saw a single ant here.

Afiya
Cleaning is why you never saw a single ant here, Leyla.

Leyla
Amir loved those nights—I did, too,
All together.
The TV was smaller then.
Always those violent American movies, with your brother.

Afiya
Yes.

Leyla
Bruce Willis would be shocked, the hours he's spent in this apartment.
. . .
And for a few months, remember who came with Taroon?

Afiya
Oh, don't start.

Leyla
Jeff.

Afiya
Please, don't say that name in my house.

Leyla
He was beautiful, Afiya.
Admit it.

Afiya
They all looked the same to me,
The Americans.
A string of Jeffs.

Taroon *scratches a second time.*

Afiya
I'm so sorry, it's disgusting.
Jawid's getting a trap.

Leyla
One trap? Get ten!
There's never just one mouse.

Afiya
That's true,
I'll tell him.

Leyla
They were like brothers,
The two of them, weren't they?
Taroon and Jeff.

Afiya
Yes, yes.

Leyla
I hope they find each other again.
That they have a way of communicating—

Afiya
(*barely listening*)
Of course.

Leyla *scrutinizes her.*

Leyla
Are you okay?

Afiya
Oh,
Just this headache coming back.
It's nothing.

Leyla
You never took the medication!

Afiya
You're right.
I didn't.

Leyla
Here, I'll get you some water.

She gets up to get **Afiya** *a glass of water.*
Afiya *turns on the second fan.*

Afiya
I'm so warm, I'm sorry.

Leyla
I hope you're not really coming down with something.

She hands **Afiya** *a glass of water.*

Afiya
(*taking it*)
Thank you.

Leyla
Imagine getting Bibi sick,
Or the baby!
God forbid.

She reaches for more work from the basket.
She happens to pick up the shirt that **Taroon** *was mending.*

Afiya
Jawid's—
He ripped it in the shop.

Leyla
But Afiya your stitches have gotten so straight!

Afiya
Oh!

Leyla
How did you do this?

Afiya
You know,
I've been—
Practicing

Leyla
This new technique
You have to teach me.

Afiya
I will
Another time!
When there's less to do!
I've really let things pile up.

Leyla *nods, thoughtful.*
After a moment, she rubs her arms.

Leyla
I'm a little cold.
Do you mind if I get a sweater?

Afiya
Bedroom.

Leyla *goes into the bedroom.*
Afiya *quietly moves to the closet and kicks it, hard.*

Leyla
(*offstage*)
God, your room is always so neat.

Afiya
Well, I don't have a five-month-old!

Leyla
(*offstage*)
I wish I could blame him!

Afiya *moves back to the couch as she speaks.*

Afiya
You're lucky
Being messy is part of your charm, Leyla.

She sits back down where she had been.

Leyla
(*offstage*)
Can I tell Amir you said that?

She comes out.

Leyla
Where's the one I like?
Is it in—?

She moves towards the closet.
Afiya *shakes her head suddenly and motions to the bedroom.*

Afiya
Behind the door.

Leyla *goes back into the bedroom, and returns with a sweater.*

Leyla
I don't even know where you keep your things anymore!

Afiya
We'll have to do this more often, then.

Leyla *sits back down and starts sewing a patch onto a uniform.*

Afiya
You're putting that on backwards.

Leyla
Oh, shoot.

Afiya
You seem tired, Leyla.
I don't want to keep you.

Jawid *opens the door.*
Stocky and strong, he looks worn down and is wearing a large jacket.

Jawid
Leyla, how are you?

Leyla
(*putting her headscarf back on*)
Me?
How is the new uncle?

Jawid
Good, good.
Long day.

Leyla
You were at the hospital?

Jawid
The boy is well.

Leyla
And Bibi?

Jawid
She is well.
She won't let go of him.

Leyla
Why should she?

Jawid
You're right, of course.

A moment.

Jawid
I have to be rude, Leyla.
If you'll excuse me,
I need to lie down.
Today has felt like ten days.

Afiya *looks at* **Leyla**, *expectantly.*

Leyla
I'm sure.

Jawid
. . .
Stay, of course, Leyla.
You are welcome, you are always welcome.

Leyla
Thank you.
Amir isn't home yet,
Nabil is sleeping,
I get to enjoy.

Afiya
Can I get you tea?

Jawid
Coffee.
But I will get it myself.
Stay with your friend.

The women sit back down.

Leyla
(*smiling*)
Coffee.
Very American.
Should we call you Joe, Jawid?

Jawid
Please don't.

Leyla *grins.*

Leyla
I remember that night,
We were all here—
Maybe someone's birthday
And Taroon and Bibi,
They came in
Holding the Nescafé container
Like it was . . .

Afiya
Gold.

Jawid *picks the milk up from the counter.*

Leyla
Jawid, was that your birthday?
With the Nescafé?

Jawid *turns around, holding the milk, out of* **Leyla**'s *line of sight.*

Jawid
I don't know.
There have been so many.

He pours the milk down the sink.

Leyla
Yes, yes the elderly man I forgot.
I was just telling Afiya,
I miss those nights,
All together.
We don't do that anymore.

Afiya
No.

Jawid *re-enters, with an empty glass bottle.*

Jawid
No milk?

After a split-second hesitation:

Afiya
I forgot to go to the store, with everything.

Afiya *turns and looks at* **Leyla**, *expectantly.*
After a slight hesitation:

Leyla
I can see if we have some.

Afiya
Thank you, Leyla.

Leyla
It's no problem.
I'll be quick.

She leaves.
Afiya *and* **Jawid** *turn to each other at once.*

Jawid
Are you / alright?

Afiya
He's trying to leave.

Jawid
(*sharp*)
What?

Afiya
He got it out of me,
Taliban at the hospital
Help me keep him here.

She opens the closet door.
Taroon *bursts out.*

Afiya
Bedroom.
Now.

Taroon
Is Bibi safe?

Afiya
Yes.
Leyla is coming / right back.

Taroon
She's still at the / hospital?

Jawid
Yes.

Afiya
Leyla is coming right / back.

Taroon
(*to* **Jawid**)
I'm going to see her. / Now.

Afiya
You think this is a game, / Taroon?

Taroon
Get off me.
I have to go.

Afiya
Where?
Where are you going?
You don't even know what room / she's in.

Taroon
He'll tell me.

Jawid
Taroon.

Taroon
(*threateningly*)
You're going to tell me.

Afiya
He's helping you,
And you talk / to him like this?

Taroon
Where is my wife?

Jawid
You'll be with them tonight.

Taroon *stops struggling.*

Taroon
Tonight?

Jawid
Yes.
I'll explain.
But if Leyla sees you—

Taroon *rushes, silent, into the bedroom.*
Afiya *turns to* **Jawid**.

Afiya
Tonight?

Jawid *shakes his head no.*

Jawid
Has anyone been here?

Afiya
Only Leyla.

Jawid
Other than Leyla?

She shakes her head.
He moves to the kitchen and starts the hot water.

Afiya
Jawid, I had to tell him.
He wouldn't stop.
But not that they hit her
Not that they pushed his Bibi, full of life
Down the steps
Stone steps, Jawid
Seeing her fall
It's all I can think of

Jawid
We are blessed she was far enough along.
The child is healthy.

Afiya
But they thought he'd left Kabul,
They thought he'd left the city.
What else could it have been?
Three months of quiet.

Jawid
Afiya.

Afiya
What happened?
What changed?

Jawid
I don't know,
But I think we need your brother out.

Afiya
What?
Why?

Jawid
Whoever did this,
They expected him at the hospital.
And when he doesn't turn up . . .

A moment.

Afiya
No.
He stays.

Jawid
Just to the plum field.
He can stay with your aunt a few days, maybe a week, until this passes.

Afiya
No.
No.

Jawid
Afiya

Afiya
He's so reckless tonight
If I'm not with him—

Jawid
Afiya these men pushed a pregnant woman down stone steps
In public, in the middle of the day
We can't keep him here.

A moment.

Afiya
Stupid, he's so stupid!

Jawid
Lower your voice.

Afiya
Not to cover his face.
We told him, cover your face when you translate, Taroon.

Jawid
He did not want to cower.
He was tired of cowering.

Afiya
He was prideful.
He doesn't think.
He never thinks.

A knock at the door.

Jawid
Afiya, we need him out.
But remember, a baby was born.

Jawid *plasters a smile on and looks at* **Afiya** *expectantly until she does the same. He opens the door.*
Leyla *comes in, holding a jar of milk and a bottle of peppermint oil.*

Leyla
Ta-da!

Afiya *takes the milk from her.*

Jawid
Thank you.

Leyla *walks to the closet.*

Leyla
Peppermint oil!
For the vermin.

Afiya
Please, Leyla.
We don't want mice all over.

Leyla
I'll be quick.
Just a trick of my mother's.

Afiya *motions, tired, to the door.*
Leyla *opens the closet.*
A tense moment.

Leyla
The strangest thing just came over me.
I felt Taroon would be right there.
Isn't that bizarre?
. . .
I must have wanted him there
To see him safe
To stop imagining . . .
. . .
She turns to them.
. . .
Lately, my mind goes to the strangest places
Not enough sleep.

Jawid
You're kind to worry for him

Afiya
The door, Leyla!

Leyla
Oh!

She shakes the peppermint oil into the closet,
Then closes the door.

Jawid
Thank you.

Leyla
It's nothing, nothing at all.

A moment.

Afiya
You must be exhausted,
Wrangling the child all day

Leyla
I'm never too tired to sit with friends
The night their nephew was born!
Besides, what am I going to do, celebrate with Nabil?

Afiya *gives a tired laugh.*

Leyla
Come talk to me, Jawid.

Jawid *reluctantly follows* **Leyla** *to the couch as* **Afiya** *anxiously mills about in the kitchen.*

Leyla
So, big day, uncle.

Jawid
Yes.

Leyla
Did you get to hold him?

Jawid
I did.
He's very small.

Leyla
A baby.

Jawid
I don't think I've held one so small before.
At least, not in a long time.

Leyla
That's right.
No one got to hold my little Nabil as a newborn.

Jawid
We didn't.

Leyla
Poor thing, in the hospital for weeks.
I tell Amir, these are your genes.
Problems with lungs, who heard such a thing in my family?
Remember how well I could sing, Afiya?
You need full, healthy lungs for that.

Jawid
That's right.

Leyla
But he's healthy, your nephew?

Jawid
He is.

Leyla
What a blessing.
I remember those were the first words Amir said
"Is he healthy?"
. . .
So will you send word to Taroon?
I'm sure he's worried sick.

Jawid
I wish we could.
I really do.

A long moment.

Jawid
Do you hear that?

Leyla
What?

Jawid
I think it might be Nabil crying.

Leyla
I didn't hear anything.

Jawid
Do you want to go / check on him?

Leyla
No, no.
He's probably just fussing.
Best to leave them alone when they fuss.

Jawid
You know better than me, I suppose.

Leyla
If I jumped for every whimper . . .

Jawid
Yes, yes.

Leyla
You men,
You really know nothing about children!
Do you remember,
The night we brought Nabil home?
Amir was panicking,
So scared to pick him up
Like he would shatter or something.
Now he won't put him down!
Five months old,
I tell him,
Amir,
Nabil has to learn to walk!
He looks at me, why?
Why does he have to walk?
Can't I carry him forever?
. . .
Becoming a father, it isn't real
Not until he holds the child.
I pray that moment comes soon, for Taroon.
He was so good with Nabil,
With his own son, I can't imagine.

Afiya
You know,
I think I am coming down with something.
I have these chills.

Leyla
Well, it is cold in here.
Here let me—

She turns off both fans.
An eerie silence.

Leyla
Better?

Afiya *nods, weakly.*

Jawid
Leyla, we couldn't keep you from Amir, not so late.

Leyla
I'll tell him to come by when he's finished!
Won't that be nice?

Jawid
. . . Yes.

Leyla
Moments with friends,
With *family*, I should say,
They're rare now, with the child.

Afiya
Amir won't be too tired?

Leyla
No, just hungry!
But I could make us something simple!
We can have a little celebration.

Jawid
Oh, we couldn't ask you to—

Leyla
Jawid, I would love to.
It's a baby, we have to celebrate!
And you know me, Afiya,
I can make a dinner out of anything
Isn't that right?

Afiya *manages a small smile.*
As **Leyla** *starts to rummage in the refrigerator, Nabil starts to cry from across the hall.*
Leyla *freezes.*
She lets Nabil cry just a moment too long.

Afiya
Leyla?

Leyla
Well
That's my evening gone then!

Jawid
Don't worry,
Tomorrow, we'll celebrate tomorrow.

Leyla
If you need me
I'll be pacing the hallway like a ghost again.
Oh—and congratulations, my friends.
A boy,
What a blessing.

Leyla *leaves.*
Afiya *turns both fans back on.*
Jawid *listens at the door.*

Jawid
How long will she be out there?

Afiya
I don't know.
Sometimes it's hours.

Jawid
Hours?

Afiya
Back and forth,
It's all she can do to quiet him.
Taroon can't leave now,
Not till she's back inside.

Jawid
Okay.

He goes to make coffee.

Afiya
I love Leyla, but my God,
The way she talks.

Jawid
Coffee?

Afiya *shakes her head.*

Afiya
We weren't rude, were we?
Too strange?

He shrugs.

Jawid
It's late.
You can make our apologies tomorrow.

Seeing **Jawid** *take out two cups for coffee:*

Afiya
I said I didn't want / coffee.

Jawid
For your brother.
He'll need it.
We have a long night ahead.

Afiya
You'll drive him to the plum field, then?

He nods.

Afiya
And if you're stopped?

Jawid
These men know me, Afiya.
No one gives me problems on the road.

Afiya
Just the same, he'll wear the chadaree.

Jawid *nods.*

Afiya
He shouldn't need his pack.
We left enough food at my aunt's / for a week.

Taroon *peeks out, hopeful.*

Taroon
So?
When are we leaving?
How are we . . .

He trails off, seeing their serious expressions.

Afiya
Taroon.

Taroon
It's not true, is it?
I'm not seeing them in a few hours.

Afiya
I'm trying, Taroon.
We're trying.

Taroon
Trying?
All I see is the two of you—

Afiya
Lower your voice!

Taroon
—standing there, when there was a man—

Afiya
Shh

Taroon
—at the hospital?
Is my wife safe? My son?

Jawid
Taroon, we're sorting it out.

Taroon
Sorting it out?
You're making coffee!

Afiya
When you don't go to the hospital
They might come look for you here

Taroon
Where is Bibi?
Where's my son?

Afiya
Once Leyla's asleep,
Jawid will drive you out of the city
To the plum field

Taroon
Is that where Bibi is?

Afiya
She's still at the hospital

Taroon
Unbelievable.

Afiya
You have to lie low, Taroon!

Taroon
No!

Afiya
For a few days—

Taroon
Tonight!
I am seeing them tonight, understand?
You don't decide! I decide!

Afiya *laughs bitterly and shakes her head.*

Taroon
What?
What is it?

Jawid
Please, be quiet.

Taroon
Look at me.

Afiya
I will not look at you.
I don't know why I bother anymore.
And making noise, so Leyla would hear?
You're a child.

Taroon
(*to* **Jawid**)
Do you hear how she talks to me?

Jawid
Taroon, not now.

Taroon
(*rounding on him*)
And you!
Was it one of your friends, threatening my wife?
Was it the same hand that pays you?
That held the gun in the hospital
Pointed at my son?

Afiya
Get out.

A stunned silence.
She points to the door.

Afiya
Get out, now.

Jawid
Afiya.

Afiya
I mean it.
Get out of my house.

Taroon *is frozen.*
An awful silence.
Finally, he retreats into the bedroom.

Jawid
He's scared.

Afiya
I know.

Jawid *goes to listen at the door.*
Nothing for a moment, then crying.

Jawid
When she stops,
I'll take him with me.
I'll keep him safe.

She nods.
A moment of stillness.
Then, gentle:

Jawid
The baby.
He's got a lot of hair.

Afiya *smiles, despite herself.*

Jawid
Did you see it sticking straight up, after they dried him off?

Afiya
(*softening*)
No.
I must have left already.

They listen.
Leyla *is still out there, pacing.*

Afiya
I hope, this child—
He'll have a bit more sense than his father
That he'll know how to keep his head down
That there's more than enough trouble to go around
That he shouldn't add to it.
. . .
How can I teach him that?
Should I whisper it in his ear when he sleeps?

Jawid *smiles.*

Afiya
I'm being serious.

Jawid
I know.

A moment.

Jawid
You're sure he'll be in Kabul, then.

Afiya
What do you mean?

Jawid
You don't think Taroon's son will grow up in America.

Afiya
Jawid, come on.

Jawid
I don't know.
. . .
When I was holding him, Afiya
In the middle of it all, at the hospital
For the first time, I thought
This child has two lives.

Afiya
Two lives?

Jawid
Think.
If this visa doesn't come
The child stays here, in Kabul.
He speaks our language
Hums our music . . .
But with the visa, Afiya,
He'll be an American.
He'll live somewhere like . . . Rochester.

Afiya
Rochester?
What do you know about *Rochester?*

Jawid
That's where Taroon's friend ended up, no?
And that's where this child may go, too.
And if he does,
Maybe he would still know our language
Hum our music
But he would be completely different.
Unrecognizable to us.

Afiya *makes a pff sound.*

Jawid
He would be, Afiya,
Unrecognizable, I'm sure of it.

Afiya
He has one life, and it will be here.

A moment.

Jawid
Just in case, to prepare him—
Maybe you'll teach him English.

Afiya
I've forgotten my English.

Jawid
That's a lie.

Afiya
It isn't.

Jawid
I've seen you,
Correcting Taroon's visa application when he isn't looking.

Afiya
I don't.

He looks at her.

Afiya
(*unable to resist*)
I'm not correcting it.
I'm just improving upon it.
Sometimes it's a just a choice of words—
One word makes you sound educated,
Another, a little less so.
It's nothing,
I barely looked at it.
. . .
He's done a good job with it.
He's really applied himself.
I can't really find fault with it.
What am I saying?
I barely looked at it.

She stands to listen at the door.
Leyla *is still pacing.*

Jawid
That soldier said you didn't have an accent, you know.

Afiya
What?

Jawid
When he was here, he told Taroon
That when you spoke English, you didn't have an accent.
He was impressed.

Afiya
That's flattery.
I barely spoke to him.
He just said that because he knew I didn't like him.

Jawid
Okay.

Afiya
Don't look at me like that.

Jawid
Like what?

Afiya
Like I'm a precocious child.

Jawid
Afiya, don't speak like that.

Afiya
Well, it's all amounted to nothing, hasn't it?
Everything my mother taught us.
She was dreaming of universities abroad,
That her son and her daughter would make names for themselves.
And what has it brought her?
A son hiding for his life,
And a daughter with a party trick
For an American soldier to clap at.

Jawid
I didn't mean to upset you.
I was proud.

She looks at him, moved, and hugs him.
He draws back away from her, sharply.

Afiya
What?

Jawid
Nothing.

Afiya
What's wrong?

Jawid
Nothing.

Afiya
Jawid.

Jawid
I'm fine.

A moment.

Afiya
What did they do?

Jawid
Nothing.

Afiya
(*trying not to let her voice crack*)
Show me your back.

Jawid
I'm fine.

Afiya
Show it to me.

Jawid
No.

Afiya
Show me your—

Jawid
Lower your voice!
You want him to hear?

Afiya
You need medical help—

Jawid
I stopped by Karim's.
He put on an ointment.

Afiya
And bandages?

Jawid
Some.

Afiya
But when—?

Jawid
When I was leaving the hospital.
It was nothing.

Afiya
I don't understand
Who did this?

Jawid
Boys.
Not old enough to grow beards.

Afiya
What did they want?

Jawid
Nothing.

Afiya
What did they say?

Jawid
Nothing!
It was nothing.

Afiya
Did they ask about Taroon?

After a moment too long, betraying the answer:

Jawid
You're making this more than it is.

Afiya
They asked about Taroon.

Jawid
You weren't there.

Afiya
Did they know who you were?

Jawid
They were boys.
It was nothing.

Afiya
Did they know you work for Taliban?

Jawid
Afiya.

Afiya
Did you tell them?

Jawid
Taroon is going / to hear you.

Afiya
(*quieter*)
Did you tell them you worked for them?

Jawid
Listen to me.
When the men I work for
When they find out what these children did to me

Afiya
Did you tell them you work for Taliban?
Yes or no?
Did you tell them?

Jawid
They didn't care.
They were children.
You think they listen to reason?
They don't listen to anyone!

A still moment.

Afiya
Did you call?
Did you call the men you work for?

Jawid
Of course I called,
What do you think?

Afiya
What did they say?

Jawid
They're busy.
What, they can't pick up every phone call.

Afiya
Did you leave a message?

Jawid
Enough / Afiya.

Afiya
Did you leave a message?

Jawid
To say what?
To say, these children are in the city.
They pushed her.
They bothered me.

Afiya
Of course!
Of course to say that!

Jawid
I'll call them back.

Afiya
Jawid, why wouldn't you leave a message?
You have an understanding, call them back.
(*He makes a dismissive gesture.*)
You call them now and you leave a message.
(*He doesn't move.*)
. . .
Jawid.

Jawid
The line was dead.

Afiya
What?

Jawid
The line was dead.

A moment.

Afiya
Did you go past their building?

Jawid
The lights were off.

Afiya
Jawid.

Jawid
It's late.

Afiya
Did you knock?

Jawid
Did I knock?
I'm not a dinner guest.

Afiya
Go down there now.
You go down there and tell them what's happened.

Jawid
(*shaking his head*)
There were people outside the building.

Afiya
Who?

Jawid
I didn't recognize them.

Afiya
So?

Jawid
So I didn't recognize them.
They didn't look like people to walk up to
If I didn't recognize them, okay?

A moment, despair mounting.

Afiya
And the other number?

Jawid
Afiya.

Afiya
You have two numbers, you tried the other number?

Jawid
Afiya.

Afiya
Are both lines dead?

He looks at her.
Her worst fears realized.

Afiya
Oh my God.

Jawid
Afiya.

Afiya
It's happening.

Jawid
Stop

Afiya
They're here for Taroon.
It's happening.

Jawid
You aren't listening.
This will pass.

Afiya
He has to go.

She claps her hand over her mouth, disbelieving her own words.

Afiya
Tonight.
He has to leave the country tonight.

Jawid
You're inventing stories.

Afiya
First Bibi, now this—

Jawid
You're inventing stories in your head.

Afiya
Taroon goes in that truck,
He leaves the country tonight.
We have to text Mohammad.
Your phone.

Jawid
Afiya, listen to me.
I will drive Taroon to the plum field.
When I've resolved this,
He comes back here.

Afiya
Give me your phone.

Jawid
It's a misunderstanding
When the men I work for—

Afiya
Jawid, we don't have time.
We have to contact Mohammad,
He has to ready the truck.

Jawid
Men die on this journey, Afiya!
You don't put your brother in the bottom of a truck
For nothing!
Because this was nothing,
It was nothing!

Afiya *looks at him.*
Then, quiet, and calm:

Afiya
Jawid you look me in the eye and you swear to me
You swear on my head that if my brother stays in the country
He's not dead by the end of the night.

Jawid
Afiya.

Afiya
On my head, swear it.
Swear Taroon survives this night.

A silent moment.
He can't swear this.
He pulls his phone from his pocket.
They both look at it.

Afiya
Mohammad said he needed two days' notice,
But I know he's done it before.
We'll pay extra.

Jawid
He might not agree.

Afiya
He has to.

Jawid
And Bibi?

Afiya
She'll have to follow, when she can,
With the child.
A newborn won't survive the journey.

They look at each other.
Then, **Jawid** *turns to the door.*

Jawid
She's stopped.
Listen.

Afiya *listens.*
Leyla *has stopped pacing.*

Jawid
I could take him to the plum field now.
No one would see him.
I could take him.

She shakes her head.

Jawid
You're sure?
Taroon, out of Afghanistan?

Afiya
I'm sure.
Text Mohammad.

After a moment, he takes out his phone and sends a text.
She watches.
Then he sets his phone in front of them.
They sit there.
They listen.

Afiya
Once we hear from him, we can move.

Jawid *is collapsed into himself.*
Afiya *looks at him.*

Afiya
Have you eaten?

Jawid
No.

Afiya
I didn't have time to make—
There's the rice and meat?
From yesterday?

Jawid
I'm fine.

Afiya
You should eat.
It might be a long night.
I'll warm it.

Jawid
No, no.
I'll have it cold.

Afiya
You're sure?

Jawid
Cold is fine.
I don't have much of an appetite.

She brings him a bowl and sits with him.

Jawid
You're not eating?

Afiya
No.

Jawid
Do you want some of mine?

Afiya
No, no.

Jawid
What have you eaten today?

Afiya
Some bread.

Jawid
You must be hungry

Afiya
I'm not.

Jawid
But Afiya,
You need to eat.
It's very important for you to eat.

He puts a hand on her stomach.
Reflexively, she bats it away.
A sad, frozen moment.

Afiya
I'm sorry.

Jawid
No, that's / okay.

Afiya
I didn't mean / to

Jawid
That's okay.

A moment.

Jawid
It's important that you keep your strength up,
That's all.

Afiya
Jawid, I bled.

Jawid
Oh.

Afiya
I'm sorry.

He shakes his head.

Jawid
You should rest.

Afiya
No, no.

Jawid
I can handle Taroon.
You should lie down.

Afiya
It was a few days ago, Jawid.

Jawid
Oh.

Afiya
So
I'm fine.

A moment.

Afiya
Finish your food.
When he answers,
We'll have to move quickly.

He blinks, then takes a bite.

Afiya
I'm sorry,
I should have told you sooner.

A moment.

Jawid
We have the money, Afiya.
You can go to anyone,
Any clinic.

She looks down at his bowl.

Afiya
Here.
I didn't mean to give you
All rice
I'll add more meat.

Jawid
Taroon picks out the meat, and eats it.
I saw him at it yesterday.

Afiya
Manners.
He doesn't have manners.

Jawid
He's restless.
He's stuck here.

Afiya
I'm stuck here.
You don't see me ruining everyone's food.

The sound of text message.

Jawid
Mohammad can take him tonight.
He's getting the truck ready.
I have to pay him.
Help me.

Jawid *and* **Afiya** *work seamlessly together to move various household items.*
They ultimately reach a small, hidden box—
Within which lies the bulk of their savings.
Jawid *counts out what he needs and puts on his jacket,*
Before turning to **Afiya**, *serious.*

Jawid
Afiya
When I'm gone,
Be careful.
Close the window, lock it.
Don't answer the phone
Or make any calls.
Not even to Leyla,
Or your mother.
Keep Taroon hidden.
We can't take any chances.
And don't answer the door
Lock the door.

Afiya *nods.*

Afiya
You should go.
Be safe.

With **Jawid** *gone,* **Afiya** *takes a moment to gather her bearings.*
She finishes rearranging **Taroon**'s *pack.*

She removes various things stashed around the apartment—
A bag under the sink, items from the cabinets—
And everything goes in its designated place in his pack.
She removes everything from the refrigerator, and adds this to his bag.
When this is completed,
She takes a moment to be sure she hasn't forgotten anything.
She tidies up whatever mess **Jawid** *made pulling out the money.*
She is satisfied that everything is in its right place.
Then, she knocks on the bedroom door.
Taroon *comes out.*
He looks around, suspicious.

Taroon
Where's Jawid?

Afiya
He's going to pay Mohammad.

Taroon
Pay Mohammad?

Afiya
He's going to take you in his truck.
You're leaving Afghanistan tonight.

Taroon
What?
Why?

Afiya
This night has become too dangerous, Taroon.
We can't keep you safe.

Taroon
But we said—
The plum field—

Afiya
(*shaking her head*)
They're looking for you.
Asking around.

Taroon
Asking around?
They're always asking / around.

Afiya
It's different tonight.
Men no one has seen before,
From outside the city.

Seeing him about to protest:

Afiya
They're hunting you, Taroon.

Terror.

Taroon
Bibi, they didn't hurt Bibi?

Afiya
No.

Taroon
You swear?

Afiya
I swear.

Taroon
And my son?

Afiya
Safe.
I swear on his own head.
They'll follow you.

Taroon
No
Afiya, I can't leave without them.

Afiya
He's an infant, Taroon.
He won't survive the journey.
They'll follow as soon as they can.

Taroon
When?

A moment.

Afiya
Months?

Taroon *starts to pace.*

Taroon
But why should I leave?
Bibi and the child, they can come here
Jawid can keep us, until she can travel!

Afiya
They can't come here.

Taroon
Do you know how dangerous it will be, for Bibi to make that journey alone?

With a child?
Afiya, I have to stay here
Jawid will protect us.

Afiya
He's a tailor, Taroon.

Taroon
He works for Taliban!
What, is he afraid to keep us here?
Is that it?
He's afraid?

Afiya
They beat him, outside the hospital.
. . .
You have to go.

A moment.

Taroon
And you're sure they can't come with me?

Afiya
A newborn, Taroon?
In the bottom of a truck?
He'll cry, he'll get sick,
Besides, Bibi isn't strong enough.

Taroon
Strong enough?

Afiya
She just gave birth, Taroon.
She needs time.

Taroon
And until you can send her,
She's safe?

Afiya
She's safe.

A moment.

Taroon
So I'll meet her—

Afiya
In Europe.

Taroon
When?

Afiya
I don't know.
I promise, Taroon
We're keeping her safe.
As safe as we can.

A moment.

Taroon
You would tell me?
If you thought there was another way?

She nods.
Taroon *looks around the apartment, helpless.*

Taroon
Can I—
Can I help with anything?

Afiya
No.

Taroon
The pack is—

Afiya
Ready.

Taroon
And everything in the kitchen—

Afiya
Packed.
Everything is ready.

She goes to stand by the window, to look for the truck.

Taroon
 . . .
So I go in this truck
And it takes me to—

Afiya
Tehran.
Mohammad drives you to Tehran.

Taroon
Okay, and then from Iran to Turkey.

She nods.

Taroon
And from Turkey to Greece?

Afiya
No, Mohammad's friend goes by land.
He says it's safer.

Taroon
By land?
So
. . .
What comes after Turkey?
Why did I learn the periodic table
When I don't know what comes after Turkey?

Afiya
Bulgaria.

Taroon
Don't say Bulgaria, like it's so obvious.

Afiya
I looked it up.

Taroon
And then to . . . Germany?

After an almost imperceptible hesitation:

Afiya
God willing.

Taroon
Germany.
(*Trying to wrap his head around it:*)
Germany.
Someone will speak English, in Germany?

Afiya
I think so.

Taroon
And for work?

Afiya
There are other Afghans there.
You'll figure it out.

Taroon
And money?

Afiya
We'll send you some.

Taroon
I'll need a bank account.

Afiya
You'll open one.

Taroon
They'll let me?

Afiya
I think so.

Taroon
And where will we live?

Afiya
The other Afghans there.
They'll help you.

Taroon
We don't know them

Afiya
They'll help you.

Taroon
And this is if I even *make it* to Germany?

He gets up suddenly and fiddles with the router.

Afiya
Taroon.

Taroon
Why didn't you repair this?
Imagine if my visa,
If the Americans have sent it.
. . .
No.
I can't leave!
I won't leave without it!

Afiya
Taroon,
You will leave without your visa
Or you will stay without your head.

This hits him.
He becomes still.

Taroon
And what if it comes, after I leave?
And I can't find a computer?

Afiya
I'll call.

Taroon
You promise?

Afiya
I promise.

Taroon
You swear on—

Afiya
My head, your head, Jawid's, your son's.

A moment.
Then, **Afiya** *returns to the window.*

Taroon
Bibi
. . .
She wanted our children to be engineers in Afghanistan.

Afiya
What?

Taroon
Bibi, she wanted our children to be engineers in Afghanistan.
Engineering, that's what *she* wanted to study,
She wanted to be an engineer,
Before they pulled her out of school.

Afiya
She never told me.

Taroon
(*nodding*)
Someone needs to fix the roads, she said.
The bridges.
And I would say,
Bibi,
We're not having children to put them to work.
And she'd give me that look:
Why not?
Why not put children to work?

He looks off.

Taroon
Well, when we get to America
Bibi—
She can be the engineer.
. . .
Though they probably need less help with their roads.
The roads are better in America, aren't they?

He looks at **Afiya**, *still standing sentinel by the window.*

Taroon
Do you have to stand there?
It's making me nervous.

Afiya
I want to know when Mohammad gets here, Taroon.
That's all.

Taroon
Seriously, Afiya
Can you please come sit down?

Afiya *moves away from the kitchen.*
Taroon *goes into the kitchen.*
Afiya *sees him.*

Afiya
(*sudden*)
What are you doing?

Taroon
Making coffee.

She ushers him out of the kitchen, frantic.

Afiya
Get away from the window.

Taroon
The curtain.

Afiya
It's dark out
If anyone is watching the building

Taroon
You think they're counting bodies behind curtains?

Afiya
We can't take any chances.
We can't take any chances.

A moment.

Taroon
I'm sorry.
I didn't know I couldn't make coffee

Afiya
You need coffee,
I'll make it for you, okay?
You need coffee?

Taroon
No, no.

A moment.

Taroon
Afiya,
How do they even know I'm in Kabul?

Afiya
I don't know.

Taroon
How do they know I didn't leave?

Afiya
I don't know.

Taroon
We were so careful
Did someone tell them?
Did someone see me?

Afiya
I don't know.

Headlights flashing.
Afiya *rushes back to the window.*

Taroon
Is it?

Afiya
No.
He's across the city
It will take longer

Taroon
Then why are you standing there?

Afiya
To be ready, Taroon.

Taroon *goes back to the router.*
He begins clicking and unclicking the button.

Afiya
That's making me crazy.

Taroon
If we're waiting here

Afiya
It's not going to work.

Taroon
You don't know that.

A knock at the door.
They freeze.
Another knock.
They spring into action—
Taroon *goes into the bedroom.*
Afiya *shoves the pack into the closet.*

Leyla
It's me.
. . .
Come on, I can see the light's on.

Afiya *goes to open the door.*
Before the door is even all the way open,
Leyla *has slammed it open.*
She is desperate.

Afiya
(*startled*)
Leyla!

Leyla
They took Nabil.

Afiya
What?

Leyla
They took Nabil.
They have my baby.
Where's your brother?

Afiya
What?

Leyla
Where's Taroon?

Afiya
Leyla, I—

Leyla
All night they've had Amir
With a gun to his head in the shop
All night they've had my husband.

Afiya
But—

Leyla
They want your brother, Afiya.
And I tried everything
I looked
I looked everywhere
And I told them,
I don't know where Taroon is
And now they took my baby
And now they took my baby from me
My Nabil

Afiya
Leyla, I don't understand—

Leyla
Afiya,
They want Taroon!
They want your brother!
If you tell me now,
I can get my baby back.

Afiya
Oh my / God.

Leyla
Tell me now, Afiya
Where is he?
Where's Taroon?

Afiya
I—

Leyla
Tell me where he is.

Afiya
I don't know.

Leyla *pushes* **Afiya**.

Leyla
You do.
You do.
I have eyes!
Those stitches?
That's Taroon,
I know it's Taroon.
I know he's been here

Afiya
He hasn't.

Leyla
And I looked!
The closet, the bedroom!
I tried
If he's not here now
Tell me where he is

Afiya
Leyla

Leyla
Where is he?

Afiya
I don't know.

Leyla
You're lying.
Afiya, tell me!

Afiya
I don't know.

Leyla
They have my baby.

Afiya
I'm sorry,
I can't help you.

Leyla *suddenly grabs* **Afiya** *by the neck.*

Leyla
You listen,
My son hasn't even lived a full year.
Tell me, why should he have to pay?
Why should he have to pay for your brother's choices?

Afiya
He shouldn't.
He shouldn't.

Leyla
He's done nothing.

Afiya
I know.

Leyla
So where is Taroon?

Afiya
I can't.

Leyla
How can you say that?
He's a baby.
Tell me where.

Afiya
I can't.

Leyla
Afiya, tell me!
Please, tell me!

Taroon *opens the bedroom door, unseen by* **Leyla**.
Afiya *locks eyes with her brother, and terrified, blurts:*

Afiya
On the plum field
My aunt's cabin!
Where we used to go
My aunt's cabin
That's where he is

Taroon *retreats back into the bedroom.*

Afiya
That's where he is.

Leyla *looks at* **Afiya**, *hard—*
Then releases her.
For a moment, they are suspended, then:

Leyla
I'm sorry.
I'm sorry.
I—

Leyla *runs out.*
A terrible silence.
Afiya *reeling.*
Taroon *cracks open the bedroom door.*
Afiya *puts out her hand, without looking at him.*

Taroon
Afiya, I—

Afiya
No.

Taroon
What was—

Afiya
No.

Taroon
Are you / hurt?

Afiya
Stay.
Stay under the bed.

The phone begins to ring.
Taroon *and* **Afiya** *both startle,*
Then **Afiya** *realizes:*

Afiya
That's probably Mama.

Taroon
Afiya, I—

Afiya
Now.

Taroon *goes into the bedroom.*
The phone stops ringing.
Afiya *goes to retrieve his pack from the closet.*
The phone rings again, interrupting her.
She stops for a moment,
Then continues packing as it
Rings, rings, then stops.
The phone rings five times before stopping completely.
She continues packing.
Jawid *enters.*

Afiya
(*alert, ready*)
Mohammad is here?

Jawid
No.

She turns back to the pack.

Jawid
But Afiya
The boy is downstairs.

Afiya
The boy?

Jawid
Taroon's son.
I brought him with me.

Afiya
Where?

Jawid
I left him, with Salima.

Afiya
But why wouldn't Bibi—?

Jawid
She . . .
. . .
She hasn't woken up.

Afiya
She hasn't woken up?
. . .
Should we wait?

Jawid
(*shaking his head*)
They don't think she will.
. . .
They hit her too hard.
She lost too much blood.

Afiya
Bibi
. . .
. . .
Taroon won't leave now.

Jawid
We don't tell him
We tell him Bibi will still follow, when she can.

This shakes **Afiya** *awake.*

Afiya
We can't.

Jawid
We have to.
Otherwise, he won't go.
I'll go tell him.

Afiya *nods.*
As **Jawid** *is about to leave the living room:*

Afiya
Wait—
Jawid—

Jawid
What?

Afiya
Leyla
She has to go with Taroon.

Jawid
What?

Afiya
She has to go with Taroon.

Jawid
Leyla?
What do you mean?

Afiya
They sent her, Jawid
She was asking for Taroon.

Jawid
(*sharp*)
Who was here?

Afiya
Only Leyla
I'm fine
(*He moves as though to inspect her.*)
I'm fine!
But I lied to her—

Jawid
(*livid*)
Coming into this house
You alone

Afiya
I said Taroon was at the plum field
She lied to them
She lied
She needs our help

Jawid
The *moment* that truck is downstairs
I want your brother out.

Afiya *goes to the hiding place again,*
Haphazardly displacing their belongings to get back to their box of savings.

Jawid
What are you doing?

Afiya
How much did it cost?

To get him out of the country so quickly
How much?

Jawid
Double
Afiya, she is not going / with him.

Afiya
(*doing mental math*)
Double, okay
Then for Leyla

Jawid
Afiya

Afiya
And Nabil . . .

Jawid
(*incredulous*)
And Nabil?

Afiya
(*triumphant*)
We'll have just enough!

Jawid
We'll have nothing left!

Afiya *looks at* **Jawid**, *stunned.*

Jawid
Be reasonable, Afiya.
At the first sign of danger
We don't smuggle someone out of the country!
She can go outside the city, hide with family
I'll help.

Afiya
They'll find her

Jawid
You don't know that

Afiya
Open your eyes, Jawid
The way this day has gone
She won't survive the night

Jawid
We'll try to hide her

Afiya
No
She leaves the country, tonight
I'm going to tell her.

Jawid *blocks the door.*

Jawid
Tell me, what do you envision, Afiya?
Sending Leyla with Taroon, who just betrayed him.

Afiya
Yes.

Jawid
With her child, in the back of a truck?

Afiya
Yes.

Jawid
A child who will scream the entire journey,
Endangering your brother?

Afiya
They'll drug Nabil
They'll have to

Jawid
And if Leyla won't go?

Afiya
She will
She will

Jawid
It's too dangerous
Too reckless

Afiya
We have no time

Jawid
This is reckless like Taroon
No regard for any plan
For anything we've agreed to
Or worked for

Afiya
You listen to me.
If we don't use this money for Leyla,
I will never touch it again.
Not for a home, not to have a child.

Jawid
Forget the child, Afiya
I'm thinking of you!
What happens if they come after *you*?
What then?
Then we have nothing left
No truck, no way out, nothing!

Afiya
You've done this for me?

Jawid
Yes.

Afiya
(*motioning to the uniforms*)
All of it?
All of this?

Jawid
Yes, to protect you

Afiya
Then listen to me.
For me.
To protect *me*, Jawid
We take everything we have
We sell what we have to sell
And we put them in that truck,
Understand?
I will not have blood on my hands.
We end this night clean.

A terrible moment.

Jawid *gives a small nod.*

Afiya
I'll go tell her.

She looks at the bedroom door, behind which **Taroon** *still hides.*

Afiya
Make sure he'll go.

She leaves.
Jawid *goes to another hiding spot.*
Removes a stack of bills—
Bills for her fertility treatments, for their future, for their security—
And pockets them.
Then he moves to retrieve **Taroon**.

Jawid
You will meet your son tomorrow.

Taroon
Tomorrow?

Jawid
(*nodding*)
They've already left.
They're halfway to Farah.
Bibi and the boy.

Taroon
But—
I thought they were following me?
Afiya, she said—

Jawid
This was safer, Taroon.
She was strong enough,
I saw the opportunity and I took it.

Taroon
Who is she with?

Jawid
A friend of mine.

Taroon
So I'll see them both tomorrow?

Jawid
Yes, tomorrow.

Taroon *is elated.*

Jawid
And Leyla is going with you.

Taroon
(*incredulous*)
Leyla?

Jawid
And her son.

Taroon
She was just here,
Threatening my sister.

Jawid
And your sister has decided,
Leyla goes with you.

Taroon
If you had seen her, / Jawid—

Jawid
Tomorrow you will be
With your wife and your child, Taroon.

Taroon
(*giddy, despite himself*)
Tomorrow.

Jawid
You should look through your pack.

He does.

Taroon
I am already packed.
Your wife has seen to it.

Jawid
Good.

Taroon
I wish I hadn't eaten those bars.

Jawid
I will check for more.

Taroon
It's no use.
I've eaten the reserves.
. . .
Doesn't it bother you?
That she's always right?
Ever since I was small—
My mother would smack me on the back of the head
She would say,
Afiya got two portions of sense.
Her own, and yours.

A moment.

Jawid
You're ready?

Taroon
She's a good planner, my sister.

Another moment.

Taroon
My folder, of course!

Jawid
That's right.

Taroon *retrieves it.*

Taroon
It would be stupid to leave this

Jawid
Yes.

Taroon
If I left it here,
Afiya would burn it.

Jawid *gives a terse smile.*
Taroon *packs the binder.*
An awkward moment between the men.

Taroon
Listen, Jawid.
I want to thank you.

Jawid *puts up his hand.*

Taroon
I know it hasn't been easy.
To keep me here.
And I want you to know that
Your kindness, and your hospitality,
It isn't lost on me.

Jawid
Okay.

Taroon
Okay.

Jawid *checks his watch, then begins to look around the room.*

Taroon
(*getting progressively giddy*)
You're a man of few words, Jawid.
I remember you, when we were younger.
Never picking sides.
Quiet.
Afiya said she liked that.
She knew other people had less patience with you
But she said—
That's a man who doesn't have to be the center of attention.
I guess, growing up with me . . .

He looks at **Jawid**, *beaming.*

Taroon
I don't know what I'm saying anymore, my brother.
I can't believe it.
I'm going to meet my son tomorrow.

Jawid *hands him a bundle.*

Jawid
Put this on.

Taroon *unfolds the bundle.*
It's an Afghan army uniform.
A long, long moment as **Taroon** *stares at the uniform.*

Jawid
You'll wear a chadaree over it.

Taroon *stares at the uniform for a while longer.*
Then, finally,
He removes his pants and starts putting on the uniform pants.
Taroon *puts on the uniform top over his t-shirt.*
He looks down at himself, then at **Jawid**.

Taroon
Are you gloating?

Jawid
Why should I gloat?

Taroon
After all the trouble I have given you
For making these uniforms.

Jawid
You weren't wrong.

Taroon
I called you a coward.

Jawid *shrugs.*

Taroon
Now I am a man dressed up as a soldier
About to be dressed up as a woman.
Two layers will separate me from the world.
Who is the coward now?

Jawid
You're not a coward.

Taroon
All that time berating you.

For keeping your family safe.
For keeping my sister comfortable.
For keeping me hidden away.

Jawid *shrugs again.*

Taroon
You can be angry with me, Jawid.
Please.
Let loose an uninhibited word!
You're a good man,
Who has been made the guardian of a coward.

Jawid
I am not a good man.

Taroon
No modesty, please.

Jawid
I have no right to modesty, Taroon.
I have sold Kabul for a television set.

Taroon
What?

Jawid
All you have told me.
All the spite
All the insults.
All the provocations.
I don't answer because it's all true.

Taroon
Jawid, no
Listen.
I didn't mean anything by it.
I've been lonely, and agitated.

Jawid
It's all true.
Will my wife be safe?
I think so.
And our children, God willing?
I think so.
But my country?
I have willed myself not to think of it.
I have given up my right to opinions.
I experience only shame.

Taroon
I'm telling you,
You shouldn't.

Jawid
If my father could see, Taroon, what I am doing.
He would die twice over.
If he could retrace his footsteps from the grave
He would have never moved inside my mother.
He would have drowned me quietly when I was born.
He would take back the gunshots in the city, celebrating my birth.
He would tell the neighbors, hush.
Let no sounds escape your lips
In celebration of this thing.
Who is not my son.
Who has sold Kabul for a television set.

Taroon
For my sister!
To have a child!

Jawid
And how is a child different than a television set, my brother?
Vanity, all vanity,
And nothing more.

Taroon
You don't say this to Afiya.

Jawid
No.

Taroon
Thank God.

A moment.

Jawid
All I can tell you, Taroon.
Is that next time there is an opportunity.
I will not cower behind my store,
Talking about protection and providing,
Watching braver men risk everything.

Taroon
I hope that isn't true.
For my sister's sake.

Jawid
Your sister can't sleep for the shame.

A long moment between the men.

Taroon
Bibi, I would sneak into her father's house to see her.
And we would talk about Afghanistan.
Kabul in ten years.
One night, her cousin Srosh had just signed up.
To interpret, for the Americans.
And I saw how strong she thought him, and how brave.
So the next day, I signed up.
I signed up for the way I saw her look at her cousin.
And that night, I saw Bibi and her father in the street.
I told them the news.
He looked from me to her and he said, quickly,
That's it, you're getting married tomorrow.
He was nervous about the way she was looking at me.

Jawid *smiles.*

Taroon
All of this to say, Jawid.
I am not a pillar of strength.
It is Bibi, only.
Bibi, who wanted the Taliban gone.
Bibi, who was tired of war after war.
Bibi, who wanted more than this.
And now, she will see me in this uniform.
Reduced to hiding in a truck, with the neighbor and her son.
What will she think?

Jawid
She will think
This is my brave husband.
Who has risked everything
And deserves some peace.

Taroon
God willing.

Jawid
Besides, the uniform—
It is very becoming.

Taroon
You're just saying that because you made it, eh?

Jawid
Maybe.

An easy moment between them.
Suddenly, the door bursts open.

Leyla *enters, enraged.*
Afiya *follows, panicked, carrying* **Leyla**'s *swaddled infant, Nabil.*

Leyla
You!
You piece of shit!

Taroon *lunges back, alarmed.*

Leyla
You piece of stinking human garbage!

Jawid *struggles to hold her back.*

Leyla
They took Amir with them!
They said that if you weren't hiding there
At the plum field
That Amir would pay.
You killed my husband!

She spits at him, enraged.
It lands in his face.
He doesn't wipe it off.

Afiya
Ley / la—

Leyla
And for what?
For what?

Jawid
Ley / la—

Leyla
You piece of garbage.
I could smell your stench across the hall.

She pulls hard and **Jawid** *moves to restrain her better.*

Leyla
Let me kill him.
If Amir can't breathe,
He shouldn't breathe.
You are taking air that doesn't belong to you.
It belongs to Amir!

Taroon
I don't understand—

Leyla
Fuck you!
What right do you have to talk?

Taroon
I—

Leyla
Garbage!
First to help the Americans, of course!
Taroon, strutting through the town.
Amir said—
He said, he likes the attention.

Taroon
Leyla—

Leyla
Shut up!
I want you dead!
I want you dead!
It should be you!

She collapses in **Jawid***'s arms.*
A stunned moment passes.

Taroon
Amir—
Instead of me?

Afiya *nods.*

Taroon
I have to go.

Jawid
You are not at the plum field, Taroon.
There's nothing to be done.

That hangs there.
Then **Afiya** *disentangles herself from her husband and* **Leyla**.
She stands in front of **Leyla** *and* **Taroon**.

Afiya
The two of you are getting in that truck together,
And you are leaving Kabul tonight.
. . .
I am going to go pack up Nabil.
There is no time.

She leaves to go across the hall.
A long, long time during which no one speaks.
Suddenly, **Leyla** *raises her head from her hands.*

Leyla
His medicine.

Jawid
What?

Leyla
Nabil, he will need his medicine.

Jawid
I'll go tell her.

*He leaves **Leyla** and **Taroon** together.*
They don't move.
***Taroon** stares at the ground.*
***Leyla** stares off into the distance.*
They are alone together like this for a while.
*Then, **Jawid** reappears.*

Jawid
We can't find it.

Leyla
Under his bed.

Jawid
Okay.

A moment.

Jawid
You should come check his pack, Leyla.
We don't know what he needs.

She nods, then stands.
Walking as though completely disconnected from the world, she leaves.
***Jawid** follows,*
*Leaving **Taroon** alone, frozen.*
He does not move.
After several moments,
***Afiya** re-enters.*

Afiya
Taroon.

She sits next to him.
They stare forward, in silence.

Taroon
I watched the television.
Every day, I watched it.

Afiya
I know.

He looks at her.

Taroon
What have I done?

Afiya
Your best.
Everyone is doing their best.

Taroon
My best?

A light from outside—a truck passing by.

Afiya
That's Mohammad.
Quick.
Your pack.
Listen to me, Taroon.
You are going to take care of this boy.

He looks up, confused.

Afiya
Nabil.
You are about to set out on the road with him.
He will be missing his father.
You have to be strong for him.
At this age, children don't see men weep.
Do you understand?

Taroon *nods.*
Afiya *suddenly hugs him, and holds on very tight.*

Afiya
I love you.

They stand like that for a long time.

Taroon
And Bibi?
She will be there.
I will see her.

Afiya
Yes, yes.

He looks at her.
A flash of uncertainty.
Jawid *opens the door.*

Jawid
Let's go, he's here.

Taroon
I will see her?

Afiya *pulls the chadaree over him.*

Taroon
Afiya, will I—
Will I see her?

Afiya
Go! Go.

Taroon *hesitates, then is rushed out of the door.*
Afiya *slams the door shut behind him.*
Then, all at once—
She is alone in her apartment.
She stands, frozen, in the spot where she hugged her brother.
A long, long moment passes.
Then, impossibly, **Afiya** *turns off one fan, then the other.*
Silence.
She pours out what was meant to be **Taroon***'s cup of coffee.*
She makes her way to the floor and sits amidst the sewing and the baskets, barely breathing, barely moving.
Then finally,
Footsteps outside.
Jawid *enters.*
A long silence.

Jawid
His son.

She doesn't answer.

Jawid
His son is downstairs.

She doesn't answer.

Jawid
Afiya.

Afiya
Find someone else.

Seeing him about to protest:

Afiya
Find someone else.

A moment.

Jawid
He needs you.

Afiya
Me?
He doesn't need me.

Jawid
He does.

Afiya
I killed him.
I killed Amir.

Jawid
Afiya

Afiya
A man is dead
And it was me.

There is nothing to say to this.
Jawid *and* **Afiya** *stand,*
Her self-indictment vibrating throughout the room.
They stand and they stand—
Until gradually, it lessens,
And lessens,
And then:

Afiya
It's cold tonight.

She looks suddenly at **Jawid**.

Afiya
Does he have a—

Jawid
Blanket.
Yes.
He has a blanket.

She nods, less distant now.
After a moment:

Jawid
He's downstairs, with Salima.
. . .
She held him up to the window, you know
When they left.

Afiya
(*a bit hopeful*)
Did Taroon see?

Jawid
I don't know.

Afiya
You can't know, he was under the chadaree.

Jawid
I know that his son did see him.
He saw his father.

A moment.
Afiya *looks around her home, the impossibility of the years ahead washing over her.*

Afiya
What will we tell him?

Jawid
We have time to sort that out.

A quiet moment.

Afiya
All this time I pictured,
When we came home with a child.
It would be to fanfare and joy.
. . .
A crib over there.
Clothes folded in neat little piles.
A basket.
Blankets.
Bottles.
A toy train, or a ball.
Not even a ball.

She closes her eyes and leans back against the couch.
Jawid *leans over to her.*

Jawid
Keep your eyes closed.

Afiya
What?

Jawid
Afiya, you keep your eyes closed.

Afiya
Why?

Jawid
Aren't you tired?

Afiya
Yes.

Jawid
So rest.
Keep them closed.

She closes her eyes.
Quietly, **Jawid** *leaves the room, keeping the door ajar.*
He starts to bring items in from **Leyla** *and* **Amir***'s apartment.*
It takes a long time.
First a crib, then blankets, then a few toys.
Then clothes and a basket.
He folds them neatly and arranges them in little piles.
Then he sits next to **Afiya***, who, feeling him there, opens her eyes.*
She sees what he has done and stifles a sob.

Afiya
This isn't—
It's not ours.

Jawid
It's what we have, Afiya.
Don't you see?
. . .
This child isn't just your brother's child.
He has his father's eyes
His mother's nose
Your shoulder to cry on
My arms to be carried in
Salima's warmth
The crib that Amir built
The clothes that Leyla picked
And something new that we all need.
Something new and untouched.

Afiya *hugs her husband, hard.*
They stand like that for a while, in the middle of their new life.

Jawid
Should we go get him?

Afiya *nods.*
He takes her hand and leads her out of the apartment.

End of play.

Grand Horizons

Bess Wohl

Introduction

The initial inspiration for *Grand Horizons* came when my best friend's parents suddenly announced that they were getting a divorce after fifty years of seemingly happy marriage. My friend—their son—was completely blindsided. Although he was nearly middle-aged, the loss of what he'd always believed to be a secure foundation plunged him into a kind of second childhood. He found himself struggling to accept the new reality, full of questions and regret, fundamentally unable, even as an adult, to cope with the idea that parents didn't love each other anymore. That his solid family of origin could break apart. That his dad might be dating again. The entire situation was awful and painful, so of course the play would be a comedy.

By the time I began my writing process in earnest I was on the verge of getting married myself. My brain was full of questions about commitment and what happens to love over the longterm. I poured into the play my own fears and anxieties about relationships, finding shades of myself in each member of my now fictionalized French family—Nancy's longing, Bill's stoic fortitude, Ben's desire for things to "make sense," and Brian's feeling of never quite fitting in.

I realized that I had intuitively marooned Nancy in a family of men, and the play began to take on feminist overtones for me. What does it take for a woman to self-determine in a world constructed for and by men? How much strength does it take for Nancy to step outside of the box that's been created for her?

As I continued to work on the play, I became pregnant with my first child and the character of Jess came into focus, an in-law wondering whether Bill and Nancy's marriage presages her own. Jess provided an opportunity to look at the particular challenges women face from the point of view of a younger generation. In spite of enhanced opportunities, women's struggle for full and equal status in society continues. The assertion of female selfhood is still, unfortunately, a radical act.

In this way, the play utilizes a traditional structure and form—the family comedy—to contain a subversive, feminist message. Like Nancy herself, the play both inhabits a familiar structure and fights to break it, at moments quite literally, like in a theatrical coup at the end of Act One. And it's no accident that Bill is studying to be a stand-up comedian. Comedy, in the play, is a serious thing. It contains its own set of rhythms, pressures and expectations—which can be both imprisoning and liberating. Much like marriage itself.

Ultimately, though, for me the heart of the play transcends questions of gender, form, and politics, and simply comes down to Nancy's fervent desire to be seen as a whole person. Now that I have a family of my own, I am struck by how often the ones we love the most are the ones we really "see" the least. Is it possible for us to see our loved ones as full people? How might we begin to try? I believe that it starts, as the play ends, with true and honest conversation.

Characters

Bill
Nancy
Ben
Brian
Jess
Tommy
Carla

Time

Now.

Setting

Grand Horizons.

Notes

A double slash in the dialogue indicates the place where the next character's line should begin.

Notes on Production

Grand Horizons had its co-world premiere at Williamstown Theatre Festival (Mandy Greenfield, artistic director) opening on July 20, 2019. The play was directed by Leigh Silverman, the stage manager was Melanie J. Lisby, the set and costume designer was Clint Ramos, the lighting designer was Jen Schriever, the sound designer was Palmer Hefferan. The cast was as follows:

Nancy	JoBeth Williams
Bill	Jamey Sheridan
Brian	Jesse Tyler Ferguson
Ben	Thomas Sadoski
Jess	Ashley Park
Tommy	Maulik Pancholy
Carla	Priscilla Lopez

The play subsequently opened at the Helen Hayes Theater of Second Stage Theater (Carole Rothman, artistic director; Casey Reitz, executive director) on January 26, 2020. The cast was as follows:

Nancy	Jane Alexander
Bill	James Cromwell
Brian	Michael Urie
Ben	Ben McKenzie
Jess	Ashley Park
Tommy	Maulik Pancholy
Carla	Priscilla Lopez

Grand Horizons was co-commissioned by Williamstown Theatre Festival and Second Stage Theater.

Act One

Scene One

Evening.

The lower floor of a private home in an independent living community for seniors called Grand Horizons.

A table.
Some furniture.
Doors. Generic art.
A staircase to upstairs.

It's all contained in a box.
The box is a house.

Nancy *finishes preparing dinner.*
Perhaps it involves a very large pot roast.

Bill *fastidiously sets the table.*

This is their nightly routine, an elaborate dance that happens in total silence.

It's the dance of a fifty-year marriage.
One in which words no longer matter much.
Every need is anticipated.

For example:

Nancy *brings over two glasses of lemonade.*
Bill *is at the ready with a coaster.*

Bill *turns the little fake flower arrangement around so it faces just the right angle.*

Nancy *salts* **Bill***'s food just so.*
Bill *gets* **Nancy** *a back pillow for her chair.*

They begin to eat.

Perfectly balanced.
Pairs skaters or synchronized swimmers.

Nancy   I think I would like a divorce.

Bill *looks up.*
If he's shocked, he doesn't show it.

Bill   All right.

Bill *continues to eat.*
Nancy *does not.*

Scene Two

Nancy *and* **Bill**'s *adult children have now arrived:*
Ben *and* **Brian**, *and* **Jess**, **Ben**'s *very pregnant wife.*

Nancy *and* **Bill** *are seated with their kids.*
It's a family meeting.

Brian   Okay, Mom, Dad.
We're here, // we're here now.

Ben   Guys? Here's the thing, guys.
We just want to figure out // what's going on.

Brian   This is just—not you, this is not who you are—
We want to make sure you're okay—

Ben   And so we're going to figure it out // okay guys?

Brian   We're concerned—

Ben   Family meeting, we're going to
Hash this all out and, you know, figure it out.

Pause.

Jess   What if we just, Bill, Nancy—
What if we start the conversation, by talking about some happy memories.
I was saying to Ben, in the car on the way down here,
I don't think I've ever heard about your very first date.

Nancy   Oh, it was freezing rain,
And I remember I was wearing these ridiculous high heels
My feet were killing me.
I have very long toes.

Bill   She has toes like fingers.

Nancy   I just remember the shoes.

Bill   She had a steak.
I picked up the check.
Been doing it ever since.
Check please.
Check please.

He gets up and begins to pack his things.

Ben   Dad, where are you going? Dad, sit back down—

Brian   Mom? Hi. I'm here. I'm here.
You can tell me, what did Dad do.

Nancy   Ask him yourself.

Bill Nothing.
She's the one who brought up this whole divorce thing, not me.
I would have just slogged it out.

Brian Nice, Dad, that's really nice.

Ben It just doesn't add up, you don't fight.

Brian Did you guys get in a fight?

Ben They don't // fight.

Brian Well, maybe they did, we don't know, // how do we know—

Ben Look, at the end of the day
We're going to support whatever you want—

Brian Is this what you want?
Mom, is this actually // what you want?

Bill She doesn't know what she wants.

Jess Your plants look wonderful, Nancy.

Nancy Thank you, Jess.
They're surprisingly hearty.

Ben (*a mental checklist*) Okay. Okay.
Is somebody sick?
Is everyone getting enough sleep?
Are you getting out of the house, taking walks,
Are you, I don't know, drinking enough water—

Brian Is anyone feeling anxious, or sad or scared or
Is anyone forgetting things, or, like,
Putting, like, the telephone in the fridge?

A crash from where **Bill** *is packing.*

Brian Dad, what was that?
// Dad?

Ben Dad?
What are you doing?

Bill I'm packing the car.

Brian Oh my God, Dad, you're not packing the car.

Ben Is that the toaster?
What // do you need that for?

Brian What do you need that for,
Dad.

Bill Toast.

Nancy He doesn't know how to make toast.

Bill I'm taking the toaster.

Ben Okay, okay, guys guys guys guys.
Nobody's taking anything,
Nobody's packing up.
Nobody's going anywhere.

Bill I'm taking my chair.
The TV.
(*To himself.*) I'm going to need a U-Haul.

Brian Dad, you're not getting a U-Haul.

Nancy He can't drive a U-Haul.

Bill I can operate a U-Haul.
I'm not dead yet.

Ben What if we all, like, // sit back down and—

Jess Let's all sit back down and—
Nancy, if you could—

Nancy I really don't have much time.

Jess Okay, okay, that's fine,
(*Rhetorical.*) Where do you have to be, Nancy?

Nancy // I have things to do.
I do, I have things to do.

Ben Dad, let's // put that down.

Bill It's mine, I paid for it—

Ben Dad, Dad—

Brian Everyone! Sit down.
Just sit back down!

The others all make their way back to their seats.

Brian Sorry.
I've just—
I'm just—
I'm just a little . . .
Anyway,
I'm fine, I'm fine,
I'm just,
Going through some personal stuff, and
I'm also, I happen to be under a lot of stress right now,
At work.

Bill Work?

Brian What.

Bill Aren't you a theater teacher?

Brian Yes,
And I'm smack in the middle of our big // spring show.

Ben Okay, okay everyone.
This won't take long.
Bri's got work,
We've both got work—

Nancy I don't have much time.

Jess // That's all right, Nancy.

Bill Don't skip work on my account.
I worked my whole life, never missed a day
At the pharmacy.

Brian That's not healthy, you realize that, Dad.

Bill I'm perfectly healthy.

Brian The fact that you spent your whole life at work
Is probably half the reason we're having this insane conversation
About splitting up in the first place.

Nancy Or maybe it's why we never had it sooner.

The sudden sound of several sharp gunshots.

Ben Jesus Christ, // what is that—

Jess Oh my God—

Now it's recognizable as the TV next door.

Bill The lady next door watches crime shows all day.
Over there, they've got a dog, yappy little thing.
Nothing to be done 'til they ship them off to Rose Court.

Jess Rose Court?

Bill This is independent living.
Rose Court is the next stop on the line,
It's more of an assisted situation.

Jess Got it.

Brian There's a medical facility—

Bill You stay until you . . . (*Die.*)

Ben Okay, Dad, let's come sit with Mom—

Bill It's one stop shopping.
And then in the cafeteria
They put your picture up there on the bulletin board
With all the other news.
So it's like, "Okay, everyone, so it's gonna rain Friday,
Ed is this week's Bingo champion,
Sheila's started a new book club,
Sam and Joanie are dead."

Jess Okay, Bill—

Bill I'm taking a class.
They got classes here.
I've been doing stand-up comedy.
I'm starting to think, if I wasn't a pharmacist,
I would've been a stand-up comedian.
Anybody want to hear a joke?

Ben No, Dad, definitely not.

Brian Not right now, Dad.

Nancy God, no.

Jess One thing I've been thinking about is the fact that
You've both been through a lot of transitions recently.
Moving here, packing up the old house—
Also, fifty years, that's a big milestone.
And I don't know if we marked that enough,
Or, like, celebrated enough—

Brian I made a video.

Jess That's right.

Brian Did you guys even watch it?

Jess Yes.
Yes,
We did.

Nancy I watched it, Brian.

Brian Thanks, Mom.

Nancy It was very good.

Brian Thanks.

Jess Obviously talking about all this stuff
Can feel awkward, even painful.
Communicating.
Honestly, when I work with couples in my practice
We often start with just trying to make eye contact, or hold hands—

Bill (*with great disdain.*)   Hold hands?

Jess   When was the last time you two held hands?

Nancy   // I don't know . . .

Bill   I don't think so.

Ben   Guys, hold hands.

Jess   Don't push them.

Ben   They can hold hands.

Jess   But they don't have to right now.
Fear is normal.

Bill   Fear? I'm not afraid of it.
I can hold anybody's hand.

Ben (*sharper, like a coach*)   Guys. Guys.
Come on.

Bill   Fine, what do I care.

Bill and **Nancy** *very awkwardly hold hands.*
It's agony.
Ben *looks to* **Jess** *like: "This is progress."*

Jess   Okay, how does that feel?

Nancy   Fine.

Bill   Stupid.

Jess   Now, Nancy, if I were your therapist—which obviously—
But I have done this a lot,
I have helped a lot of people avoid a lot of loneliness and regret—
So, anyway, the next exercise would be for you to try telling Bill,
What you want—

Nancy   I want a divorce.

Jess   Sorry if I wasn't clear—I meant physically.
I meant, what kind of touch do you want?
What feels good? Hard? Soft?
With just the fingertips or the entire hand.

Nancy   Um . . .
Soft.

Ben   Go ahead, Dad.
Touch her hand softly.

Nancy (*laughing*)   It tickles.

Jess (*a breakthrough*)   This is great.

Humor is fantastic.

Bill My arm is getting tired.

Jess Okay, that was great, that was actually great,
You both tried, and, you know,
I know a lot of couples that couldn't even do that.

Ben Good job, guys.

Jess And just to say, holding hands, rubbing a loved one's back, cuddling—
These are just a few ways to be intimate in the later years—
We could also talk about exploring the imagination, fantasy, role play—

Ben Okay, babe.

Jess All I mean, is I don't imagine they ever—
Did you and Bill ever talk about that kind of—

Nancy // No, I don't think so.

Bill Nope.

Ben Okay.

Nancy I'm happy to.

Jess Sure, wow, okay, that's very brave—

Brian Mom, if you want us to leave, // so you can—

Ben Yeah, we'll be . . . Somewhere else.

Nancy It's fine.
I'd like you to stay in fact.
I'd like you to stay.
So. Okay . . . Um . . .
My biggest fantasy is.
Well . . . I would . . . I would like . . .
(*Thinks, then.*) I'd like to eat dinner alone.
In a restaurant.
I've never done that before.

Bill Are we done?

Jess Okay, Bill, I can really feel your anger.

Brian *exhales.*

Jess Yours too, Brian, // if I'm being honest.

Brian Thanks, that's great.

Jess And that is some of what you are going to have to unpack,
If we're going to understand what's happening here.
In any marriage, there are lots of little disappointments over the years.

Ben Yep.

Jess Ben?

Ben That was just me agreeing with you, just saying yes.

Jess Right.
My point is, anger is understandable.
Nancy sort of threw out a hand grenade, by jumping right to divorce
Didn't you, Nancy?
Nancy?

Nancy I'm sorry,
I just don't understand what we're doing here.

Bill Neither do I, neither do I.

Brian Wait. Hold up.
What is it, Mom?
Mom? Are you okay?
Is it that . . .
You don't remember what you did?

Nancy What do you—

Ben You don't remember what you did, // Mom, is that it?

Brian (*to* **Ben**) Shhh. (*More gently.*) Mom.
It's okay, now, did you forget what happened?
Did you forget what // you did, Mom?

Jess Let her speak.

Brian Mom.
Do you know who this is?
Do you know who this person is?

Nancy I, um . . . I think . . . I think . . . It's . . .

Jess It's all right, Nancy.

Nancy That's Cousin Lou.
That's Louise's son.

Brian Cousin Lou? No, no, this is, this is—

Ben She's fucking with us.
Mom, you are fucking hilarious, you still got it,
I love you.

Brian That's funny. That's really funny.

Jess Brian, please—

Bill Was she kidding?

Act One, Scene Two   379

Jess   // She was kidding.

Nancy   I was kidding. It was a joke.

Brian   It's not funny, Mom, we're very concerned.

Bill   Since when does she kid.

Nancy   I kid.

Bill   She does not kid.

Brian   Who is cousin Lou?

Nancy   You don't have a cousin Lou.
It was a joke.

Bill   What is she joking for?
I'm the funny one,
I've always been the funny one—

Nancy (*preparing to go*)   Well, this has been great.

Brian   Mom, Mom, sit.
Where else do you have to be right now?

Nancy   I have a meeting about my clothing drive.

Brian   What is that?
You never told me about// a clothing drive.

Nancy   I'm telling you now.
People around here have a lot of old clothes.
And then after they die
They really don't need their clothes anymore.

Brian   Mom.

Nancy   So we're sending the dead people's clothes to refugees.
// All kinds of refugees, from Syria, Afghanistan, Sudan.
War refugees, climate refugees,—

Ben   Okay, but Mom?
Okay okay okay,
Those people are very far away—

Brian   Ben—

Nancy   So?
We can still do things for them.
With all due respect, that is exactly the kind of attitude
That exemplifies everything wrong with the world today.
Nobody cares about anybody anymore.
Nobody cares.

Brian   I care, Mom. I care.

Tell me about your clothing drive.

Ben You can wait five minutes, Mom.

Nancy No, I can't.
I can't actually, Ben, because I organized it myself.
I'm . . . I'm leading the meeting.

Brian That's really impressive, Mom.
You've never done anything like that before.

Ben Five minutes.

Bill Let her go.
She's made up her mind.
She wants to split up, fine.
Big whoop.
What's the big deal?

Ben (*losing his cool*) The big deal is,
It's a fifty-year marriage,
You can't end it without a conversation.
I'm not even sure you can end it at all at this point,
I mean, if you wanted to get divorced
You should have done it after we went to college,
Like normal people.
Like a mid-life crisis kind of a thing.
I mean,
You're almost eighty.
Like.
How much else—
Even is there?

Jess Ben—

Brian What we're trying to say is—
Life can get really lonely—
You can't see it, you've had each other but—
You could be
Making a really—
A, just, a
Terrible mistake—and so all we're asking is—
Can we just talk about this?
Do you guys have anything to say for yourselves?

Bill There's a bunch of nuns all trying to get into heaven.

Ben Dad, come on—

Brian Are you serious, Dad—

Bill And St. Peter says to them, you know, St. Peter at the gate, so he says . . .

Okay, line up, ladies, you're nuns, of course you're getting in,
I'll let you all right through the pearly gates as long as no part of your body
Has ever touched a man's . . . member.
So, Sister Sarah is first in line.
St. Peter says, has any part of you ever touched that part of a man?
She says, "Well, one time I touched one with my little pinky finger."
He says, that's fine, wash your pinky finger in this holy water and you can go on in.
So, next in line is Sister Elizabeth.
St. Peter repeats the question, "Has any part of you ever touched blah blah blah."
She says, "My whole hand."
He says, "Okay, that's fine, wash your hand in this holy water and go ahead in . . ."
Next is Sister Christine,
But before anyone can say a word someone comes running up from the back of the
line like gangbusters and shoves her way all the way to the front—
It's Sister Susan.
And she goes, "Hold on! If I'm going to have to gargle with that stuff,
At least let me do it before Sister Christine puts her ass in it!"

Nancy Well, I'm off.

She quickly escapes out the door.

Ben Mom—wait—

And now **Bill** *escapes upstairs.*
Ben *and* **Brian** *look to each other.*

Scene Three

It's now the middle of the night.

All around are overflowing bags of clothing from **Nancy**'s *refugee drive, and huge piles of loose clothes, the clothes of the dead.*

The toaster is missing, along with a photo or two.

Next door, the TV is playing another crime show.

After a moment, **Jess** *comes downstairs, still in her clothes.*

Jess Ben?
What are you doing?
// You're still working?

Ben Hey, babe.
I'm so behind—
The judge on this case is like monumentally unsympathetic,
What are you doing up?

Jess I just did four back-to-back phone sessions—
And then my sleepwalker needed an "emergency call."

Jess   What happened to Brian?

Ben   Who?

Jess   Your brother?

Ben   Oh, yeah, he went out for a drink.

Jess   Sounds kind of lonely.

Ben   I think he was lonely and that's why he went.

Jess   And your parents?

Ben   Went to bed hours ago.

Jess   In the same room?

Ben   I thought it was kind of a good sign.

Jess   Sure, if you block out the part where they barely spoke to each other,
And then your mom pretended to have dementia
And then your dad told a dick joke.

Ben   No, I know, it's insane, they're children.
Come here. Come here come here.

She goes to him.
Leans down to kiss him.
He kisses her stomach.

Jess   It's not even that.
It's more how you get when you're around them.

Ben   Wait, how do I get?

Jess   And what's going on with your hands?

Ben   It's my eczema, you know // and I don't have my cream—

Jess   Where's your cream?

Ben   I don't have it.

Jess   Okay, it's fine, let's go to bed, we'll be home in the morning.

Ben   Babe.

Jess   What?

Ben   We can't // leave them like this—

Jess   Wait, no, Ben, no no no I already canceled today's sessions to be here //
I have like a million things to do before this baby comes—

Ben   They need us—
They need us—

Jess   They need professional help—

Ben And, look, Brian is obviously useless, and—

Jess They don't even want us here—

Ben Trust me, I get it—you don't think, you don't think it pisses me off?

Jess What?

Ben I mean none of this makes any sense.
Are they serious?
Is it a cry for help?
Is it even real?

Jess Wait, no, people crying for help is real, Ben.
It means they need help, it means help me.

Ben No, I know, all I'm trying to say is.
Just look at the facts, okay?
They never fought.
They always got along.
They have stuff in common—they're about to have a grandchild together.
What else do they want?

Jess I don't know.
Love.

Ben Sure, whatever that means.

Jess Do you not know // what it means?

Ben No, I know what it means for us, obviously—

Jess Okay.

Ben I'm saying for them, at their age—
And anyway, I'm not even talking about love,
I'm talking about marriage.

Jess What are you talking about?

Ben I don't know what we're talking about.
All I'm saying is,
Sure maybe they never had some like great marriage,
But I always thought they had like a regular marriage.

Jess A regular marriage?

Ben Uh-huh.

Jess And what is that to you?
What's a regular marriage?

Ben A marriage, I guess,
That doesn't end.
Sorry, babe,

I'm not in a place to be like super-articulate or deep right now—
I'm getting crushed.

Jess Could you—
Could you maybe just not call me that anymore.

Ben What?

Jess Babe.
I'm not a baby.
I'm not an actual baby you do realize that.

Ben It's a term of affection.

Jess Right, but when somebody doesn't like it
Then it's hostile.

Ben Okay.
Goodnight.
Love you, babe. I love you.

Jess Good night. I love you too.

She goes.

He sits alone.
Scratches his hands.
After a moment, he rushes upstairs after his wife.
From outside, a car pulls up.
Car doors close and, "Thank you, sir!" can be heard.

Brian (*from off*) . . . I hope this is the right house—
I know it's the corner house but—
They all look exactly the same.

Tommy (*from off*) I know, our Uber driver was like // what is even happening?!

Brian (*from off*) I know, he was like . . .
He's probably still just like driving around like . . .
Aaaaah!
(*Then, flirty.*) Ouch! Wait. Stop that—

The door swings open.
Brian *and* **Tommy** *enter.*

Brian Go in, go in, the whole thing is even sadder inside—

Tommy No, I'm so sorry about my roommate situation.
She just freaks on me when I bring home random strangers.

Brian Do you do that a lot?

Tommy Do you?

Brian No, actually, I'm just, I'm having a weird day.

Tommy Great, let's get weird—

Brian Come in, come in, come in, come in, come in—
Don't mind the pile,
That's just the clothes of the deceased.

Brian So, wait—what was I saying, before, in the—

Tommy You mean about the play, your school play—

Brian Right, so—right, so—I'll give, like . . .
I'll give, like, what I do is . . .
I gave Abigail a best friend,
John Proctor has a sister,
Reverend Hale has a sort of assistant reverend,
Danforth has a clerk and there's a court stenographer—

Tommy Am I supposed to know
Who those people // are.

Brian No, they're not people, they're parts,
They're // parts in a play—

Tommy (*teasing him*) Ohhhhh.

Brian The point is, I rotate.

Tommy Mmmm, you rotate.

Brian So, and then like, like a third of the way through,
The first Abigail switches with a new Abigail
But we all know it's still the same Abigail because she takes off her locket
And gives it to the other Abigail.
// And, like, John Proctor hands over his glasses to the new Proctor—
And the Reverend has a collar and you know, and so on and so forth—
And then it all happens like three more times
And of course I've added extra girls and more spectators in the courtroom and—

Tommy No idea.
No idea what you're talking about.
No idea. No idea.

Brian I can seriously—
I've managed to get, like, over two hundred kids,
Into the show—

Tommy Wow, I am so hot for teacher // right now.

Brian // Okay, okay—

Tommy What's your last name?

Brian French,
Brian // French.

Tommy   Mr. French, ooooh la la, come here—

Brian (*enjoying the attention*)   All right, hold on—
Do you want a drink?

Tommy   Sure, why not.

Brian *starts to make drinks.*

Brian   I've been mixing vodka with Crystal Light.

Tommy   Yum.

Brian   The point is, the way I do it—
Every kid who wants a part gets one—
Because, like, do you remember how painful it was
To like,
Audition for the school play and not get a part?

Tommy *shakes his head.*

Brian   It was a popularity contest.
And you know, I guess I just.
I love these kids.
And I . . . I don't know.
I don't want anyone to be disappointed.

Brian   What.

Tommy   No, just
You seem kind of amazing.

Brian   Really? Come on, I'm blushing.

He comes over with the drinks.
Tommy *starts to make out with him.*

Brian   I feel bad
I haven't asked you anything about yourself.

Tommy   I'm fascinating
I swear, ask me later—

They kiss.

Brian   Okay, okay
Wow.
That is . . . Wow.
Okay wow.

Tommy   Are you nervous?
// Are you?
That's so cute.
You are so cute.

Brian No! I'm not, nervous!
It's just, I think—thank you—
This place is kind of throwing me off—
I don't usually—

Tommy Wait,
Are you married?

Brian What?
No.

Tommy 'Cause way too
Many of the dudes online are.

Brian No, I know—

Tommy And it's funny 'cause, it's like,
The single ones just want sex,
But it's always the married ones who want intimacy.

Brian I don't want intimacy.
I don't know what's wrong with me.
You know what?
Let's go in the garage.

Tommy Okay. Is it less sad in there?

Brian It's more sad, but also maybe more . . .
Soundproof?
I mean, my brother and sister-in-law are—
And my mom and dad are literally right . . .

Tommy (*points straight up*)

Brian Right.

Tommy Then I guess we should be *very quiet*.

Brian Yeah.
I don't even know if it's possible . . .

Tommy You mean, because, like . . .
What if they come down?

Brian That's my point.

Tommy (*as a very bad kid*) We could get in trouble again.

Brian Right . . .

Tommy Remember last time?

Brian Last time?

Tommy Dad was so mad he spanked me
Until I was sore for days.

I still have a mark, see?

Brian Um . . .

Tommy And remember the time Mom caught us a
And sent us to bed without supper?

Brian Ah . . .

Tommy I mean we weren't doing anything wrong.
Just playing, right?
Our favorite game.
"Penis to penis."

Brian What is that?

Tommy Don't you remember?
Come here. I'll show you.

Tommy *arranges himself.*
Brian *comes closer.*

Tommy But be very quiet
So Mom and Dad don't come downstairs and punish us again . . .
Because it's wrong, I know we're not supposed to, but I can't help it . . .

Brian (*starts, then pauses*) Wait, I'm sorry—are we—
Are we pretending to be siblings right now?

Tommy Shhh.

Brian Okay, I'm not—

Tommy Shhh.
Mom and Dad might hear you and spank you silly.

Brian I don't want to—um—just—

Tommy That's so naughty!

Brian Let's not role play.

Tommy Oh. Okay.
If you can't, like, go with it.

Brian I can go with it,
I can go with a role play—
I just don't want to do—incest.

Tommy Incest?!

Brian "Mom and Dad"?

Tommy *My* Mom and Dad.
My Mom and Dad.
It was "Sleepover."

It wasn't *our* Mom and Dad.

Brian Okay, 'cause I said, "Siblings,"
And you didn't correct me.

Tommy I was in the moment.

Brian I'm sorry I'm sorry—
Shit. I feel like an idiot—

Tommy It's fine, hey, it's fine.
Let's start over.
You want to just tell me what you want?

Brian I, um . . . I actually . . .
Will you just,
Could you maybe just give me a minute?

He tries to recover.

It's totally not you.

Tommy I didn't think it was.

Brian Just—did I mention my parents—

Tommy You said a lot, I don't know.

Brian My parents are getting divorced.

Tommy Okay.

Brian Okay?!

Tommy Lots of parents get divorced—
It sucks when you're like, *eight*,
But you seem pretty middle-aged.

Brian Thanks.

Tommy So, like, whatever,
Let them do what they want.

Brian Let them do what they want?

Tommy They're adults.
They can do whatever the fuck they want.

Brian Are you kidding me? Are you kidding?
Adults cannot do what they want.
That's like—
The defining feature of adulthood is that you never get to do what you want.
Children do what they want.
Adults struggle to meet the needs of other people,
Make a living,
Satisfy a thousand obligations

And still fall short and wind up disappointing everyone.

Tommy Are you sure you're not married?

Brian No, I'm not married.
This is my family.
As disappointing as they are, as disrespectful as they are
About like pretty much everything I do . . .
As unwilling as they are to, like, see me . . .
I don't have another family,
I don't have "my family."
I have fish.

Tommy Look, all I'm trying to say is, having gone through this myself—
It's not the same because I was a child—
But I did feel like the world was ending.
I thought it was my fault, all the typical stuff,
But I can also tell you, you realize that you can survive this.
And it's sad, it's really sad—
But also, maybe not everything is meant to last forever.
And, well, how amazing that your parents are still reaching for happiness,
Even at their age,
I mean how brave, and kind of inspiring actually.

Brian That's not what's happening here.
My parents are just being shortsighted, and honestly a little bit selfish.

Tommy I kind of think you're the one being selfish.
That's what I think.

Brian How am I being selfish?
I've put my whole life on hold just to be here for them.
Just at the moment, just at the worst possible moment—

Tommy Right.

Brian And it's not just my show, I also, just got out of a
Kind of a, like an almost relationship thing for the first time in a very long time—

Tommy Got it.

Brian And, so I mean, to have this all happen right now—
And to be, like the only one here with any emotional intelligence—
No, seriously my brother has, like, all the emotions of a rock—

Tommy You know what?
I actually can't do this.

Brian Do what?

Tommy I just, like, promised myself I would stop caretaking in relationships—
// And, like, put myself first, fly my freak flag—

Brian What are you even—

Tommy You couldn't hang with my role play, that's fine,
I can't do yours.
I can't take care of you.

Brian That's not what I'm even asking for.

Tommy Yeah, but it is.

Brian Wow, okay, wow.

Tommy And I'm so tired of dealing with, like, needy guys—

Brian That's not // even who I am—

Tommy Fine, whatever, I have to go.

Brian Great, fine, go.

Tommy Good luck with your parents.

Brian Thanks, you're an asshole.

Tommy Well, you're ridiculous.

Brian By the way, you're going to get lost—
The houses all look the same—

Tommy This place is literally designed so people with Alzheimer's can navigate it.
I think I'll be fine.

Brian Great. Go be fine!

Tommy I will!
You're a fucking baby.
You are a fucking baby

Tommy goes.
Brian is alone.
He feels suddenly devastated.

A voice, from upstairs:

Nancy Brian?
Are you okay, sweetheart?
I heard voices.

Brian I think—
You were imagining it, Mom.

Nancy flips a switch and the fluorescents flip on.
Everything is suddenly much too bright.

Brian *quickly runs some water over his face.*

Nancy Oh, Brian.
What's gotten into you?

Brian What's gotten into *me*?
What's gotten into *me*?!

Nancy Shhh.
Shhh.
You are so sensitive.
You always were.

Brian You used to say it made me special.

Nancy It does.

Brian Thank you.

Nancy But it's also a bit ridiculous . . .
It's all going to be okay.

Brian It is?

Nancy I promise.

Brian Good.
And I'm sorry if I don't visit enough, Mom,
If that's all this is.
I'll visit more.
Okay, I'm going to bed.

He gives her a long hug.
Then he starts to arrange his bed on the sofa.

Nancy Your father has something on the side.

Brian What?

Nancy I want to say that outright
Because I feel like I'm getting blamed about all this and it's not fair.

Brian What do you mean he has something on the side?

Nancy What do you think I mean? A woman.

Brian What?

Nancy A girlfriend.
He has a girlfriend on the side.
Carla.

Brian Carla?

Nancy Yes. She lives in Vista View.

Brian Vista View?

Nancy It's the set of homes near the highway.

Brian Near the highway?

Nancy Why do you keep repeating everything I'm saying?

Brian I'm having trouble understanding.

Nancy I'm only telling you
Because he's saying I'm the one who suggested a divorce,
Which is true, in a way, but he's hardly blameless in the situation.

Brian How did this . . .
How did they . . .

Nancy Stand-up comedy class, at the rec center here.
Apparently she thinks he's a "real hoot."
He parades her around the rec room, the cafeteria, that kind of thing.
She's much younger.
A real floozy, you know the type.
Very provocative.

Brian Uh-huh.

Nancy And I think they "sext."
That's what you call it, right?
Sexting? Sending pictures?

Brian Okay, Mom? Mom?
I actually don't think I can have this conversation with you.

Nancy You're a grown man, Brian.

Brian What's that supposed to mean?

Nancy You're old enough to contemplate
The fact that your father sexts.

Brian No, I know that. I just don't want to.

Nancy You've certainly put us through enough.

Brian Right. Okay.
(*A bit colder now.*) Mom. I'm sorry this is happening.
If it even is happening.
It's, it's, it must be very embarrassing for you.

Nancy More for him, I would think.
Carla.
He's not funny. He's not.

Brian Well, this is good information,
And now I'm going to get him to stop.

Nancy I'm not taking him back.

Brian What do you mean?

Nancy I'm not taking him back.
I love him—I mean I must on some level—
But I don't think I'm in love with him.

Brian What does that even mean?
Of course you're not "in love" with him anymore.
That's not a feeling that lasts.

Nancy That's a very depressing attitude, Brian,
And I think it explains why you're alone.

Brian I'm only trying to say that . . .
Even if you don't feel fully "in love" right now . . .
Whatever that even means.
I think you can honor the time,
The memory of the time when you were.
I know you were.
Once.
I know it.
Weren't you?

Nancy I suppose I was.

Brian Of course you were.

Nancy With Hal Barrow.

Brian Who?

Nancy Hal Barrow.

Brian Who is that?

Nancy He was my high school sweetheart.

Brian What are you talking about?

Nancy Then he went away to college,
And then he joined the Peace Corps to pay for it,
And then he got a full scholarship to law school
And then he became a lawyer in Chicago.
He was very smart.
He's dead now.
Stroke.
I saw that.
On Facebook.

Brian And you, what, you still think about this, this, this . . .
Hal person?

Nancy I've always thought about him.
Sometimes I wonder
If I only married your father to try to get Hal out of my heart.

Brian What?

Nancy I know, it was silly, really.
Everyone knows that doesn't work.

Brian You only married Dad because of, of, of—

Nancy Hal.

Brian I don't care what his name was—

Nancy I'm not saying it was the only reason, it was just part of it.
Anyway, people get married for much less.

Brian Right.

Nancy But whatever got you into it, you try.
You go on.
You try to make the best of it.
You divide things up over time.
He'll have the soup. I'll have the salad.
Unless there's fries.
I'll have fries over salad but if the choice is soup or salad I'll have salad over soup.
I find soup depressing, don't you?
It's so wet.
I like to chew.

Brian Mom.
What you're saying is, it's not making any sense.

Nancy So, then the years went by and finally, I thought, if I have a child, maybe.
Maybe that will help. So I had children.
Ben, and then you because I wanted Ben to have a companion.
And also I thought maybe at some point something will click
And my heart will do the things it's supposed to be doing.
But my heart never did.
And so then I just sort of . . . Gave up.

Brian Gave up on . . .

Nancy On getting out of love with him.
I probably still love him right now.
Hard to say.

Brian Hal.

Nancy Stop saying, "Hal" like that.

Brian Is it not his name?

Nancy I don't like it.

Brian You don't like his name.

Nancy I don't like the way you say it.

Brian I don't know how else to say it.
Hal. "Hal."

Nancy The point being,
I realized it was impossible for me not to love him,
So I just learned to live with it.
Sort of the way people live with back pain.
Or a limp.
Don't act like it's some big deal.

Brian Why didn't you marry him in the first place?

Nancy The timing was always wrong.
Oh, I waited and waited for him—
For years, I waited—
And then
I just panicked.
I wasn't getting any younger and,
In those days, you know,
It was very uncommon for a girl not to be married.
And your father seemed nice enough.
And stable.
A pharmacist is a very respectable job.

Brian Jesus, Mom.

Nancy And then by the time Hal finally came home from all his adventures—
It was too late.
So, there you go.

Brian And that was it?

Nancy Well, no.
I would see Hal from time to time.
He would come 'round every now and then to see his parents—
This was before they died.
His mother had terrible Alzheimer's.
It was so sad, by the end she didn't even recognize Pepper—
They always had terriers, I don't know why.

Brian So, every few years you would grab a cup of coffee with Hal.

Nancy Mmm hmm. He was married too. He had daughters.

Brian But he felt the same way.

Nancy Oh, yes.

Brian But you'd just, like, go to Pete's Coffee at the mall.

Nancy A bit further out.
I'd tell your father I was getting my hair done or something.
He'd never notice if I had my hair done or not, so.

Brian   And you'd just grab a coffee.

Nancy   One time we had dinner.
Your father was off on a fishing trip
And Hal's mother happened to have broken her hip
The exact same week so, you know, for once in our lives our timing was good.

Brian   Uh-huh.

Nancy   And Ben was old enough to watch you by then,
So I put you both in front of the television set,
And I told him if he was good I'd buy him baseball cards and then I just . . .
I snuck out.
Like a teenager.

Brian   Where did you go?

Nancy   We drove, we drove a few hours away
And had dinner at a steak place in Philadelphia.
It was delicious.
One of those places where the butter is shaped like roses.
And then, after dinner, he asked me if I wanted to go on a drive.
We drove and drove.
And he parked down under a bridge,
By the banks of the Schuykill.
I was wearing my first dress of the summer—
I remember it was short, with no stockings on—
Purple and green and black.
Do you remember it? You wouldn't.

Brian   No.

Nancy   It had these tiny flowers and it was one of those halter tops,
My shoulders were bare in it, and it was so
Short that when we got out of the car,
I worried it would blow right up.
But I kind of liked that feeling too
Because I was wearing my best underwear.

Brian   Mom.

Nancy   And we just sat down, out there, by the water.
I could feel the wind blowing up on my legs, and
I could feel the cold ground underneath me.
Nobody was around—it was the middle of the night.
I had lost all track of time.

Brian   You're lucky Ben and I didn't die.

Nancy   I know, I know.
But really, he was old enough to look after you // at this point.

Brian This is Ben we're talking about, Mom.

Nancy You were fine.

Brian And you're out in fancy underwear.

Nancy I didn't say it was fancy, I said it was my best.
It wasn't all that nice.
And then later that night . . .
He gave me the most incredible . . .

Brian What?

Nancy How do you say it . . .

Brian What,
Flowers?

Nancy Head.

Brian (*a pause, confused*) What?

Nancy He gave me the most incredible head.

Brian WHAT?

Nancy I lay back // and he just went up under my skirt—

Brian Mom mom mom mom mom mom mom—

Nancy I had never felt anything like it in my entire life.

Brian Mom. You have to stop.

Nancy I had never felt anything like it.
He told me—he loved my, you know . . .
He said, "I love your pussy."

Brian Mom, please—I'm begging you—

Nancy Just like that. Just like that.
And. The truth is?
In my entire life with your father, he never said anything like that to me.
He never said anything like that.
In our entire married life he never once even mentioned my pussy.
I mean we never discussed it.
God knows, I praised his penis to the high heavens—
I went on and on about how wonderful it was—

Brian (*trying not to hear this*) Aaaaaaaaaaah.

Nancy (*sudden, forceful*) No.
You have to hear this.

She turns to him with ferocity.

I will be a whole person to you.
I will.

Brian *looks at her, stunned into silence.*

Nancy The point is, your father never praised me that way.
And then this man . . . Hal . . .
Well, it was very powerful.
And then afterwards, he didn't ask me for anything.
We just lay together, in the dark, side by side.
Staring into each other's eyes.
And you know, I didn't feel guilty at all?
Not for a second.
Because—I felt like something this beautiful—
A moment this perfect—that's why we were put on the earth.
He was looking at me and he was
Tracing his finger along my shoulder.
Just gently tracing my shoulder.
And then he noticed—I never even noticed this before—
But, he noticed this group of five freckles.
I have five freckles on my shoulder that—if you connected the dots—
Would make a perfect line.
It's sort of back here, so, you know, I had never even noticed it myself.
But he traced it over and over again, this perfect line.
Nobody had ever seen that about me before.
But once he pointed them out, I would look for them every time I got undressed.
That little line of five.

Brian *is suddenly full of grief.*

Brian You should have run off with him.

Nancy You're angry that I left you and Ben alone for one night—
A night you don't even remember.

Brian Still, I would have wanted you to be happy.

Nancy Children don't care if their parents are happy.
You just want us to be there.

Brian Well, I didn't want this.
I wouldn't have wanted—this.
Growing up surrounded by—
You want to talk about why I'm alone?
You want to talk about why I can't ever, like, find intimacy—
I never saw it.
I never actually saw it.

Pause.

Nancy Well, maybe you're seeing it now.

Nancy *walks back up to bed.*
Brian *reels.*

Scene Four

Night has turned into day.

Bill *is alone, puttering and packing.*

Some furniture is missing.
More huge piles of clothes fill the living room.

From across the way, a neighbor's dog.
Whimpers tragically, left alone.
It might even howl.

Bill *pauses to listen.*
Maybe he considers murdering the dog.

Instead, he continues to pack as he works on his stand-up.

Bill   . . . I've been married fifty years . . .
We each had a very happy twenty years.
After that, we met!

I'm the kinda guy who.
I'm the kinda man who.
I'm a guy who.
I'm the kinda husband who.
I'm a gentleman, ladies and gentlemen!

Oh no.
That doesn't work.
I'm a gentleman, folks.
Folks. Hey there, folks.
Thanks for coming out.
I'm from Delaware.
Delaware.
Think of a joke about Delaware.

He tries to think of something.

Bill   There's nothing funny about Delaware.
Maybe that's the joke.
"There's nothing funny about Delaware!"
Work on it.
I worked my whole life as a pharmacist, folks.
Let me tell you what that's like.
Nobody much cares that you're there 'til they need you—
It's not like being a doctor, ooooh doctors,
Nope, the pharmacist, well,
You're just expected to be there, twenty-four seven—
But make one mistake, you could kill someone!
(*He tries again.*) Make one mistake, you could kill someone!

Nope.

So, recently, my wife kicked me out . . .
The wife and I split up.
She walked me to my car and said:
"I hope you die a miserable death."
I said, "So you're asking me to come back?"
So you're asking me to come back?
(*A sudden plea.*) So you're asking me to come back?

Ben *comes in from running.*

Ben   Is that your U-Haul?

Bill   Yeah. What about it.

Ben   Where's Mom?

Bill *looks around like:*
How the fuck should I know?

The dog across the way barks sharply.

Ben (*scanning the room*)   You took your chair?
Where are you even taking that stuff?

Bill   That's my business.

Ben   Okay, okay.
(*Starting over.*) I'm actually glad we have a quick sec here, um . . .

Bill   Uh-oh.

Ben   Nope, not going to be intense, just—
I actually had a quick check in with Bri this morning
And, uh, he seemed pretty upset, but you know, that's Brian.

Bill   That's Brian.

Ben   Obviously, we all know that
Mom is the instigator of all this—

Bill   I would have slogged it out.

Ben   Right.
And now she's throwing around blame.

Bill   Typical.

Ben   And, and, and according to Brian,
She's got something stuck in her head
About a new friend of yours named Carla.

Bill   Who is that?

Ben   You don't know who that is.

Bill No idea.

Ben Okay, great.
'Cause Brian said that Mom said
You guys "sext."

Bill What is that?

Ben You send each other
Text messages
Of a sexual nature.

Bill Brian is not a reliable narrator.
He's like your mother that way.

Ben So you've never sexted with a "Carla."

Bill Nope.

Ben Do you even know a Carla?

Bill Nope. Not that I know of.

Ben You don't know a Carla that you know of.
Do you know a Carla that you don't know of?

Bill Ben, for God sakes.
There's no Carla.
There's no sex messages.
You know I don't text.
I don't even know how.

Ben Can I see your phone?

Bill What?

Ben Can I see your phone?

Bill What phone?

Ben Just show me your phone.

Bill I don't even know where it is.
I hardly use the thing.

Ben You don't have it.

Bill Can we let this go?
Can I get off the witness stand please?

Ben You're right you're right you're right.
I don't know what's wrong with me.
I'm under a lot of pressure and it's a very stressful time and . . .
Come on.
Come here, Dad.
You know, I think you're right,

I think Mom's imagination gets the best of her sometimes.

Bill She was always a dreamer.

Ben Still is.

Bill Exactly.

Ben Didn't mean to make you feel like I was cross-examining you.

Bill No harm done.

Ben Come here.

They hug.
Ben *tries to feel in all of* **Bill***'s pockets for a possible phone.*
They get in a weird tussle.

Bill What the hell are you—
Stop that—// stop it stop it stop it, get off of me—

Ben I felt it! I fucking felt it in your—
Chest pocket—give me that—

Bill That is a box of Tic Tacs!

Ben Fine, give me a Tic Tac.
Give me just one Tic Tac.

Bill *does not.*

Ben Hand over the phone.
Dad?
Hand over the phone.

Bill What am I, twelve years old?
No. No, I'm not handing over my phone.

Ben GIVE ME THE FUCKING PHONE.

The dog across the way starts wildly yapping again.

Bill Quiet down.
We'll be the talk of the entire neighborhood.

Ben I would love to make you the talk of the neighborhood.
Do you want me to see if I can?

Bill There's nothing on it anyway.
You're not going to find anything.

He hands the phone to **Ben**.

Ben What's the password?

Bill Our anniversary.

Ben *types it in.*

Bill   What's going on with your hands.

Ben   It's my eczema, Dad,
You know I get eczema when I get stressed.

Bill   Don't get it all over my phone.

Ben   You know what?
You know what?
Never mind.

Ben *glares at his father.*
He stares at the phone.
He looks into the mid-distance for a while.
He walks around.
For a while he has no idea what to do.

Ben   Okay. Okay.
So.
This is . . . Pretty disgusting.

Bill   Well, you looked, so.

Ben   Did you actually do all the things in these—
No, forget it forget it forget it—

Bill   It can't shock you.
You were in a fraternity.

Ben   This doesn't shock me.
The thing that shocks me is . . .
Not this it's . . .

Bill   What?

Ben   I just, I never realized how, like,
Completely full of shit you are.

Bill   It takes two to tango.

Ben   I mean you were . . .
You were . . .
You were a veteran, you signed up to go.
And work—
You worked your ass off—
And you were so hard on anyone who dared to falter—

Bill   I love your mother.

Ben   How can you say that?
Come on, you lied and now you're running away—

Bill   I do love her.
I do.
I always have and I always will.

Ben   Then I guess you've got a pretty fucked-up idea of love.

Jess *comes in, still in her robe.*

Ben *makes a decision.*

Jess   Hi, what's // going on—

Ben   We are leaving, Jess,
We're going home.

Jess   What?
// What are you talking about?

Ben   This is too fucked-up—
This is way too fucked-up—
Are we packed?

Jess   No we're not packed.
I'm in my pajamas.
Last night you said we couldn't leave.
What is happening here?

Brian *enters with a Starbucks coffee.*

Bill   // Nothing.

Ben   Nothing.
(*Then, to his dad.*)
Stop that. Stop that.
We are not the same.

Bill *shushes him as* **Ben** *starts finding any of his things that have been left around and packing them.*

Jess (*to* **Brian**)   Do you have any idea
What is going on // here?

Brian (*to* **Ben**)   Wait—did you say something to him?

Ben   I *saw* the sexts.

Brian   Jesus Christ—

Bill   Oh toughen up, Brian.
We're all grown-ups here.

Brian   // Toughen up?
Toughen up?!

Jess   Is there an infidelity issue?

Brian You were supposed to wait, Ben—
I only even told you about the sexts because I was upset—
I just needed somebody to talk to—like a friend or, hey, maybe a brother—

Ben Dude.
What difference // does it make?

Brian Because I trusted you—and you just went ahead and, and, and—

Ben So what,
Who cares
About the order of operations here—

Brian Because we should all talk about this together,
Like a family.

Jess // Both of you, both of you—

Ben (*to* **Jess**) Babe, this doesn't involve you.
// Brian, it's over.
Let's go.

Jess It doesn't involve me?

Brian (*to* **Ben**) You are not leaving!

Bill Keep it down.

Ben Bri, I took care of it, just like
I take care of everyone // all the time.

Brian Wait, you take care of everyone.

Ben I take like seventy-five to eighty percent of everything
And it should be fifty-fifty.

Brian How does he calculate that?
What is that even based on?

Jess Okay, Ben, you know it doesn't // work like that.

Brian I am the first responder.
I do all of the emotional labor of this entire family.

Ben I'm talking practically speaking, Brian, I'm saying financially,
I'm saying every time anything goes down—

Bill What goes down?
Nothing goes down.

Ben And I, I have other priorities right now,
My own life,
(*Re* **Jess**) her,
My own *family*—

Jess Her? Her?

Brian Oh right, I must not have any responsibilities
Because I don't have kids.
Guess what, I have over *two hundred kids* counting on me right now—

Ben   // It's not the same, dude, it's not the same.

Brian Nobody in this family has ever taken what I do seriously—

Jess   // That's not true.

Ben   Oh come on.

Brian And I find it insulting when honestly
I can't think of a job out there more meaningful
Than molding America's future.

Ben   Bri, Bri, I don't care, I don't care.
I'm just saying I am the one who found this place for them,
Got them in here, paid for the move,
But there is a limit, even to Mr. Nice Dependable Nice Guy.

Jess Will you both stop?!

Brian Mr. Nice Guy?
What is this, opposite day?

Ben Opposite day?
Opposite day, are you serious?

Brian You used to sit on my chest until I couldn't breathe.
You made me walk a million steps behind you on the way to school—
You said Mom and Dad were putting me up for adoption—

Ben I was a kid.

Brian You told everyone at school I had a terminal illness,
And then you made fun of me when I was excited
Because people were noticing me and I thought maybe I suddenly got popular.

Jess Is that true?

Ben (*explodes at her*)   Jess, get in the fucking car.

From next door, the neighbor's dog barks wildly.
Jess *does not move.*

Ben Shit.
Shit

Nancy *comes in,*
Holding bags of clothes.

Everyone stops.
Nancy *looks to* **Bill.**

Nancy Is that your U-Haul?

Bill I have to return it at noon.

Nancy Then you'd better get going.

Bill I'd better.

Pause.

Nancy Do you have a long drive?
Wait.
I'll make you a sandwich.

Nancy *carefully makes* **Bill** *a sandwich.*
It's excruciating.

Ben, **Brian**, *and* **Jess** *can hardly bear it.*

Finally, **Nancy** *is finished.*
She wraps the sandwich and gives it to **Bill**.

Bill Thanks.
I'm sure we'll talk.

He looks at **Nancy** *one last time, and goes out.*
The kids are devastated.

Ben Mom, are you okay?
Mom?

Nancy *does not respond.*

The sound of the U-Haul starting just outside.

And then the U-Haul crashes violently and spectacularly through the kitchen wall.

The sound of the truck's horn stuck on.

Blaring.

End of Act One.

Act Two

Scene One

Everything is just as it was at the beginning.

Except it's very quiet.

And **Carla** *is there.*

Carla *is nothing like the floozy we may have imagined. She's cheerful, frumpy, warm, an easy laugher.*

The kind of person who wears themed outfits for holidays.

Nancy *and* **Carla** *stand awkwardly, neither quite knowing what to do.*

Nancy Can I get you anything, Carla?

Carla Oh, I think I'm fine.

Nancy You're sure?

Carla Oh, yeah.
If you had a donut or something, I'd take that.

Nancy I don't think I have donuts.

Carla I'm a donut freak!

Nancy Really?

Carla Yeah.

Nancy Sorry, I don't think I // have donuts . . .

Carla That's okay.

Nancy I have crackers?

Carla Nah, that's okay.
What kind?

Nancy Saltines, I think?

Carla Yeah, no, that's okay.

Nancy Bill likes to crumble them in his soup.

Carla Okay.

Nancy If you want you can take them.

Carla I'm sure they have 'em at the grocery store.

Nancy I won't eat them, most likely.

Carla Oh yeah? Okay. Okay.

Pause.
Carla *looks around.*

Carla It's great that they could get you in a new unit so fast.

Nancy It is.

Carla Is it much like where you were?

Nancy Yes, in fact.
But quieter.
Our old unit had a lot of—
You know, those kind of obnoxious loud neighbors.

Carla Oh yeah, that's the worst.
And the thin walls.

Nancy What's that?

Carla THIN WALLS.

Nancy Right.
Here the people are much, much better.
We barely hear a peep.

Carla Well, so it's all for the best!

She laughs nervously.

Oh, I didn't mean . . .

Nancy No, I know.

Carla Obviously, it's a tragedy.

Nancy Yes.

Carla Although they've said he may improve, yeah?

Nancy It's hard to know, a bit early to know.
But yes, they're hopeful that, with therapy . . .

Carla He could walk again.

Nancy Oh sure, that's the idea.
(*Insinuating.*) I don't know how "agile," he'll be.
They'll know more once the rehab gets going.

Carla Oh that's okay that's okay.
We mostly just like to sit around all day and laugh.
He's such a funny guy.

Nancy Sure.

Carla And right now he's . . .

Nancy He's just upstairs, getting ready.

He likes to do what he can on his own.
It's not much, but I let him take his time.
Then he calls me up to help out with the rest.

Carla I can help too.

Nancy I think you'll have plenty of time for that.
But yes. If you want to, be my guest.

Carla We'll wait for him to call down.

Nancy Okay.

Carla He's probably nervous about seeing me, since . . .

Nancy Since?

Carla Since the accident and everything.
He's probably worried what I'll think.
Not that I would think anything but. You know.
(*On a brighter note.*) And your kids are still around, that's nice.
I don't mean "around" like "alive,"
I mean here, in town, still staying with you and stuff.

Nancy Yes, well, yes, now, ever since the accident, we can't get rid of them.
They're relentless.

Carla Oh.

Nancy Did he have a stroke?
Was the U-Haul defective?
Should we sue?
Like there needs to be some grand explanation for driving a U-Haul through the wall of your home. They're over at the medical center now getting a fold-up wheelchair. They'll be by with it, I guess, or I'll have them drop it off.
You're not far, are you?

Carla No, just over in Vista View.
You know, it's . . . By the highway?

Nancy I don't know it, but it sounds very convenient.

Carla *laughs.*
Neither one of them quite knows what to say.

Nancy I like your scarf.

Carla You do?

Nancy Mmm hmmm.

Carla Thanks, I hardly ever wear it.
It's just been sitting on the floor of my closet for ages.
And then this morning I don't know why, but I grabbed it.

Nancy If you want to donate it . . .

Carla Excuse me?

Nancy If you want to donate it, I'm running a clothing drive.
It was my idea,
And now suddenly
We've got over thirty boxes, all for refugees.
We're driving it all down to D.C.—

Carla We?

Nancy Linda Warburger and I.
We all just have so many old things
We never wear anymore and it turns out others do too.
When you get here you realize all the things you really don't need.

Carla Like your husband!
Sorry, I don't know why I said that.
I got a weird sense of humor sometimes.

Nancy No, it's a very good point.

Carla Anyway, I think I'll keep my scarf.

Nancy Sure. I understand.

A crash from upstairs.

Bill? You okay?

Bill (*from off*) I'm fine.

Nancy What was that?

Bill (*from off*) Just a lamp. I'm FINE.

Nancy Well, hurry up, Bill, your girlfriend's waiting.

Bill (*from off*) I'm *fine*.

Nancy and **Carla** *look at each other.*

Carla Do you got to . . .

Nancy Probably best to let him have his independence, if he can.
Tea?

Carla Sure.

Nancy *busies herself making tea.*

Carla So you said you got over thirty boxes!

Nancy Yes, people's generosity has been extraordinary.

Carla Must feel good to be making a contribution, yeah?

Nancy I mean, it's just some old clothing, really.
But, you know, it is sort of wild
To think about some complete and total stranger half way across the world
Wearing the same coat I wore just last year.
It makes me feel a little bit more like I exist.

Carla I get that.

Nancy You do?

Carla I do this thing where—
I mean it's not exotic like your clothing drive—
But you know, sometimes I go over to Rose Court and I just hold people's hands.
The sick people, the hospice people?
'Cause some of them don't have anybody, you know?
And so I just go over and hold their hands.

Nancy And it's not awkward? Holding a stranger's hand?

Carla I think they like it.
I mean I can't tell honestly, most of 'em are pretty out of it.
But nobody's ever socked me in the face.
Of course most of 'em are probably too far gone for that.
This one lady there, this lady, Irma, she's got Alzheimer's pretty bad actually.
And one day the nurses notice, she's saving her cookie.

Nancy Her cookie?

Carla The cookie she got from lunch every day.
She leaves it right on top of her chest of drawers,
Right in front of this little mirror she's got there.

Nancy Why would she do that?
Nobody knows.
And then she starts leaving little pictures there too, stuff she drew at the craft table.
And then she leaves little cards, notes that say things like, "Hello," and "Nice to meet you."
And the nurses can't figure it out.
They don't know why she's doing this,
Leaving all these little treats and presents and everything in front of the mirror on her dresser.
Until one day, they realize:
Irma thinks the woman in the mirror is somebody else.
She thinks it's some other woman, trapped in there.
And she's trying to make a friend.

Nancy You mean she's so far gone . . .

Carla That's right.
She doesn't even recognize herself anymore.

They both sit with that for a moment.

Nancy I don't think I've . . .
Ever really recognized what I saw in the mirror.

Carla Oh yeah?

Nancy I think I can count on one hand the number of times I've looked in the mirror
And the thing I saw matched anything I felt inside.

Carla I look in the mirror these days I'm like . . . AAAAAAH!
I'm not leaving treats, I'm running for cover.

Nancy I always felt like I had these big things inside me.
I mean I did, I know I did.
But on the outside, I just looked like a librarian.

Carla You mean because . . .

Nancy Well, because I was.
I was a librarian.

Carla Oh. (*Laughs.*)
Well, that's a great job, you must get to read everything.

Nancy I did read a lot. I still do.
Sometimes I thought about writing a book.
I had this idea I could put my book on the shelf.

Carla You probably could,
I mean who's more qualified to write books than a librarian?
Write what you know.
And you know books.

Nancy Being a librarian is mostly just telling people to be quiet.

Carla Oh, sure, yeah, I could see that.

Nancy How about you?

Carla Oh, I'm a,
I *was* a receptionist—dentist's office.

Nancy Oh.

Carla I mostly tried to cheer people up
While I was, you know, finding a time for their root canal.
I'd make jokes.
Wear a bright print.
I'd dress up for holidays, you know?
Like those reindeer horns with the bells for Christmas
Or I had this axe that I would put on my head like, chopping through my head, for Halloween.
Just trying to say, "Okay, it's the dentist, but we can still have a good time."

I did the job that way for forty years.
When I was young, people thought it was cute.
When I got older I think people thought it was kinda sad and crazy.
And then, when I got even older, nobody noticed me at all.
I could have had a real axe in my head, nobody would have noticed.
You know, you get older, you become invisible.

Nancy Or you're reduced to a cartoon.

Carla I know!

Nancy You're either a cute old grandma, or you're a crotchety old bitch—
There is nothing in between.

Carla I know, and then I hear younger women complain about—
Well, anything—
And I just want to punch them in the fucking face.
They have no idea what's coming for them.

Nancy Do you still have sex?

Carla That's sort of personal.

Nancy You're taking my husband, I think it's fair.

Carla Well, I'll tell you.
I had stopped for a long time.
I was so tired of these men, bumping around down there
As I pretended to have a good time.
So I had given it up.

Nancy (*apprehensive*) Until Bill?

Carla Until I got a vibrator.

Nancy Oh, that's smart.

Carla You don't even have to go into a sex store anymore.
You just order them on the internet.
It comes in a plain box so nobody knows.
And they don't look like a penis anymore,
I mean you can get a penis one if you want, but they come in all kinds of shapes.
Mine looks like an egg.

Nancy Really?

Carla Like a little blue egg.
And it's hands-free.

Nancy Hands-free?
How is that possible . . .

Carla It just tucks right in there.
It has different speeds, different rhythms, you can do harder, softer, pulse, steady.

It's just like on a blender.

Nancy That's fantastic.

Carla I'm telling you.

Nancy Who needs marriage, right?

Carla Who needs marriage is right.
Not that—I mean—look, I don't want you to get the wrong impression—
I have the greatest respect for marriage.

Nancy Have you ever been married?

Carla No, like I said I was a receptionist.

Nancy Well, if you had been, I doubt you would respect it so much.

Carla Oh yeah?

Nancy It's not some high and mighty thing up on a hill.
It's sort of a stray dog of a thing.
Sometimes it's nice to have someone around.
Other times it's more of a box you can't claw your way out of.
It holds you. It keeps you.
But don't *respect* it because God knows it doesn't respect you—
It's a boa constrictor—
It will watch you wither and keep going and going for generations, whether you live or die.
Are you getting married?

Carla Who?

Nancy You and Bill.

Carla I never thought of myself as the marrying type really.
And I don't cook or anything, so . . .

Nancy Well, you'll have to cook a bit now.
Bill likes to be cooked for.
I can send you some recipes.

Carla Oh yeah? I don't want to trouble you.

Nancy It's no trouble at all. It's the least I can do.
You're doing me a great favor.
(*Then, off* **Carla**.) What?

Carla I just . . .
I guess I didn't expect you to be so nice.

Nancy I'm just practical.

Bill (*from off*) Nancy? NANCY.

Nancy (*calling back*) Are you ready?

Bill (*from off*)   Why do you think I'm calling you?

Nancy (*calls back to him*)   All right then. Coming right up.
(*To* **Carla**.) Excuse me.

Carla   Sure. I'll be here.

Nancy *goes up.*
Carla *looks around.*

Slowly she takes off her scarf.
Folds it.
Puts it in the donation pile.

And goes.

Scene Two

The next day.

Bill *slowly enters.*
His neck is stabilized with a medical brace.
One leg is on a scooter.
One arm is in a sling.

He tries to navigate his scooter over the carpet:
It's impossible.
He gets stuck.
It's sad to watch.

Brian *follows him in.*

Brian   Dad, Dad, here, let me help you.

Bill   I'm fine.

Brian   // You're stuck.

Bill   Stop that. Stop that.

Brian   Okay. There you go,
There you go.

Nancy *enters.*
She's carrying an overstuffed purse.

Nancy   The emergency numbers are all on the fridge.

During what follows, **Nancy** *is brushing her hair, putting on lipstick, earrings, making sure she has everything in her wallet, doing other things to ready herself for leaving.*

Nancy   You can also just pick up any phone and dial zero,
Because it's all part of one system.

They come very quickly—obviously.

Ben Okay, great.

Nancy Also if the phone's left off the hook, they just show up.
So if you think you're having a heart attack or a stroke?
You can just knock over the phone.
And somehow they know it's Bill and Nancy French.
Rona Norberg was telling me at lunch the other day.
I guess she and Arthur knocked the phone off the hook
While they were, you know . . .
Medics showed up and walked right in on them.
So be careful about that.

Brian *is trying to put a blanket around* **Bill**'s *feet.*
It's driving **Bill** *crazy.*

Bill Stop that.

Nancy Physical therapy is every day at ten and three.
And a nurse will come in the morning.
And again in the evening . . .
The staff here do a very good job, he really won't need a thing.
(*Remembering.*) And oh!
There's no need to water the plants—they're fake!
This whole time, I had no idea!
I thought I had such a green thumb.

She looks down at her shoes.
She looks up to her family.

And before any of you can say anything,
About how cruel it is for me to leave him this way,
I'd like to say . . .
(*She takes a few steps forward.*)
It's not my fault Bill is in this state.
The U-Haul shenanigans were not my fault,
And I can no longer be tied to every stupid thing
That he does.
And yes, I do realize that's what marriage is,
A contract to be tied to each other's stupidity,
But I don't think that's what love ought to be.
Anyway, no need for a grand speech.

Ben Great.

Jess You should give a speech if you want, Nancy.
You should say whatever you want.

Ben Okay, Jess.

Nancy No.

That's fine.

She looks down to her feet again.
Stops.

These shoes are very uncomfortable.
(*Pause, then regaining momentum.*)
I've left all the numbers and the name of the hotel . . .
Where am I staying . . .
Let's see.

Ben Here, Mom, I have it here.
I'm going to put it in my phone, too.
Bri, do you want this number?

Brian No.

Ben I've got it, so, if you need it.

Brian I won't.

Nancy Brian, I'm sorry, I know this is hard for you—

Brian Please just . . .
Let me have my experience over here.

Ben So, just to recap,
Jess and I will stay 'til tomorrow, Bri will be back for the weekend—

Bill They're going to make me move to Rose Court.

Brian Don't you dare say that, Dad.

Nancy Not if you can handle things here on your own.

Bill Rose Court is where you go to die.

Jess Bill, nobody's dying.

Ben Dad, please.

Nancy There's no need to be so dramatic.

Bill Me? I'm dramatic?
You're the one who scared away my girlfriend.

Nancy I scared away his girlfriend, that's right.

Bill She was ready to take me off everyone's hands.
This one talks to her for five minutes and . . .
(*Hurt, pained.*) I never hear from her again.

Nancy Okay. That's what I did.

Bill Not that I blame you.
Jealousy is normal.

Nancy Why would I want to scare away your girlfriend, Bill?
She was the answer to all of my hopes and dreams, quite frankly.

Bill Keep telling yourself that.
You keep telling yourself that.
I know you, Nancy, I got your number.

Ben Okay guys?
Guys?
Nobody is going to Rose Court.
All that's happening is, Mom is going to D.C.
For a few days to drop off the clothes and meet with the—the—what is it?

Nancy The ladies from the charity.
I want to make sure this whole thing isn't a scam.
If I could, I'd go drop off the clothes with the refugees myself.
Maybe I will one day.

Ben Okay, well, you're not going to Syria.

Nancy It wouldn't be Syria, Ben.
They're not in Syria, obviously, because they're refugees.
The camp is in Lebanon.

Jess She could go to Lebanon, why not?

Brian Sure, it's fine, Mom, go to Lebanon.
Leave your injured husband of fifty years and have a great time.
Hopefully he'll still be alive when you get back here.
Also my fish are dead so I hope everyone's happy.

Nancy Oh, I'm not coming back here.

Brian What?

Nancy (*to* **Ben**) You didn't tell him about this?

Ben I thought I would address that—

Brian Tell me about what.

Nancy I've found an "Airbnb."

Ben Okay, okay, see,
I thought I would address that after the D.C. trip.

Brian You what?!

Nancy It's only about forty-five minutes away.
Ben helped me find it.

Brian You helped her find an Airbnb?

Nancy It's only until I can get a new unit.

Ben There's a huge waitlist—

Brian You helped her find an Airbnb?

Ben Jess, do you want to jump in here?

Jess Not really, no.

Ben Jess, come on.

Jess Remember what we've been talking about?

Ben Jess, I'm doing exactly what you asked, //
I'm listening, I'm taking the people's—needs—seriously—
What more do you want from me?

Jess Don't act like it's for me, Ben,
I've been here over a week now,
So don't act like you're doing me some big fucking favor.

Nancy It's very reasonably priced, just a room in somebody's house.

Jess That's great, Nancy.

Bill Great, that's fine by me.

Brian You're not moving into some random room in some random stranger's house.

Ben Bri, calm // down, dude, let's just—

Brian She could slip and fall, she could get robbed, she could get raped—

Nancy Oh for the love of God.

Brian An Airbnb?
Our mother in an Airbnb?
At her age? It's . . .

Nancy And Ben said the next thing is, I need to open my own bank account
So I can "establish my own financial identity."

Ben Mom? Mom mom mom.

Jess Don't shut her down.

Brian I can't believe this.

Nancy I know!
I never had my own bank account before.

Ben I think that's pretty normal, Mom.

Jess No, that's insane, Nancy.

Nancy He's right, plenty of women of my generation didn't have them.

Ben All I meant.

Jess My mother always had her own bank account.
I mean, she's a little bit younger than you—

Ben Babe—

Jess But also she ran her own business—
And she *still* tells my dad what to do.

Ben Babe—

Jess What?!

Brian She is literally heartless,
Do you know how it feels—
To realize your own mother // is heartless?

Jess Oh, come on, Brian,
She's not literally—

Ben Babe, come on—

Jess And stop fucking calling me babe.

Ben Shit.

Jess All I was trying to say is—
She's not literally heartless, Brian,
She's not literally heartless because if she were?
If she literally had no heart?
She would literally not be alive, that's all I'm trying to say.

Brian Okay, fine, everyone knows what I meant.

Jess Which is—actually—
That actually makes sense.
Something finally makes sense.
Because, like, maybe that's how you all feel about her.
Like she's not alive.

Nancy Thank you, Jess, but—

Jess Like she's not an actual person, with real actual needs
She's just, Mom.
Mom, fix my boo boo.
Mom, make it better.
Mom, you missed my baseball game!
Mom mom mom mom mom.

Brian Thank you, this doesn't involve you.

Jess It does involve me,
Because I am standing here,
I have somehow found
Myself here, with all of you assholes and, it's like,
I've been here for over a week and I can't even sleep—
And I am so not doing this,
I'm not doing this.

Ben Not doing what?

Jess Like, first I was "babe" and now I'm going to be "mom" and it's like,
You're not even taking that in
I am so not waiting fifty more years
Only to find myself, only to find myself in this
Kind of a shit situation.
Or I guess it would be forty-three.
Because, we've been together seven, so.

Ben Wow.
You've done the math.

Jess I subtracted seven,
That's not doing the math.

Pause.
Ben *might put his head in his hands.*

Brian So . . . Just to clarify . . .
Mom's not going to Ben's Airbnb.

Jess She's going to do
Whatever she wants.

Nancy Jess—

Brian I am not okay with that.

Jess You're not in charge of her life.
She's not, like, some stupid kid in one of your stupid plays—

Nancy Jess, it's okay—

Jess No, Nancy, I got this.
She has articulated something she wants
For maybe the first time in her entire life,

Brian Oh, come on.

Jess And it's something that doesn't make the rest of you *comfortable*—
But you are going to suck it up—

Brian Suck it up? // Seriously?

Jess And listen to her,
Listen to her,
And let her lead the way.
Why don't both of you you grow the fuck up
And have a little compassion—

Brian I have plenty of // compassion.
You have no idea, no idea—

Jess Or at least understanding

For the fact that this is a woman
Who has worked her ass off to satisfy your
Every need—

Nancy That's okay, Jess.

Jess And who has *never*, *ever* in her whole entire life
Asked you for anything—
What about *her* needs?
What about her getting her own needs met?

Brian Oh,
I think our mother got her needs met.

Nancy Brian.

Brian She was getting her needs met,
Don't you worry.

Jess What is that supposed to mean.

Ben What the fuck are you talking about, Bri.

Nancy Brian.

Brian I'm not keeping your precious secret, Mom.
You're leaving this family?
You forfeit the right.
Our entire childhood she was in love with a guy named Hal.

Ben Hal?

Jess Who is Hal?

Brian Mom loved him,
And he loved her pussy.

Ben What?!

Brian And I'm sorry if that's painful to hear, Dad.
But you taught us to be tough.
So. There it is. Toughen up.

Pause.

Ben Mom?
Is that true?

Nancy In a way.

Ben Oh my God—

Jess Ben.

Bill It's fine, I know all about it.

Brian What?

Bill That thing with Hal Barrow.
Yeah, I always knew about that.

Pause.

Nancy You did?

Brian You did?

Jess Okay,
Okay.

Ben This is so crazy.

Brian You knew?

Bill Of course I knew.
It was obvious.
Every time she saw him she lit up like a Christmas tree.

Nancy Why didn't you . . .
Say something.

Bill I guess
I liked seeing you happy.

Everyone takes that in.

Ben Great, so great, so now it's official,
The whole thing was a joke.
No, great, no, that feels good.
To finally get that out in the open.
Nobody was happy, nobody was honest, everyone was suffering and compromising.

Hallelujah.
What a relief to know that nothing was anything other than
Pure, unmitigated, bullshit.

I mean, every Christmas.
Every birthday.
Every baseball game.
Bullshit bullshit bullshit.
Every family photo, every family trip, every hug, every lesson learned, take your pep talks, your matching plaid pajamas—
Just erase it all and replace it with bullshit.
Our whole childhood.
Just blown sky high into bullshit.
(*To* **Nancy**.) And here I am, like an idiot, finding an Airbnb for you.
Because I want you to be happy
And comfortable
And making sure it has AC and Wi-Fi and is pet-friendly in case you want to get a cat—
Because Dad was always "allergic," but hey, it's a new day—

And I'm putting it all on my credit card and handling things, like an idiot—

Ben (*cont.*) (*to* **Jess**)   And then you're pissed at me,
For calling you "babe,"
When, like, you used to love that,
You used to talk in baby talk, literal sexy baby talk—
When we were fooling around—

Jess   Are you serious, are you—

Ben   Oh sorry, everyone, is this too personal now—
Sorry, Mom, Dad, Bri, fuck you all.
(*Back to* **Jess**.) You did, you talked in that high little baby talk—

Jess   I was playing around—

Ben   You wanted to be all sexy baby and now I'm the jerk,
'Cause I don't see you—
When the truth is,
You never told me, you changed your mind and you never told me.

We do not communicate!
That's the truth.

We do not communicate.

And that scares the shit out of me
Because we are about to—to—to—
Start a family.

Start a family.
That sounds stupid.
How stupid does that sound right now?

I mean, I mean,
What kind of a loving family—
What kind of grandparents are you—
You're supposed to want to be—
Knitting booties or woodworking a crib or whatever—
And now, because of you, my skin is literally like peeling off of my body—

And—
(*To his parents.*) I don't even want you.
I don't even want you around him.
You—yes, you—
With the lies and the—I—just feel like—honestly—

Honestly, it would be simpler,
It would be easier if you had just died.

Because at least that would make sense.
At least then, I could keep my memories.

You want to know what love is?
Love is commitment, love is commitment—

Ben *breaks down completely.*
Jess *goes to him, stopping him.*

Jess Shhh. Shhhh. Shhhhh.
It's okay.

He buries his head on her stomach.
A very long pause.
Nobody knows what to do.

Brian Okay.
Okay.
I'll.
I'll move in here with Dad.

Nancy We don't want you to do that.
Bill, do you want him to do that?

Bill (*pause*) No.

Nancy Maybe we haven't been clear.
We don't want you here anymore.

Bill You kids should go.

Nancy It's enough.
Brian. Ben.
Enough.
I can't take care of you anymore.
I understand that we were supposed to make you feel like the world is safe
And love is possible.
But, you know, that's an enormous responsibility.
And I'm not sure it's true.

Ben Well, the world is definitely not safe, so.

Jess Love . . .
Is possible.

Ben Jess—

Jess No, I know that for a fact.
I don't know how exactly?
But . . .
I think I . . .
I still believe in it.

Ben Okay.
Okay.
I'll go get us packed.

Jess No.
It's okay.
I got this.

She goes.
A beat.

Brian What about Thanksgiving?

Ben That's six months away, dude.

Brian Still.

Ben Maybe we'll go to Jess's family this year.
She's always wanted to do that, and we'll have the baby so . . .

Brian So I'm just, like "Ubering" by myself between an Airbnb and Rose Court?
God, that's depressing.
Are you even making a turkey, Mom?

Nancy I hadn't thought about it.

Bill I'm not going to Rose Court.

Brian I'm just like eating cafeteria turkey with Dad and some nurse?

Nancy There's a decent Chinese at the mall.

Brian Oh my God.

Ben You can come to Jess's if you want.

Brian I don't want to be your charity case, Ben.
I don't want to be, like, your good deed for the year.

Ben Please come.
We'd like you to come.
Hang with your nephew . . .
Teach him about . . . What you do.
I'm trying. I don't know what to say.
I'm trying here.

Brian I'll consider your invitation.

Jess (*from off*) Ben? I'm ready.

Ben Yep.
Coming.

*He goes to help **Jess** with the bags.*
*He and **Jess** come downstairs.*

Brian So this is it?
Are we going to see you guys together ever again?
Are we ever going to be together, like this, ever again?

Nancy I don't know.

They all look to each other.

If I can offer a little maternal advice?
I would focus on your own lives.
(*To* **Ben**.) You have a baby coming.
You should probably get things straightened out before then.

Nancy *turns to* **Brian**.

Nancy And Brian,
Two hundred kids
Seems like way too much for *The Crucible*.
I understand you don't want anybody to feel disappointed.
But it's better to be truthful, I think.
I think maybe truth is the first part of love.

Brian Yeah, well . . .
Thanks for your honesty.
(*Pause.*)
The show is actually pretty great.
It's beautiful to see all those kids' faces light up,
Feeling like they're part of something.
Maybe someday you'll come check it out.
I have to get my stuff.

He goes off to get his stuff.

Nancy I didn't mean to insult him.

Ben I didn't mean when I said—

Nancy I know.

Ben I mean I . . . I . . . love you guys.

Nancy We love you.

Bill Take care, son.

Jess Bye, Bill, bye, Nancy.

Nancy Keep us posted on that baby.

Jess Any day now.

Bill Parenthood is very rewarding.

Nancy *looks at him.*
She laughs.

Nancy That was funny.

Ben Tell Brian . . .
We said bye.

Nancy Bye, kids.
Drive safe!

And they're gone.
Brian *comes back in with his stuff.*

Brian I'm taking an Uber to the train.
I can't, I can't.
I'm sad. That's all.
It's okay.
I'll call you.
(*Into his phone.*) Yes, yes, I'm coming outside. I'm coming right now.

And he goes.

Nancy *watches from the doorway as the car drives off.*

She turns back to **Bill**.

Nancy And they're gone.

Bill Well.
Then.
That's that.
You'll probably want to head off to D.C.

Nancy *has a far away look on her face.*

Nancy I was just thinking about
When Brian went off to college.

Bill What about it?

Nancy And we dropped him off near his dorm
Because he—he wouldn't let us come too close, in case someone might see us,
And figure out he had parents.
And remember, he was wearing that sort of oversized
Maroon cowl neck sweater, with the buttons?

Bill Cowl neck?

Nancy It was such a blue fall day,
And we watched him walk off down the road and he looked so ridiculous and hopeful
And beautiful,
And my heart just flew right out of my body with him.

Bill Nancy, I . . .

Nancy (*re her ring*) I guess I should give this back.
That feels sort of strange.

She puts her ring on the kitchen table.

Bill Keep it.
Go on.
It didn't mean a thing anyway.

Nancy How can you say that?
You don't mean . . . Hal?

Bill Yeah, Hal.
Good old Hal.
Let's not talk about Hal—
I spent enough of my life thinking about that bag of shit.

Nancy Hold on.
No—you have to understand,
I thought it was just mine—
A problem I had,
I never meant for it to hurt you.
Honestly,
I'm shocked you even noticed.

Bill Oh, I noticed.
It's a lot easier being the fantasy, you know that?
You never have to do the day in, day out.

Nancy Well, I'm shocked.
You never seemed to notice me at all—
It's just like the canoe.

Bill What canoe?

Nancy I've told you this—
How my father used to take me out on the lake in the canoe—
We would paddle for hours in total silence . . .
And he taught me never to take my paddle out of the water,
Forward and back, forward and back,
So that I wouldn't even make the smallest splash, the tiniest sound.
And now I think . . . I lived my entire life that way—no splash—
No impact—
I said I would like a divorce, you just said, "All right."

Bill What was I supposed to say?
Was I supposed to fight for you?

Nancy Is that too much to ask?

Bill I can't play this game with you, Nancy,
I don't know the rules.
I was trying to be accommodating.

Nancy I don't want to be accommodated.

Don't accommodate me.
See me.
Challenge me.
Touch me.
Destroy me.
Do something to me so I know that I'm here.
I just want to know that I'm here, alive.

Bill Nancy.
I drove a truck through the wall of our house.

Nancy That was an accident.

Bill You know, for a bright woman
You can be remarkably slow on the uptake.

Nancy You're saying you did that for me?

Bill I don't know,
I don't know why I did it.
I hate this place,
"Grand Horizons,"
You try to smash it and it grows back like an octopus.
It's an octopus.
I'd blow the whole thing up if I could.

Nancy You're a maniac.
You're out of your mind.

Bill Well, if I'm out of my mind, it's because you made me this way.
You think you had no impact in your stupid canoe
With all your splashing and paddling around, that's a laugh.

Nancy What impact did I have?

Bill You were my whole life, Nancy.
You've been my whole entire life.

A pause.
Nancy *takes that in.*

Nancy How?

Bill It's just science, plain science—
Every meal you've ever cooked
Is now what makes up the cells in my body.
This stuff you picked out at the grocery store.
The pot roast you made over and over and over, the eternal pot roast,
I am literally made up of that now.
My cholesterol, well . . .
That's your fondness for eggs in the morning.

Nancy You liked eggs,

That was you—

Bill I prefer toast.
I have more wrinkles on the left side of my face, ever notice that?
How it's sort of smushed up?
That's from years and years of sleeping on my left side
Because I know you like to sleep on your left and I used to like to hold onto you that way.
So my face, my whole face is a result of how you sleep.

Nancy You can't hold me responsible for your crooked face—

Bill And while we're on the subject of romance.
Let me tell you something, Nancy.
You were no acrobat.

Nancy Oh fuck you, Bill.

Bill You just lay there expecting me to figure it out,
Well, I'm not a mind reader.
How the hell was I supposed to know what you wanted.

Nancy You could have asked.

Bill I didn't know the questions.
I would have done anything, anything to please you.

Nancy You didn't even try.

Bill I was trying the whole time.
That was me trying.

Nancy Well, you don't have to try anymore.
Doesn't that feel fantastic?!

Bill It does.
// It feels fucking great.
I'm a new man.

Nancy I'm twenty years old again.
I can't wait to get the hell out of here.

Bill Then go.
Get the hell out!

Neighbor (*from off*) Hey, quiet down over there!

Bill You quiet down.
Quiet down your goddamn self.

Nancy We will NOT QUIET DOWN.
WE WILL NOT BE QUIET.

Bill We spent enough time being quiet.

Nancy We're going to be loud.
And if you don't like it, you can come at us.

Bill Okay, that's okay, Nancy—

Nancy We will fuck you up, lady.
We will fuck you up.

A moment of release.
A shared silence.

I want to go to D.C. with Linda Warburger.
I want to be touched.
Softly,
I do.
I want my own bank account.
I want to get one of those eggs from the internet.
I might go to Lebanon.
And I . . .
I don't want to be Nancy French anymore.

Bill I don't want to be Bill French.

Nancy (*stops, then*) You don't?

Bill No,
It's just a job, it's a lousy job,
I'd quit if I could.

A beat.
Something falls away.

Nancy What else?

Bill What do you mean?

Nancy What else don't you want.
Or do you want, or . . .
Anything.

Bill You mean . . .
Okay, what the hell.
I want . . .
To tell some good jokes.
I want . . .
No, that's pretty much it.

Nancy That is not it.

Bill Okay, fine.
I want . . .
I want our kids to get their shit together.
I want to be a better grandfather than I was a father.

I want to take a walk.

I want to take off my shoes.
Just for a moment.
They're killing my feet.

She takes off her shoes.

Bill (*re his medical gear*)   I don't want to wear this stupid thing.
It's driving me nuts.

He takes off his medical collar.

Nancy   But—the doctors—

Bill (*dismissively*)   Doctors.
I'll be fine.

He looks at her feet.

Nice feet.

Nancy   Thank you.

Bill   I like feet.

Nancy   Really?
I have weird toes.

Bill   But a beautiful arch.

Pause.

Nancy   Now what.

Bill   I don't know.
Pause.

Nancy *looks to the door, her bags.*

Nancy   I don't have much time.

Bill   Neither do I.

Pause.

Nancy   What if—
What if we tell each other more things
We want out of life.
And maybe . . .

Bill   What?

Nancy   I don't know.

Bill   Okay.
You go first.

Nancy You go.

Bill Count of three.
One, two, three . . .

Nancy // A cat.

Bill Death with dignity.

Nancy Okay.
One, two, three . . .
Make a difference.
You didn't say // anything.

Bill Sorry, sorry, I was just . . .
I will.
Ready?

Nancy Yes.
You're with me this time.

Bill I'm with you.
Here we go.
One . . .

Nancy Two . . .

Bill Three.

Pause.
They look at each other.
Really look.

They take a breath in unison.

End of play.

Performance Rights

Paradise Blue

Published by arrangement with Theatre Communications Group, Inc. All rights reserved. Application for permission to perform, etc. should be made before rehearsals begin to Theatre Communications Group, 520 Eighth Ave., 24th Fl, NY, NY 10018-4156. No performance may be given unless a license has been obtained.

Cost of Living

Published by arrangement with Theatre Communications Group, Inc. All rights reserved. Application for permission to perform, etc. should be made before rehearsals begin to Theatre Communications Group, 520 Eighth Ave., 24th Fl, NY, NY 10018-4156. No performance may be given unless a license has been obtained.

Actually

All rights whatsoever in this play are strictly reserved and application for performance, etc. should be made before rehearsal to The Gersh Agency, 41 Madison Avenue, 31st Floor, NY, NY 10010 USA Att: Seth Glewen. No performance may be given unless a license has been obtained.

Where Storms Are Born

CAUTION: Professionals and amateurs are hereby warned that "Where Storms Are Born" is subject to a royalty. It is fully protected under the copyright laws of the United States of America and all countries covered by the International Copyright Union (including the Dominion of Canada and the rest of the British Commonwealth). The Berne Convention, the Pan-American Copyright Convention and the Universal Copyright Convention as well as all countries with which the United States has reciprocal copyright relations. All rights, including professional/amateur stage rights, motion picture, recitation, lecturing, public reading, radio broadcasting, television, video or sound recording, all other forms of mechanical or electronic reproduction, such as CD-ROM, CD-I, information storage and retrieval systems and photocopying, and the rights of translation in to foreign languages, are strictly reserved. Particular emphasis is laid upon the matter of readings, permission for which must be secured from the Author's agent in writing.

Inquiries concerning rights should be addressed to: William Morris Endeavor Entertainment, LLC, 11 Madison Avenue, 18th Floor, New York, New York 10010, Attn: Michael Finkle.

Selling Kabul

Published by arrangement with Sylvia Khoury. All rights reserved. Application for permission to perform should be made before rehearsals begin to Theatrical Rights Worldwide, 1180 Avenue of the Americas, Suite 640, New York, NY 10036. Amateur Licensing: licensing@theatricalrights.com; Professional Licensing: pro@theatricalrights.com. All other permissions to Creative Artists Agency of 2000 Avenue of the Stars, Los Angeles, CA 90067, USA. No performance may be given unless a license has been obtained.

Grand Horizons

Published by arrangement with Beth Wohl. All rights reserved. Application for permission to perform, etc. should be made before rehearsals begin to Creative Artists Agency of 2000 Avenue of the Stars, Los Angeles, CA 90067, USA. No performance may be given unless a license has been obtained.